egg
ON THE MENU

Luc Hoornaert and Kris Vlegels

L | LANNOO

Foreword

There are few things better at turning a house into a home than the delicious smell of a freshly fried omelette wafting from the kitchen. Eggs are eaten all over the world and so they immediately create a connection and reveal the essence of what eating can be – a social facilitator, super glue bonding cultures around a well-laden table.

Eggs have a special significance in most ancient cultures too. Reason enough to explore what chefs in different cultures have to say about eggs through their dishes. Humankind is not alone in being a consumer of eggs; many other animals also regularly eat eggs. And so the egg forms a link between us and our prehistory.

The typical shape of the egg has inspired many crafts including traditional ways of aging wine to produce a better result and our language is full of references to eggs.

An egg therefore has much more to offer than you might at first think. This book contains a selection of recipes from some of my favourite chefs.

Enjoy!

Luc Hoornaert,
author

TABLE OF CONTENTS

     5 Foreword

9. INTRODUCTION
    9 **To be or not to be**

13. CHINA
   13 **An egg is a new beginning**
   19 Fried tofu
   21 Fried milk Daliang
   23 Oyster omelette
   25 Fried scrambled egg with Jelly ear fungus
   27 Pomegranate chicken
   29 Steamed minced pork with salted eggs

33. UNITED KINGDOM
   33 **Birds' nests**
   37 Pickled eggs
   39 Deviled eggs
   41 Eggs Benedict
   43 Crème caramel
   45 Scotch eggs

47. JAPAN
   47 **Tamagokake Gohan – Mmm raw eggs**
   53 Onsen tamago
   55 Chawan mushi
   57 Okonomiyaki
   59 Tamago somen
   61 Tamago dashi
   63 Datemaki
   65 Omurice

67. KOREA
   67 **Korea**
   70 Dalgyal jjim - steamed egg with spring onion
   72 Dalgyal guk - soup with egg clouds
   76 Sogogi Jangjorim - braised beef with quail's eggs
   80 Yukhoes - steak tartar with egg yolk

83. TURKEY
   83 **Ottomania**
   86 Menemen
   88 Elbasan tava (with lamb)
   90 Cilbir - poached egg with yogurt
   92 Hamsili yumurta
   94 Mucver

97. IRAN
   97 **Sepideh Sedaghatnia**
  103 Baghlava
  105 Gojeh farangi omelette
  107 Scrambled egg khaviar divinity
  109 Mirza ghasemi
  111 Kuku
  113 **Thus spoke Zarathustra**

115. DESSERTS
- **115 The magic of baklava**
- **119 Joost Arijs**
- 121 Opéra
- 123 Chocolate macarons
- 125 Matcha cake
- 127 Lemon meringue pie
- 129 Canelés de Bordeaux
- 131 Caramel choux

133. CLASSIC DISHES
- **133 Peter Goossens**
- 136 Golden egg
- 138 White truffle omelette
- 140 Langoustine egg yolk
- 142 62°C Egg
- 144 Mandarin sabayon
- **147 Christophe Hardiquest**
- 148 Eggs and bacon
- 150 Brussels heritage: Meulemeester's quail's eggs
- 152 Infused egg yolk crème
- 154 Egg yolk ravioli with truffle
- 156 Ile flottante
- 158 Brussels heritage: Manon revisited
- **161 Giel Kaagman**
- 162 Duck egg, North Sea crab, Jerusalem artichoke, bottarga, black lovage
- 164 Veal, Zeeland oyster, 63 °C egg, kohlrabi, crystalline ice plant, hazelnuts
- 166 Cold smoked wild fjord salmon, egg yolk crème, radishes, herring roe, pork skin, salted preserved lemon, pickle
- 168 Marrowbone, North Sea sole, kaffir lime, mashua, bloodwort, mollica fritta
- 170 Egg yolk, white chocolate crumble, coconut, grapefruit, tarragon sorbet and lemon balm

175. COCKTAILS
- **175 A cocktail out of a vet's handbook**
- 180 Absinthe suissesse
- 182 Whiskey Sour
- 184 Brandy Flip
- 186 Coffee Cocktail
- 188 Ramos gin fizz

190. CONVERSION TABLE

191. ADDRESSES

TO BE OR NOT TO BE

The egg? If you stop and think about it, an egg is an incredible delicacy: fried, scrambled, boiled and so on, as well as being one of the most complete sources of nourishment. But an egg is even more than that. In many cultures it has a special metaphysical significance that usually represents a transition from not being to being.

Chaos

Ancient cultures in South-East Asia believed that in the beginning there was a sort of primordial egg. The egg contained the beginning of all things: outright chaos. The eggshell was heated by fire and the mythological figure Panu hatched from it. The weightless, light things became the heavens and the dark things formed the earth. Panu emerged to become the universe, uniting light and dark, while also creating the wind, clouds, thunder and lightning and of course the sun, because it was cold on Panu's earth. The moon served as a reminder of this cold; it shone while the sun warmed the earth.

In ancient Egypt, eggs were given as spiritual food for those who had died, as well as to placate Osiris, the god of the underworld whose job it was to guide the dead to their new lives. The ancient Greeks believed that Poseidon's sons hatched out of silver eggs. When Zeus overstepped the mark with Leda, she laid two eggs from which Castor and Pollux emerged: the birth of light and shadow. This vision is not unknown in the West either. The Kröller-Muller Museum in the Netherlands has a work by Constantin Brâncuși, created in 1924, which he called *le commencement du monde,* the beginning of the world. It is a bronze egg, perfectly beautiful in its simplicity.

Pesach

This Jewish festival, known as Passover in English, commemorates the exodus from Egypt. Prior to the journey, lamb was eaten. In present-day observances of Pesach people still eat roast meat on the bone, and ... eggs. The bone is a reminder of the exodus from Egypt, while the eggs are a symbol of the new life that the Jews were embarking upon in the Promised Land. In many languages, the words for Easter and Passover are very similar and much of the symbolism of our Easter is linked to the Jewish Passover, so it is not difficult to guess where our tradition of eating eggs and Easter eggs comes from.

Heaven and earth = egg

John of Damascus was a Byzantine theological philosopher. One of his striking assertions was that heaven and earth are similar to an egg. The shell corresponds to the sky, the membrane is the clouds, the yolk is the earth and the white is of course the water. Eggs have been found in graves almost all over the world; usually they are placed in there for the dead person or the eggs are eaten at the funeral as a symbol of new life after death. In Eastern Europe people sometimes take eggs instead of flowers to the graves of those who have recently died. Apart from real eggs, many stone, clay or jewelled stones have also been found in graves.

Ostern

Easter is called *Ostern* in Germany: neither the word *Easter* or *Ostern* resembles Pesach or Passover at all. The Saxon cultures obviously knew Ishtar or Ostara, the goddess of the returning light. Because this light always returned from the East, she was called Ostara. This Ostara had a hen with an irritating habit of hiding her eggs. Ostara was sick and tired of that and turned the hen into a hare. The hare searched among the bushes and found the eggs. Images of Ostara usually depict her with both a hare and a hen, both of which are symbols of new life and fertility. This legend eventually gave rise to the Easter Bunny. In a more sober version, birds often lay eggs in hares' forms or hollows and people therefore formerly thought that hares laid eggs.

To complete the Easter tradition, we have to take a look at Russia where *krashenki* and *pisanki* are a tradition. *Pisanki* are coloured raw eggs which, after being kept under an icon for a while, are then buried by the farmer in fields to encourage fertility. *Krashenki* are hard-boiled eggs that were painted to be given as presents at Easter.

As red as an egg

When Mary Magdalen went to Rome to visit the Emperor Tiberius, she did not follow the custom of taking jewels as a gift, but presented an egg instead. Mary Magdalen, who had once been very rich but was now penniless as a result of her belief in Jesus Christ, gave Tiberius the egg, telling him that Christ was risen. 'Arising from the dead is just as impossible as this egg changing colour from white to red,' was his answer. The egg slowly started to change colour to scarlet and, since then, red has been the symbol of the blood of Christ and an egg the symbol of the grave from which He arose. Red eggs are presented as gifts at Easter in many countries to represent resurrection. The colour red has evolved into a general symbol of love and friendship.

Matryoshka

In addition to *pisanki* and *krashenki*, Russia's rich egg tradition also has its *Matroyshka* eggs. These are eggs made from wood or papier mâché which, when opened, reveal a smaller and smaller egg inside each… Tsar Peter the Great loved these eggs so much that he brought the Moscow workshops to his new city of St Petersburg. The Imperial Porcelain factory produced 254 of them there in 1799 and 960 in 1802.

The magic of Fabergé

The Tsar summoned Peter Carl Fabergé to St Petersburg to design eggs for the Tsar's family. Fabergé's eggs were made from ivory and glass, and were of course lavishly decorated with gold, silver and all kinds of precious stones. Alexander III gave his wife a present of one every year. At the peak of

Fabergé's fame, just before the fall of the tsars, production was immense. In 1914, 3391 were made and in 1916, as many as 15,365.

Smaller Russian workshops mostly made red eggs from wood which they painted with famous icons in the orthodox Christian tradition.

An egg honoured with a statue

What would you do if you sent one of your staff to India and he ended up in the Caribbean? You'd probably sack him; but for doing just that, Christopher Columbus was rewarded with a statue in Barcelona and NYC, and worldwide fame.

Spanish dignitaries at a festive dinner hosted by Cardinal Mendoza in 1493 told Christopher Columbus that it wasn't in fact very difficult to discover India. The assumption then was that the place Columbus had landed in 1492 was India. They implied that what Columbus had done wasn't that special: any sailor with a bit of experience could do the same. Columbus held his tongue, but asked for a hard-boiled egg. He made a bet with those present that they would not be able to get the egg to stand up without help. Everyone tried but the result was the same: failure. Columbus was demonstrating out-of-the-box thinking. He banged the egg hard against the table to flatten one end, and the egg remained upright. No one said anything, but they all knew what he meant. Once someone has shown you what to do, it's easy to do it again.

No one knows whether the author of *Historia del Nuevo Mundo,* Gurolamo Benzoni, made this story up or whether it had been passed down and is actually true. What is certain is that there is a statue dedicated to the Egg of Columbus in the village of Sant Antoni de Portmany on Ibiza. I'm sure this must be the reason for the gigantic number of visitors to the island…

Eggs Benedict

The Swiss brothers John and Peter Demonico opened the first ever restaurant in the US. It was called Delmonico's and opened in 1827. Its first legendary chef was Charles Ranhofer. One of its regular guests was Mrs LeGrand Benedict. One afternoon sometime in 1860, she could see nothing she fancied on the menu. She demanded that the chef make her something new for lunch. He cut muffins in half, toasted them and laid a thick slice of ham on top. It was finished off with a poached egg richly covered in Hollandaise sauce. Mrs Le Grand Benedict was delighted and Ranhofer gave the dish an entry in the first Delmonico cookery book, *The Epicurean,* published in 1894.

The column 'The Talk of the Town' in the New Yorker magazine once contained a story about the famous retired investor, Lemuel Benedict walking into the NYC Waldorf looking for something to cure his hangover. The story dated from sometime in 1894. He placed an order with the legendary maître d'hôtel, Oscar Tschirky, for buttered toast, poached eggs and crispy bacon covered in lots of Hollandaise sauce. The staff at the Waldorf were very impressed and added the dish to their breakfast menu. And Tschirky put it in his *Cookbook of the Waldorf* in 1896. There is no mention of whether it actually cured Lemuel's hangover. There is apparently only one way to find out…

Tea eggs, a very popular snack in China.

AN EGG IS A NEW BEGINNING

While in the West eggs were usually found with the dead, in China they are given at parties to celebrate a birth. It is a tradition in China to hold a birthday party one month after a baby is born, once they are certain that the child will live. The Chinese also usually give gifts of eggs, mostly made of semi-precious stones, at Chinese New Year, on birthdays and on any occasion that symbolises a new beginning.

Tea eggs

Tea eggs are very popular snacks in China and in cities with a large Chinese community. These delicately perfumed, beautifully marbled eggs are generally a feast for the eyes and are delicious too. The idea is simple nonetheless. An egg is hard-boiled and then the shell is cracked all over at random, using a spoon, for example. The smaller and more delicate the cracks in the eggshell are, the more beautiful the final design will be. After cracking the shell, these eggs are then boiled again briefly in a mixture of strong black tea, five spice powder, cinnamon, soy sauce, star anise, fennel seeds, Szechuan peppercorns and cloves. The eggs are kept hot for half an hour and then cooled, still in the marinade, for a few days (the technique goes back to the time when conservation methods were sought for eggs to cover the periods when hens were much less productive). If you then peel the eggs, you get a fantastic result. It's an ideal snack that is incredibly popular all over China.

Pidan – hundred or thousand-year-old eggs?

Call it the hundred-year-old egg, the thousand-year-old egg or whatever you want. It is a typical Chinese delicacy born from a desire to be able to preserve eggs for the periods in which there simply aren't any.

Pidan, a typical Chinese delicacy born of a desire to be able to preserve eggs.

Obviously these eggs are not a hundred or a thousand years old, but many people think they look that old. The technique involves storing hens' or goose eggs for weeks or months in a mixture of clay, ash, salt, quicklime and rice hulls. This process gradually turns the yolk to dark green then to grey, its texture thickens and its flavours become strong with a suggestion of ammonia. The egg white becomes dark brown and transparent and its flavour becomes 'salty'. During the whole process the pH rises to a staggering 9-12. It becomes a really complex explosion of flavours for enthusiasts.

The discovery is attributed to a duck breeder from Hunan. A few months after his ducks had stopped laying, the man discovered eggs in a shallow pool on his farm, where the subsoil was a combination of his clay soil and the lime he had used when building a shed. After tasting the eggs, he naturally tried to reproduce the delicacy. And with success. There is of course no means of verifying it, but the first documents describing the process are some 600 years old, and date from the Ming Dynasty. Current knowledge of chemical processes has made the hygienic production of these very special eggs much easier. But these hundred-year-old eggs remain an experience, even for the most refined palates.

Pee on an egg

One of the traditional dishes from Dongyang is one in which eggs are cooked in the urine of very young boys aged under 10, the so-called virgin boy eggs. *Tong zi* or 童子尿煮鸡蛋 translates literally as 'boys' eggs' and it is a typical spring dish in those parts. Furthermore, it is undeniably part of the region's cultural heritage. The dish fits in with the search for preservatives for foodstuffs. Why the urine specifically has to be from very young boys is not entirely clear from a cultural point of view. The region is however known for ascribing strong health properties to urine.

The principle here is the same as that for tea eggs, except that here the eggs are first soaked in urine before being boiled in it. After that, the shells are cracked in various places using a spoon and then they are put back into the urine. Herbs and spices are added. At the end of the process, the egg white becomes golden yellow and the yolk turns green. In stark contrast to the hundred-year-old eggs which are popular all over the world, this dish is only enjoyed in Dongyang. Oh yes, in case anyone is wondering: the urine for these virgin boy eggs is collected at schools where mobile receptacles have been provided for the boys to urinate in instead of toilets. This is culturally perfectly acceptable there.

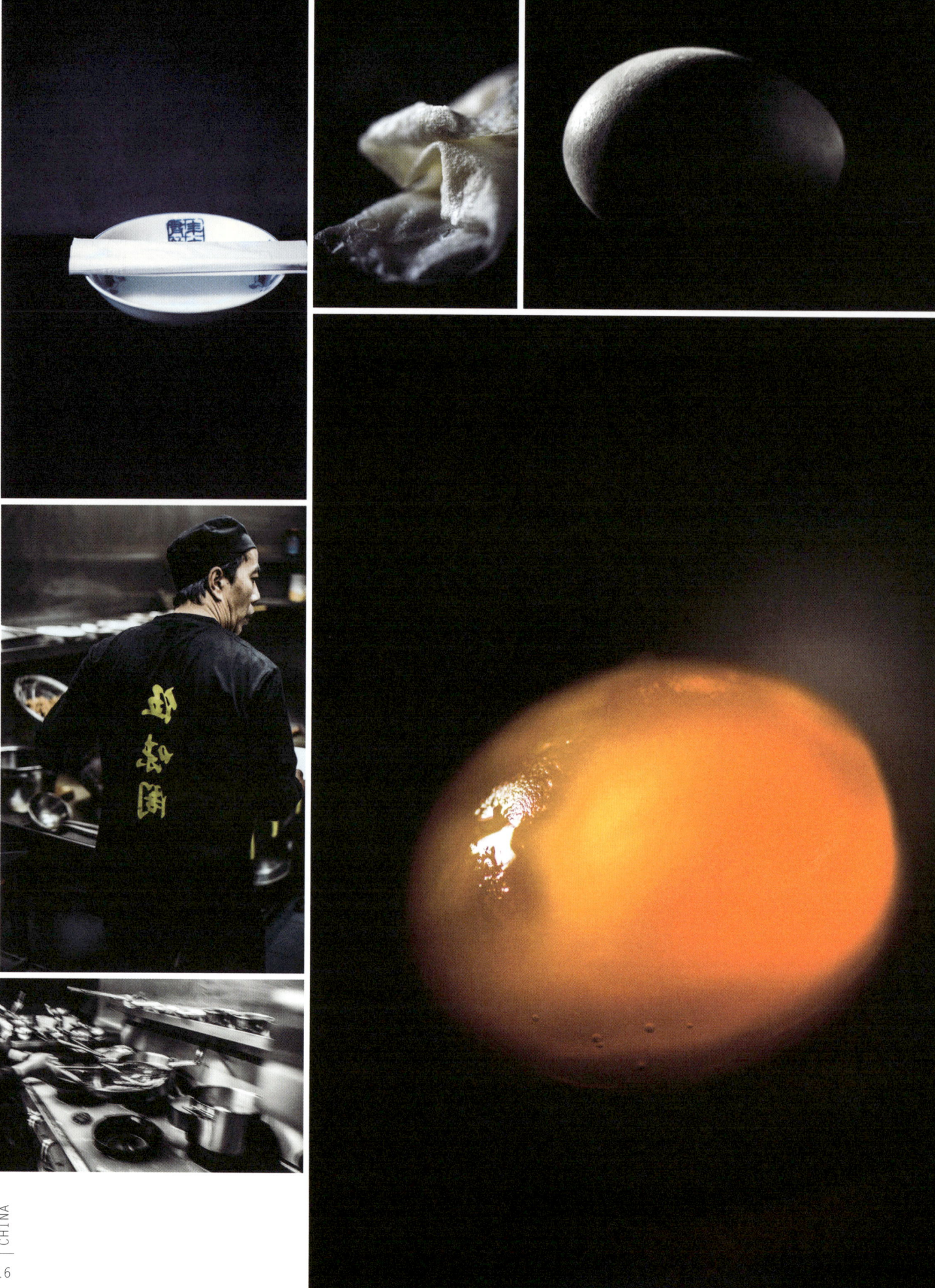

→ Leung Kwai Lam, a truly exceptional chef who conjures up one masterly dish after another.

Leung Kwai Lam

There is only one man in Belgium who comes close to emulating the authenticity and versatility of the top Chinese kitchens and that is Leung Kwai Lam, or Tai Lo for friends. This highly gifted chef is truly exceptional, conjuring up one masterly dish after another with apparent serenity. His repertoire and in-depth knowledge reveal an inordinately long period spent studying Chinese cookery and its medicinal uses. He is the type of Chinese chef who has mastered everything, and in one way or another, he reminds me of Mr Chu, the main character in Ang Lee's magnificent film, *Eat Drink Man Woman*. Not just because of the evident mastery he displays, but also because of the gratifying effect this food has on the human organism. *Eat Drink Man Woman* is an apt quote from Confucius' *Book of Rites,* which states that everything a man desires can be found in sexual pleasure, food and drink.

Leung Kwai Lam works his magic every day in the modest restaurant 5 Flavors Mmei in hip South Antwerp. He can count on a crowd of true fans who regard going to this restaurant almost as a pilgrimage to a Chinese temple of food. The Dim Sum here is an absolute must: this is where you'll find the quintessential Dim Sum and it will not fail to impress.

FRIED TOFU

INGREDIENTS

- 400 g tofu
- 1 shiitake
- 5 scampi
- 1 tsp spring onion, finely chopped
- 1 tsp coriander, finely chopped
- 3 egg yolks
- 2 Tbsp. cornflour
- 1 Tbsp. flour
- ½ tsp salt
- pinch of pepper
- 2 Tbsp. oil
- 1 Tbsp. sugar
- 1 tsp chicken powder

METHOD

Dry the tofu with a cloth.

Dice the shiitake and the scampi finely (brunoise). Add them to the spring onion, coriander, egg yolk, cornflour, flour, salt, pepper, oil, sugar and chicken powder. Mix everything very thoroughly in a food processor. Form quenelles using two spoons and fry in oil heated to 150 °C until they are nicely golden.

FRIED MILK DALIANG

●●●○○○

INGREDIENTS

6 Tbsp. whole milk or ·
buffalo milk (about 90 ml)
1 tsp cornflour ·
6 scampi ·
5 eggs ·
½ tsp chicken powder ·
pinch of salt and pepper ·

For the bird's nest
200 g potato threads ·
1 tsp cornflour ·
1 tsp flour ·

To finish
10 g Parma ham ·
(or Chinese dried ham)
1 tsp pine nuts ·

METHOD

Mix the ingredients for the bird's nest and make into equal shapes. Place them in a sieve, place a second sieve over the top and fry them in a deep fat fryer pre-heated to 180 °C until they are crisp.

Bring the milk to the boil and add the cornflour. Cool completely.

Chop the scampi finely and fry.

Separate the eggs and beat the whites. Add them to the milk, together with the chicken powder, salt and pepper. Heat two tablespoons of oil in a wok to a temperature of about 80 to 100 °C. Pour the mixture into the wok and stir gently in the same direction until it is cooked (on a gentle heat). Put the cooked milk into a bird's nest and sprinkle on the ham and the pine nuts.

OYSTER OMELETTE

●●○○○○

INGREDIENTS

15 to 20 oysters ·
1 stick of celery, finely chopped ·
1 Tbsp. coriander, finely chopped ·
1 Tbsp. onion, finely chopped ·
1 tsp garlic, finely chopped ·
5 eggs ·
1 duck egg ·
½ tsp pepper ·
½ tsp salt ·
1 Tbsp. stock ·
½ tsp sugar ·
½ tsp chicken powder ·
1 tsp cornflour ·
3 Tbsp. oil ·
1 spring onion, in julienne strips ·

METHOD

Blanch the oysters for a few seconds and drain.

Stir-fry the celery, coriander, onion and garlic in the wok and add the oysters until they are cooked. Transfer to a plate and set aside.

Beat the eggs, including the duck egg, and add the salt, pepper, stock, sugar, chicken powder and cornflour.

Pour the oil into the wok, followed by the eggs and fry them for a short time. Add the oysters. Form into an omelette and serve. Decorate with spring onion julienne.

FRIED SCRAMBLED EGG WITH JELLY EAR FUNGUS

●●○○○○

INGREDIENTS

10 g Jelly ears, dried ·
5 eggs ·
½ tsp finely chopped onion ·
1 tsp finely chopped spring onion ·
10 g minced pork ·
½ tsp chicken powder ·
½ tsp salt ·
2 Tbsp. chicken stock ·
3 tsp sugar ·
2 Tbsp. dark soy sauce ·
½ tsp cornflour ·
1 tsp sesame oil ·
pinch of pepper ·

METHOD

Soak the Jelly ears in lukewarm water for an hour. Remove the root and slice.

Beat the eggs and fry them, stirring all the time. Set aside.

Fry the onion and the spring onion together in a little oil; add the minced pork. Fry until cooked. Add the chicken powder, salt, chicken stock, sugar and soy sauce. Mix everything together and fry until the liquid has almost evaporated. Add the pepper. Dissolve the cornflour in water and add until everything thickens. Add the sesame oil.

POMEGRANATE CHICKEN

INGREDIENTS

200 g chicken fillet ·
1 Tbsp. onion, finely chopped ·
1 tsp garlic, finely chopped ·
100 g scampi ·
50 g broccoli stalks ·
20 g bamboo shoots ·
20 g carrot ·
10 g straw mushrooms ·
1 Tbsp. sake ·
8 Tbsp. chicken stock ·
1 ½ tsp sugar ·
1 tsp chicken powder ·
1 tsp cornflour ·
pinch of pepper ·
6 chives ·
10 egg whites ·
½ tsp salt ·

METHOD

Dice all the ingredients finely (brunoise). Fry the diced chicken with the onion and garlic until cooked. Add the finely chopped scampi and the vegetables. Pour the sake, the chicken stock, the sugar and the chicken powder over the top. Bring to the boil and thicken with the cornflour. Season with pepper. Set aside for later.

Blanch the chives until they are soft.

Beat the egg whites and add salt and cornflour. Fry one-sixth of this mixture in a frying pan, spreading it out in a very thin layer. Make six of these. Place some filling on each of these thin 'skins', then gather it up as in a pouch and fasten it with a chive. Place the pouches on plates and steam them together for 15 minutes. Pour a little thickened chicken stock over the pouches and serve.

STEAMED MINCED PORK WITH SALTED EGGS

INGREDIENTS

500 g pork blade steak ·
2 tsp sugar ·
1 tsp spring onion, finely chopped ·
½ tsp chicken powder ·
1 tsp finely chopped ginger ·
2 salted eggs ·

Salted eggs
salt ·
water ·
10 eggs ·
1 bottle of sake ·

METHOD

Mince the pork blade steak, preferably quite coarsely so that you get a good bite. Mix the sugar, spring onion, chicken powder and ginger through it and mix thoroughly.

Separate the eggs and reserve.

Spread the minced meat out on a board until about 1 cm thick and press it down. Spread the egg white over the minced meat and help it to soak in. Press the egg yolks flat and spread them over the minced meat. Steam for 15 to 20 minutes then serve.

Salted eggs
Make a 20-percent brine, so mix 1 part salt to 4 parts water. Boil the water to dissolve all the salt. Allow to cool completely.

Wash and dry the eggs.

Place the eggs in the salt solution and pour over the bottle of rice wine. Leave the mixture for 30 to 35 days in a sealed jar to amalgamate. Done!

31

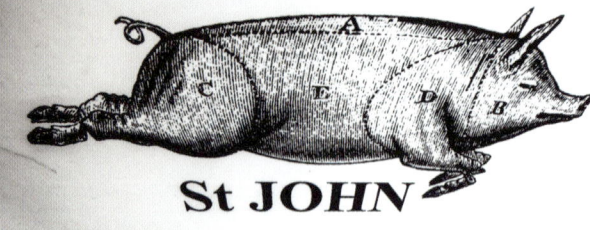

Eccles cake at St John.

BIRDS' NESTS

Who doesn't like eating a bird's nest? Or in other words, a Scotch Egg, as it's called in the UK. The dish was given the name bird's nest because there is of course an egg, large or small, in the middle. Nevertheless, the history of this seemingly simple dish turns out to contain more depth than you might initially think.

The world-famous department store, Fortnum & Mason, claims to have invented it. The dish was presented to the critical public of London for the first time in 1738. The Single Hen Scotch Egg, even then a slightly tongue-in-cheek reference to the Scots' legendary miserliness, was officially launched. Scandalmongers and realists contend that they were inspired by *nargisi kofta*, a centuries-old dish that existed between 1526 and 1857. This 'Narcissus meatball' was prepared by hiding a hard-boiled egg in a deliciously scented and lightly spiced meatball and then simmered in a spicy sauce. The dish became pure British heritage in 1809 when Maria Eliza Ketelby Rundell included the recipe in the second edition of her cookery book, *A New System of Domestic Cookery*. This book is one of the standard works in the UK, and became simply referred to as *Mrs Rundell's*. Her version is one served with the inevitable gravy.

The Scotch Egg has since evolved into the ultimate picnic snack comfort food, and is also an ideal savoury snack to accompany a few rounds of beer.

Humpty Dumpty

Humpty Dumpty sat on a wall,
Humpty Dumpty had a great fall.
All the king's horses, and all the king's men,
Couldn't put Humpty together again.

This imaginary creature saw the light of day in a children's rhyme in 1803 and exactly a century later, this popular figure was given its own black-and-white cartoon, *The Arrival of Humpty Dumpty*. It became an animated cartoon in colour in 1935, and he played a cameo role in the recent film, *Puss 'n Boots*. Somehow or other this little figure is always depicted as an egg in clothes, although its inventor probably never intended it to be so. A Humpty Dumpty is also a name for a small, clumsy person in English-speaking countries. And this is the way Humpty Dumpty appears as a metaphor in songs by Travis and Tori Amos.

Fergus Henderson – St. John

Fergus Henderson is one of the people who has my very deepest culinary admiration. Had I known of him when I was a teenager, I would probably have had a poster of him on my wall. A visit to London isn't complete for me unless I have dropped into St. John at least once and polished off a plate of home-smoked sprats at the bar. The experience is complete when, after a glorious meal in the extremely simple dining room, you sweep up the last crumbs of your Eccles cake and pop them in your mouth.

Back in October 1993, when Trevor Gulliver and Fergus Henderson decided to open a

Ricardo Van Ede, an enfant terrible in Dutch gastronomy.

restaurant, no one had expected – least of all them – that they would be changing the world and would become the face of a generation, of a movement that would sweep through the gastronomic world. Few people get the chance to do such a thing. A building on St John Street in Smithfield had caught Trevor's eye. It had been a smokehouse, a place for growing soya beans and Marxist headquarters in a previous life. It was certainly not an easy space in which to house a restaurant and moreover, it was difficult to spot from the street. There was no budget to create a real interior, but the decision to keep the walls pure white was a conscious one. No distractions! The food must and would be the main focus in this restaurant.

Fergus' food was wild, unconventional and daring right from the start, which led to an impressive number of empty chairs at first. But Fergus's fierce talent and the fact that he stuck to the concept produced a turnaround. Nose-to-tail eating became a reality: the reinvention of traditional, impressive English cuisine and the use of every part, private or otherwise, of the animal in an elegant, controlled method of preparation... the rest is history. The influences of Fergus' philosophy can be seen in a whole generation of chefs.

His concept and first cookery book became a gospel for numerous young and older chefs. Call it bistronomy or gastropub or whatever you like; I call it Fergusfood. One of his greatest merits is that nowhere else in the world, in my experience, do you see beautiful, hip young people tucking into a plate of chitterlings, a pig's trotter or his now legendary roast bone marrow. At St. John people come to absorb Fergus' stylistics in a very elegant setting. Apart from being an institution, St. John is one of the most influential restaurants in the UK whose followers have spread all over the country and beyond to preach 'His Word' in their own restaurants. I had the pleasure of working there myself twice in a holiday week. I met several people there who love eating and that was a breath of fresh air. Fergus wanted to teach us things and wanted particularly to enable his deep-rooted love for 'real food' to live on.

A good illustration of this is his tradition of serving gulls' eggs in May, poached or fried, with a simple garnish that immediately transports you to the beach. He is simply a national treasure!

Ricardo Van Ede

Ricardo Van Ede is an enfant terrible in Dutch gastronomy. He is a striking figure in all senses both in and out of the kitchen. His main claim to fame is that he is the chef who was awarded a Michelin star when he was only 21. That in itself is obviously very remarkable, but let's not reduce the career and merits of this hugely talented man to that single fact.

His cuisine is not just part of the Nouveau Rough movement; it is Nouveau Rough. I have deep admiration for chefs who are able to fully develop an unusual, personal range of ideas and use their food as a sort of style. His kitchen has a traditional look about it and his dishes can best be described as refined rustic with a refreshing lack of creativity. This bohemian puts flavour back on the menu and gives people what they really want: a delicious plate of fabulous food that usually reminds me of traditional dishes in days long past. Ricardo is an excellent chef and utterly reliable.

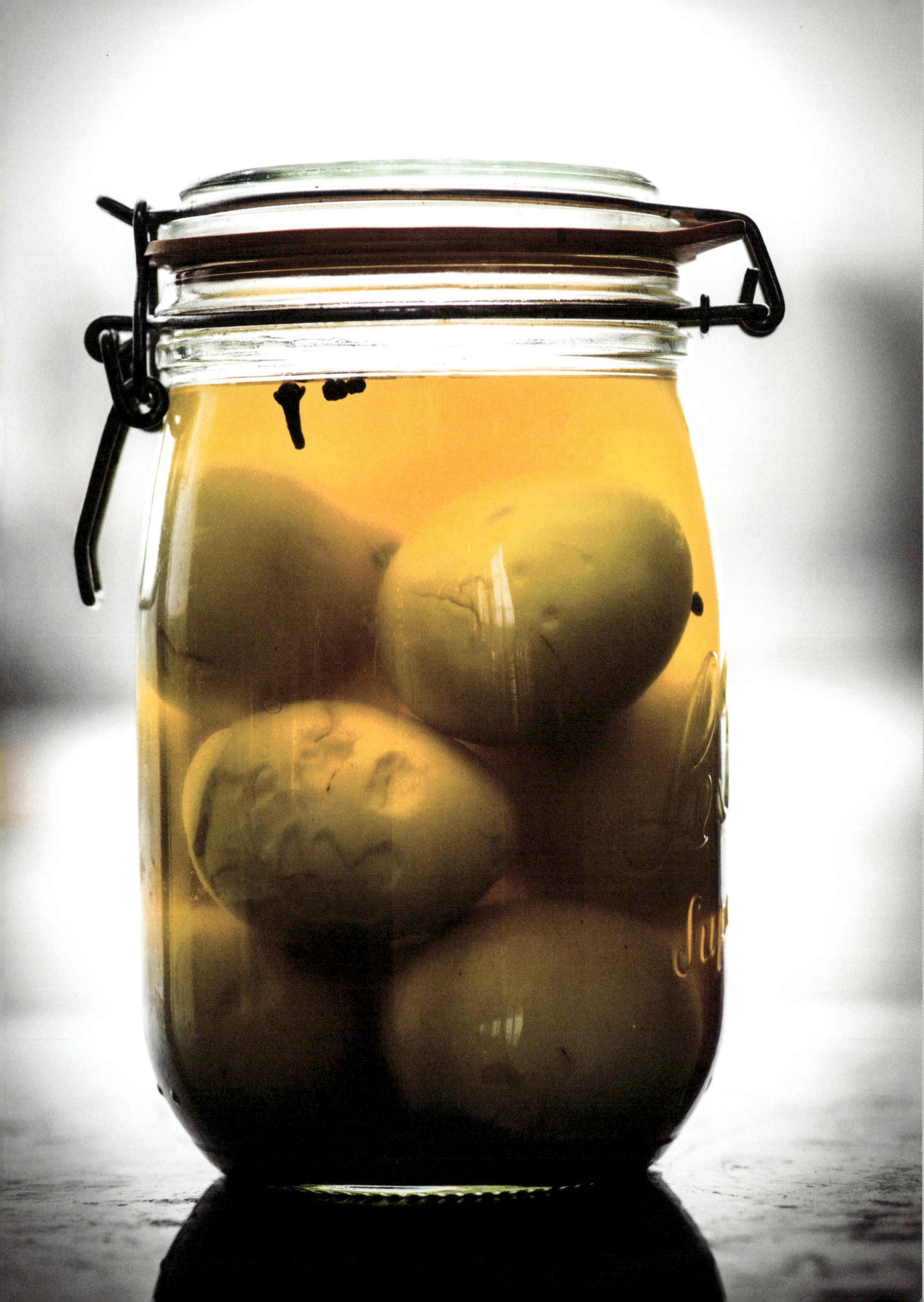

PICKLED EGGS

The ultimate pub snack: easy to eat and delicious as a snack, with cold cuts or a picnic.
Here is a recipe using hen's eggs, but quail's eggs can also be used.

INGREDIENTS

12 hard-boiled eggs

For the pickling liquid
250 ml white wine vinegar or cider vinegar
250 ml water
20 g granulated sugar
5 g salt
1 small dried bay leaf
2 cloves
12 cracked black peppercorns
½ dried chili

METHOD

How to make perfect hard-boiled eggs: place the eggs gently in a pan and pour over some cold water until it is 2 cm above the eggs. Bring to the boil. As soon as the water starts to boil, remove the pan from the heat and cover with a lid. After 12 minutes, drain the eggs under cold running water and peel them immediately.

Place all the ingredients for the pickle liquid in a small pan and bring to the boil. Gently simmer for 10 minutes then pass through a fine sieve or piece of muslin.

Put the eggs in a preserving jar and pour the hot liquid over them. Store in a cool place. Wait for at least two days before eating them.

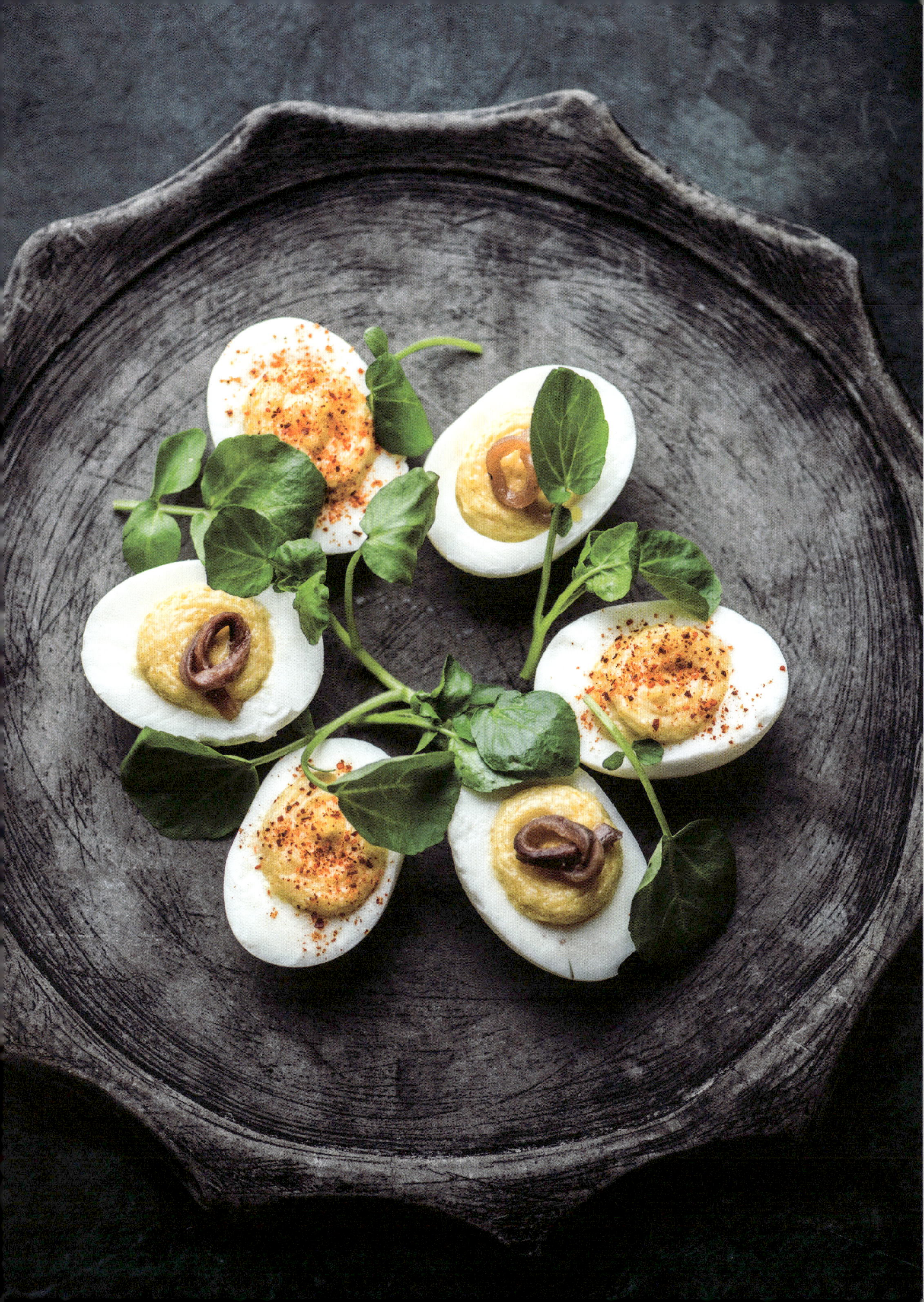

DEVILED EGGS

This dish is better known as 'stuffed eggs'.

●●○○○○

INGREDIENTS

12 hard-boiled eggs or pickled eggs ·
(see recipe on p. 37)
125 ml home-made mayonnaise ·
(if you must buy mayonnaise, go for Amora)
paprika powder, preferably pimentos ·
dulce or piment d'Espelette

METHOD

Cut the eggs in half lengthwise and remove the yolk. Place the yolks in a bowl and gently lay the empty egg whites on a plate. Mash the egg yolks with the mayonnaise and mix until smooth. Fill a piping bag with the egg yolk mixture. Pipe the mixture into the egg whites to fill them. Sprinkle with paprika. It couldn't be easier.

You can of course create endless variations:

- mix in a little grated truffle

- garnish with an anchovy

- sprinkle on some za'atar

- sprinkle on some dried tomato powder

- mix in a few chopped chives

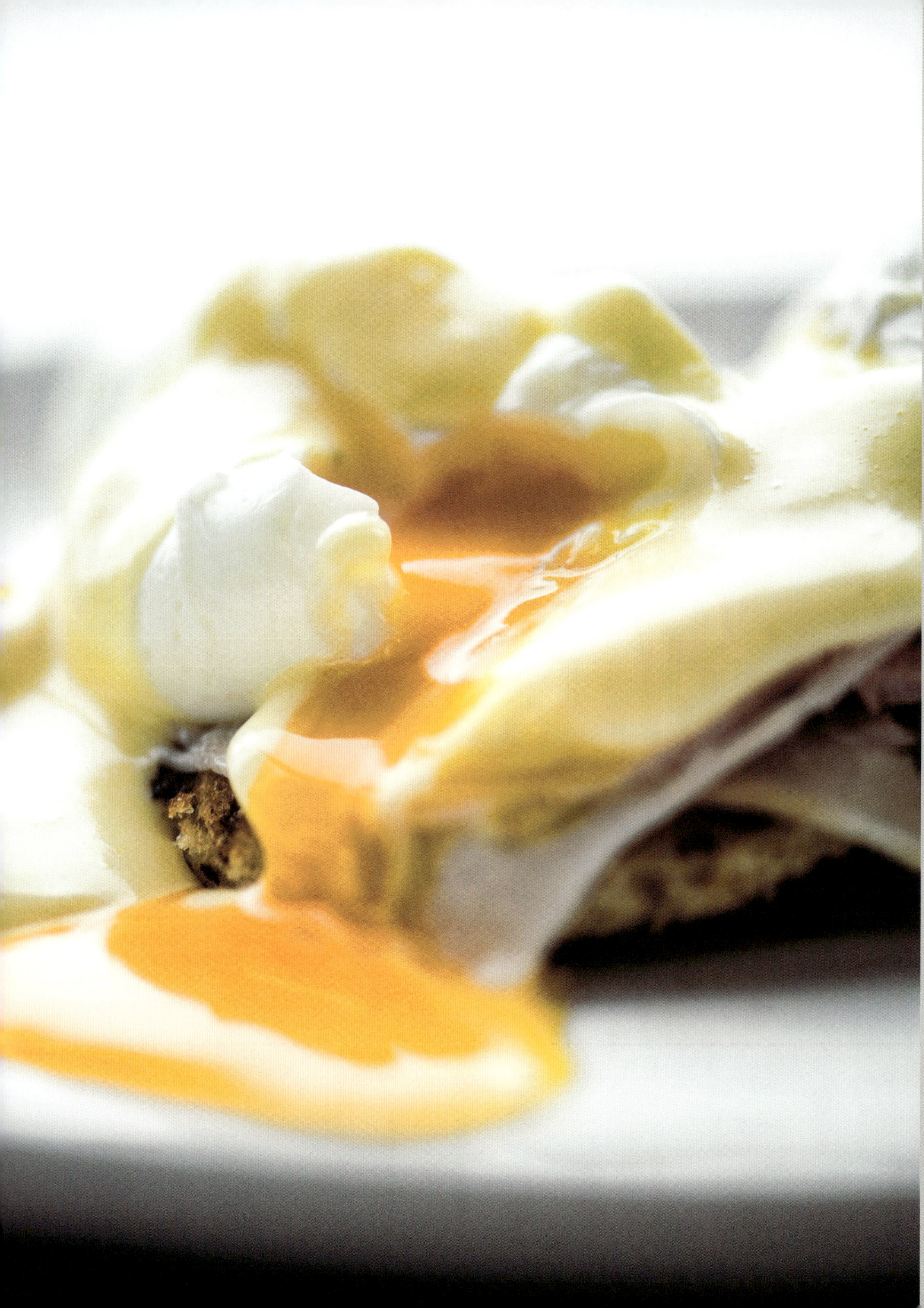

EGGS BENEDICT

●●●●○○

INGREDIENTS

1 English muffin ·
1 large slice of good cooked ham ·
2 poached eggs ·
salt and pepper ·

**For the Hollandaise sauce
(for 6 eggs benedict)**
175 g butter ·
1 Tbsp. white wine vinegar ·
1 Tbsp. water ·
3 egg yolks ·
2 Tbsp. lemon juice ·
salt and pepper ·

METHOD

Hollandaise sauce
Place a heatproof bowl on top of a pan of simmering water. Make sure the bowl does not touch the water, but two-thirds of it needs to be inside the pan. Melt the butter in the bowl then leave it to rest for a moment so that the solids and the water are on the bottom and pour off the butter from them. Keep this warm on a very low heat so that it can't congeal. Pour the vinegar and the water into the bowl and then, beating the mixture all the time, add the egg yolks. Continue to beat as the mixture doubles in size and thickens. Beat until you have a thick, stable mixture (3 to 5 minutes). Remove the bowl from the pan and now, still beating the mixture all the time, add the melted butter in a thin, slow stream. The sauce will thicken to the consistency of mayonnaise. Season to taste with lemon juice, salt and pepper.

Poached eggs
Put a pan of water on the heat and add salt and a good dash of vinegar. Bring to the boil and lower the heat; the water needs to be just below boiling point (simmering very gently). I poach eggs like this: break the eggs into a small cup, hold this cup in the hot water and gradually let the water flow in; you'll see the egg white just starting to set. Carefully turn the cup over so that the egg slides into the water. Poach for 3 to 4 minutes, depending on how you like your eggs. Spoon the egg carefully out of the water and rinse in hot water. Drain it on a cloth or a thick piece of kitchen paper. Everyone has their own way of poaching eggs, and this is mine. It is crucial to use fresh eggs, because the egg white is more stable and ensures that the egg stays together.

Eggs Benedict
Cut open the muffin and toast it; lay the ham on the muffin and place the poached eggs on top. Cover the eggs with the Hollandaise sauce. You can vary this dish to your heart's content: try it with bacon or smoked salmon instead of ham. Or something completely different, as long as it tastes good. It's very easy to make this a vegetarian dish too. Instead of ham, use two large grilled mushroom caps (the eggs fit perfectly inside them), or a fried tomato.

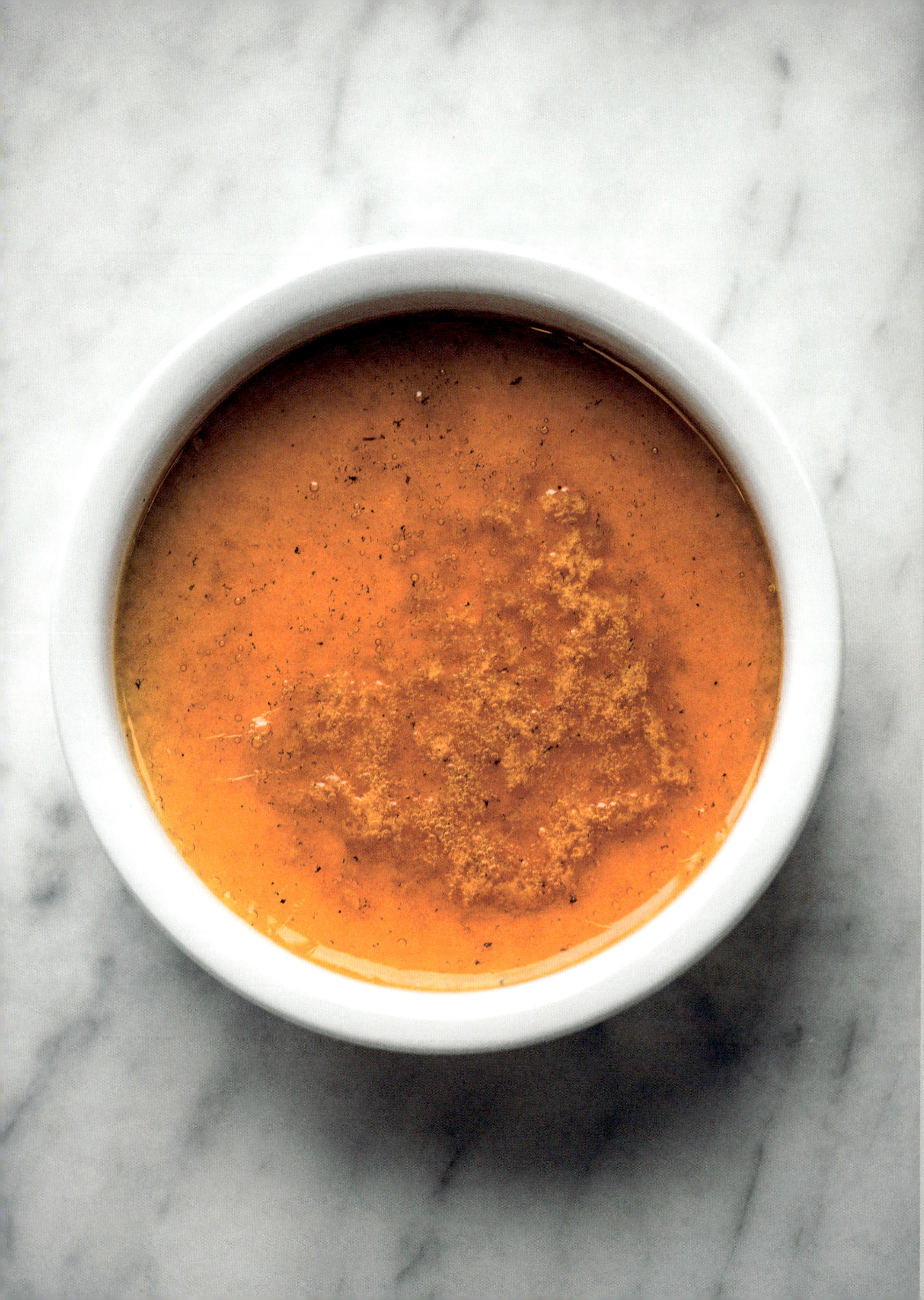

CRÈME CARAMEL

●●●●○○

INGREDIENTS

4 200-ml ramekins or metal moulds ·

For the caramel
175 g granulated sugar or demerara sugar ·
2 to 3 Tbsp. hot water ·

For the crème/custard
150 ml milk ·
275 ml cream ·
4 large eggs ·
40 g light brown caster sugar ·
a few drops of vanilla extract ·

METHOD

Caramel
Put the sugar in a pan over a medium heat. Make sure that no sugar is left sticking to the edge of the pan. Slowly dissolve the sugar, without stirring. After about eight minutes, shake the pan gently to even the sugar out. Let it dissolve some more. As soon as the sugar begins to change colour, start stirring it gently with a wooden spoon. Let it caramelise to a dark copper colour. Remove the pan from the heat and add the spoonfuls of water. Be careful, it might spit. Put the pan back on the heat and stir to remove any lumps that may have formed. Pour the caramel into the base of the moulds. The easiest way to clean the pan is to fill it with water and bring it to the boil.

Custard
Pre-heat the oven to 150 °C. Put the milk and the cream into a pan and gently bring to the boil. Meanwhile, whisk the eggs with the sugar and the vanilla extract in a medium-sized bowl. Pour the hot milk and cream onto the egg mixture, stirring all the time. Stir well. Strain through a fine sieve onto the caramel in the moulds.

Place the moulds in a small roasting tin and pour hot water into the tin halfway up the ramekins. Cover the whole lot with tinfoil and place in the pre-heated oven. After half an hour, lift the tinfoil and give the tin a little shake. If the tops are set and no longer runny, the custard will be cooked.

Chill the custard in the fridge for at least an hour. To remove the custards from the moulds, run a knife around the edge to loosen them. Turn the moulds upside down over a plate and shake gently until they loosen.

Serve with lightly whipped cream.

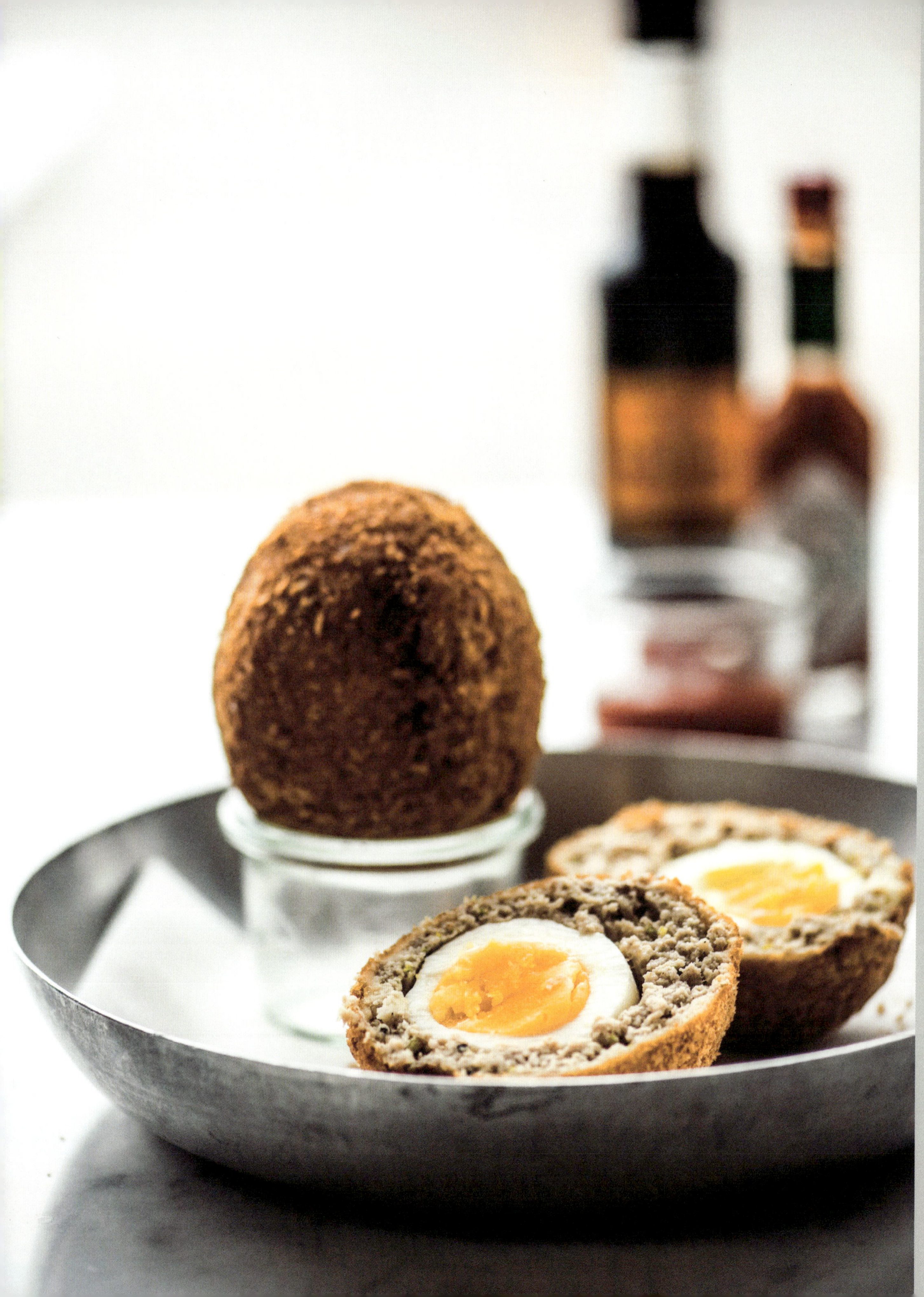

SCOTCH EGGS

●○○○○○

INGREDIENTS

6 eggs ·
200 g sausage meat; *(ask your* ·
butcher or squeeze the meat
out of a few good fresh sausages)
200 g minced pork ·
3 Tbsp. freshly chopped garden herbs ·
pinch of freshly grated nutneg ·
1 Tbsp. English mustard ·
1 Tbsp. milk ·
50 g flour ·
100 g panko, Japanese breadcrumbs ·
sunflower oil ·

METHOD

Place four whole eggs in a saucepan, cover with cold water so that the eggs are 2 cm below the water level and bring to the boil. Turn down the heat as soon as the water starts to boil and boil for 5 minutes. Plunge the eggs into ice water for 10 minutes. Peel the eggs.

Put the sausage meat, minced pork, herbs, nutmeg and mustard in a bowl and mix well. Divide into four equal parts and place each on a sheet of cling film. Flatten the meat mixture a little and then place a hard-boiled egg on each. Fold the cling film over and gently twist it tightly so that the meat mixture completely covers the egg. Do the same for each egg. Remove the cling film.

Now crack the two leftover eggs into a bowl and whisk them with the milk. Put the flour in another bowl, and the panko in a third bowl. Dredge the sausage meat parcels with the flour first, tapping off any excess flour. Dip them in the egg next and then lastly cover them in panko. Dip them once again in the egg mixture and the panko.

Fill a deep frying pan with oil and deep-fry the Scotch eggs for a few minutes at 170 °C until they are golden. Drain on kitchen paper.

Scotch eggs can be eaten hot or cold.

JAPAN

→ Okonomiyaki

TAMAGOKAKE GOHAN
MMM RAW EGGS

Japanese people eat a lot of eggs. Globally, Japan has featured regularly in the top ten in recent decades when it comes to the number of eggs per capita and in the top three in recent years. Other countries where hens have to work overtime to satisfy demand are Paraguay, Guatemala and China. Japanese people eat an average of 320 eggs a year and the most popular egg dishes are *tamagokake gohan,* a raw egg on hot rice and the obligatory soy sauce, the *omurice* or an omelette filled with rice and of course, the *chawanmushi,* a steamed savoury custard.

This has not always been the case. When chickens were introduced into Japan from China via Korea, their eggs were more usually used as sacred offerings and for medicinal purposes. To make matters worse, the consumption of eggs was forbidden from the 14th century, due to the tightening of certain Buddhist rules. Things lightened up again for egg lovers from the Edo period (1603-1867) but egg consumption only gradually gained momentum.

After the Second World War, the Japanese began eating more protein and calcium to recover from the severe public health damage the war had inflicted. The government encouraged the population to eat more eggs. By the 1960s eggs were to be found in every Japanese store cupboard. '*Kyojin, taiho, tamago-yaki*' became a well-known chant containing the three most popular things for children in the 1960s and 1970s: *Kyojin* is the celebrated baseball team (the Yomiuri Giants), *Taiho* was a popular sumo champion and *tamago-yaki* the famous egg dish that was found in every bento box. Nowhere else are so many raw eggs eaten as in Japan. That is why the checks on raw eggs are so stringent in the land of the rising sun. There is a period of 16 days in the summer and 57 days in the winter when raw eggs can be eaten safely. At other times they need to be cooked...

Apart from the *tamagokake gohan*, raw eggs are also used as a dip for sukiyaki, with curried rice, mixed with *natto,* and nowadays you can also buy *onsen tamago* in specialist shops, which is also used in the *nitamago* as a very soft egg in noodle soup.

Hinamatsuri

Japan celebrates Girls Day on 3 March every year: an ancient tradition very important to the Japanese. A meticulous arrangement of ornamental dolls is displayed on several levels in people's houses. The dolls are usually shown wearing the traditional court dress from the Heian period (794-1185). The emperor, empress, ladies-in-waiting and musicians figure on various levels. Girls are given egg-dolls in which a wish for the future has been hidden. Usually the egg wishes them a good marriage.

You can't even fry an egg

If you say to someone that they can't even fry an egg, that's a bit rude. But it wouldn't be an insult in Japan because it is extremely difficult to make *tamago-yaki*. Just ask Daisuke Nakazawa who runs one of the best sushi bars in New York City. He started as a pupil of the legendary Jiro Ono in his meticulous restaurant Sukiyabashi Jiro. 'Can I come and work here?' the young Nakazawa asked humbly. 'Make me an omelette,' Ono commanded. Nakazawa began and was ordered to stop after a few minutes. 'May I come back tomorrow?' Nakazawa begged. And so Nakazawa returned every day for 178 days until Jiro considered his egg good enough to enable him to start working as an apprentice in his restaurant. After an apprenticeship lasting 16 years, he began his own sushi bar in NY. Far too soon, in Jiro's opinion. His omelette is still a signature dish.

Making a *tamago-yaki* or *dashimaki* is a complex sequence of actions and precision work. It starts with the recipe: the right proportion of ingredients has to be added to the eggs. Every version is different. After that, the idea is to construct the omelette in wafer-thin layers which are rolled together to make a sort of scroll. All this takes place in a characteristic square pan, a *makiyakinabe*.

Gudetama

Gudetama literally means 'extremely lazy egg' *(gude gude means lazy in Japanese)*. It refers to a grumpy egg that clearly popped out of its shell on the wrong side. It's always complaining and whining and is the main character in the latest animation series from Sanrio, who invented Hello Kitty. Sanrio is obviously a master in inventing little characters that find a place in the hearts of millions of kids and even adults. His catch phrases are an invitation for personifying the Millennials: *Pah, Ugh, Meh,*

Leave me Alone, I can't, Seriously I can't... Gudetama became iconic when he pulled his blanket, a strip of bacon, up to his chin while mumbling: *'Five more minutes'*.
But why an egg? It's partly because food is important in the Japanese culture. Eggs were, and moreover are, very trendy. Egg-shaped patterns are starting to be found everywhere, especially in the avant-garde districts where fashion rules, such as Harajuku. Japanese fashion has always explored the boundaries, such as the Gothic Lolitas, Mori Girls (forest girls) and Ganguro in which make-up is applied in extreme ways. Food has recently been cropping up more and more in fashion, particularly set in motion by the *kimokawaii* trend.
Gudetama isn't the first character to come from food. His most immediate rival is Bananya, a little figure that, bizarrely, looks like a cat in a banana skin. *Shokugeki no Soma* is a popular series depicting a Harry Potter-like school for competitive cooking. The central character in *Wakakozake* is a woman who simply likes going out to eat. That's all.
Even before Gudetama there were characters based on food. There is AnPanMan, for instance, whose head is made of *anpan,* bread made from red beans. His catch phrase is *Eat My Face.* Gudetama and his friends Uncle Jam and Cheese are increasingly being cited as cultural references when referring to Japan.
Gudetama seems to be the anti-hero Japan needs, a creature who appears to be subliminally shouting: 'Whatever you do, don't be like this egg, like this character'.

Dimitri Proost

I am the first to admit that to become a fully-qualified Japanese chef, you need to invest a lot of time and acquire a huge amount of knowledge. A case in point is the son of Jiro Ono, who only received his father's blessing to stand on his own two feet after an apprenticeship lasting 40 years, and his chief apprentice, Nakazawa, was only considered good enough to start his own restaurant in NYC after 18 years. And yet there are some young chefs who seem to be the reincarnation of an ancient Japanese soul. I felt a little like that when I landed in Japan for the first time. Everyone I was with found it strange but I felt completely at home. It seems to be the same with Dimitri Proost, who would seem to possess much more Japanese blood and soul than you would think at first sight.
At the age of only 22, he has already worked at Hakkasan, Yamazato, Zuma and 't Fornuis: A very impressive record for such a young guy. Leaving Terwijl and Hakkasan waving contracts at him, he opened Dim, a tiny restaurant seating only 16 in the historic centre of Antwerp, where, with a little imagination, you could conceivably be in a diminutive *izakaya* in a nameless street in Minato-ku.
I would describe his take on Japanese food as modern Japanese with a western twist. Sometimes it tastes as if I were in the überhip Zuma in London and sometimes as if I were in Muromachi Wakuden, a classic bastion in Kyoto, because his food is bursting with tradition. In any case, he can make sushi like no one else and he leaves nothing

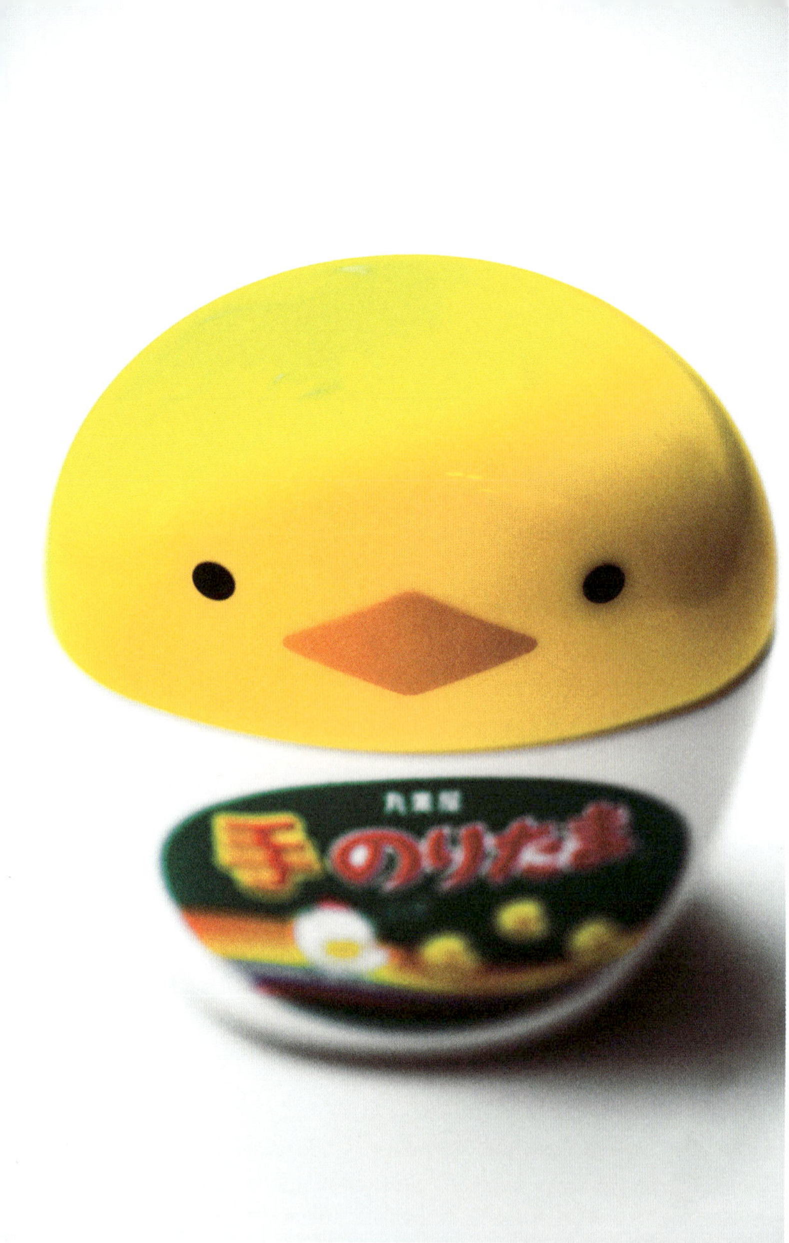
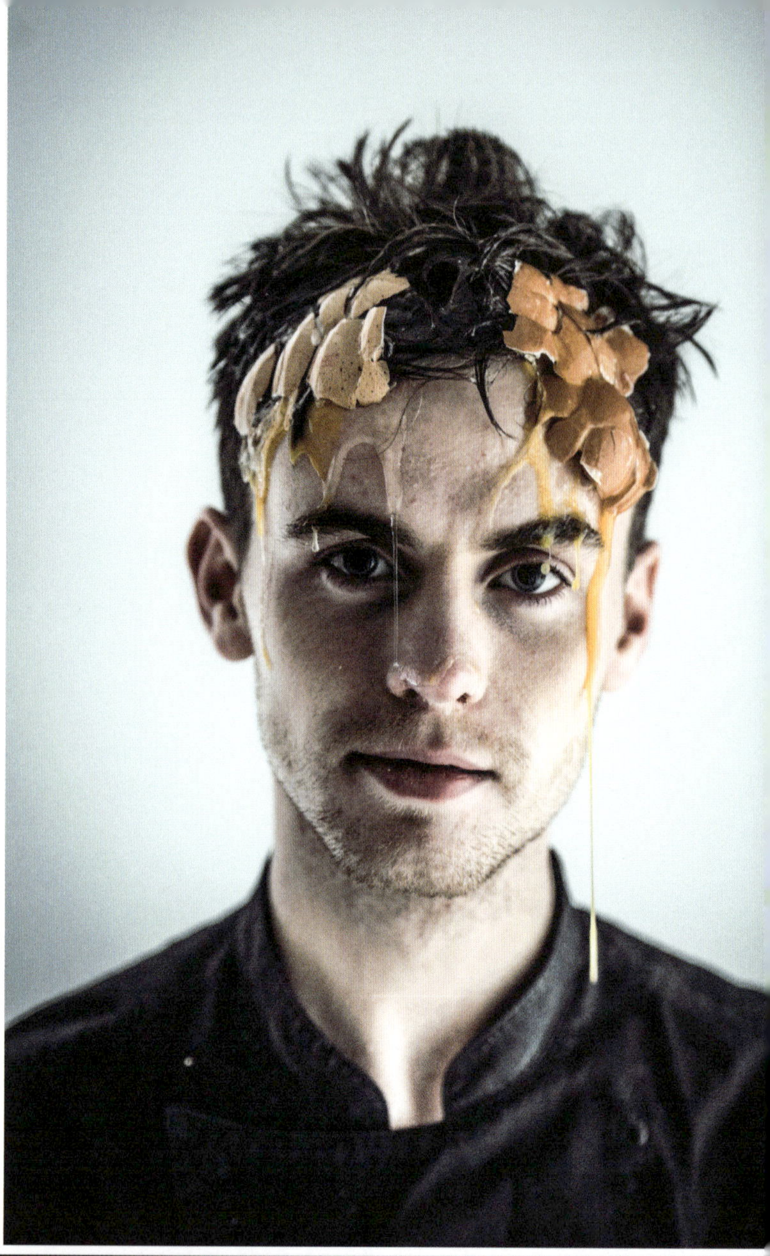
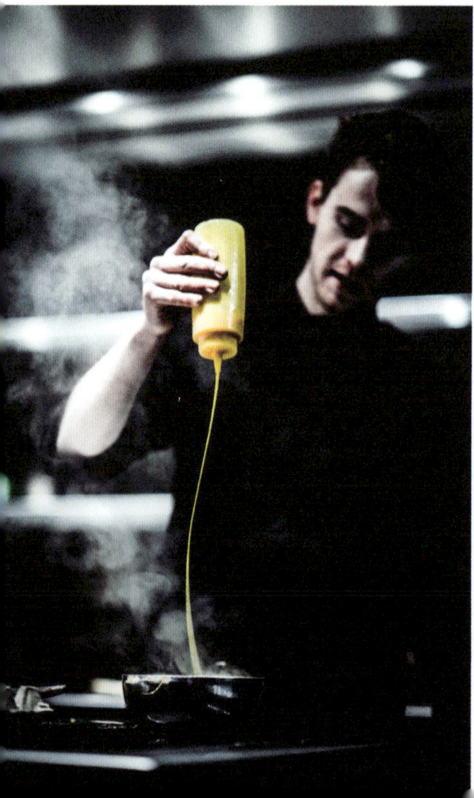
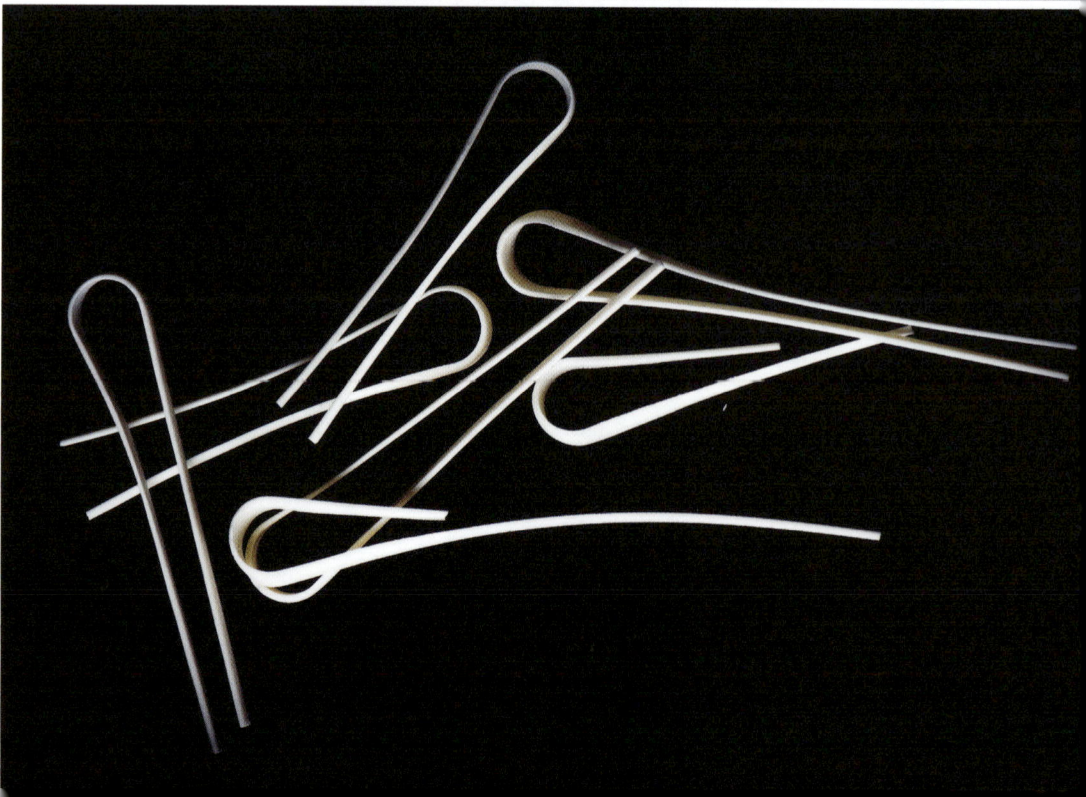

→ Dimitri Proost, a class act with a traditional knife of pure tamahagane, who has the focus and dedication of an old Japanese chef.

to chance, which is as it should be. And in doing so, if you ask me, he is continually setting new standards for food in Belgium.

A class act with a traditional knife made from pure *tamahagane,* he creates carefully-considered fundamental dishes with the focus and dedication of an old Japanese chef. Many colleagues of his age become caught up in current trends and cook as if everything is a competition: who can put the most on a plate or who is best at incorporating the most effects on a single plate to produce haphazard dissonance. Dimitri's food is exactly the opposite; it is pure and his plates tell entire stories that need very few words..

An egg from a hot spring, the onsen tamago

An *onsen* is unknown territory for many visitors to Japan because it is so typical to Japan that you can make many cultural mistakes. A visit to an *onsen* is a combination of strict and peculiar etiquette, added to the fact that most onsen are mixed and involve nudity. And don't forget the temperature of the water which is usually higher than that in an average western Jacuzzi. But don't be put off: a visit to an *onsen* is one of the things you must do when you visit Japan. Bathing in a natural hot water spring has an immensely invigorating and fortifying effect on your body and soul. It usually takes place in a very beautiful setting, and is one of the most relaxing experiences there is. All onsen waters are different, given the variations in soil structure, but they all have healing properties.

Long before cookery scientists like Harold McGee and Hervé This provided us with a better and deeper understanding of the complex chemical processes in everyday practices such as cooking an egg, the Japanese had their *onsen tamago* 温泉卵. This fits in perfectly with the characteristic food experience that usually accompanies an onsen which is of course based on extending your healthy experience at the table. An *onsen tamago* involves placing eggs in nets into the baths at a temperature of about 70 °C for about 30 to 40 minutes. The result is an egg with a unique texture in which the egg white gets a soft and delicate milky custard feel and flavour. The egg yolk is firm and tastes cooked but it retains the texture of an uncooked yolk. In an *onsen,* it is usually served in a bowl with dashi bouillon or in a light sauce of dashi mixed with mirin and soy sauce, to which chopped spring onions have been added.

If you are served this at breakfast in Japan, you're bound to enjoy the rest of the day.

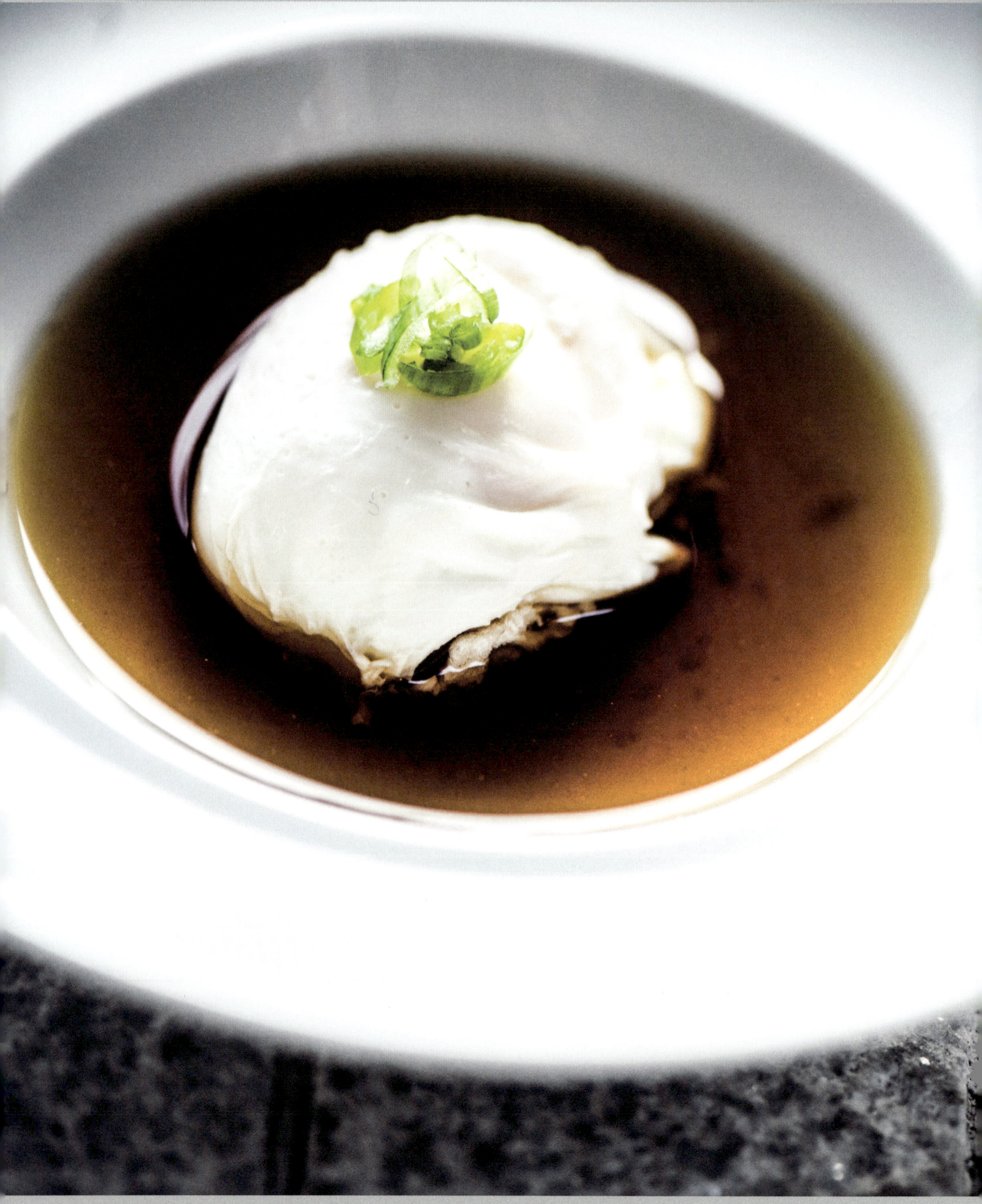

ONSEN TAMAGO

●●●●○○

INGREDIENTS

200 ml dashi stock ·
1 Tbsp. soy sauce ·
1 Tbsp. mirin ·
1 Tbsp. sake ·
spring onion ·
1 egg at room temperature ·

METHOD

Make the stock by adding all the ingredients apart from the egg to the dashi stock.

Poach the egg in water with a dash of vinegar, or in a vacuum bag for 35 minutes at 62 degrees. Pat the egg dry and pour the stock over it.

Garnish with some spring onion.

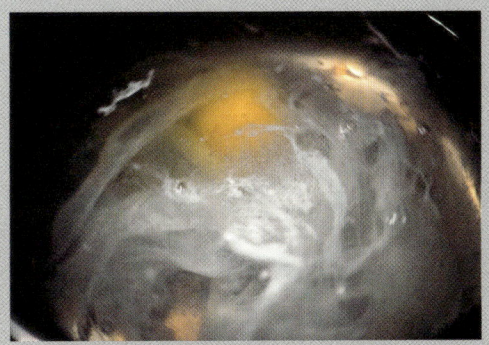

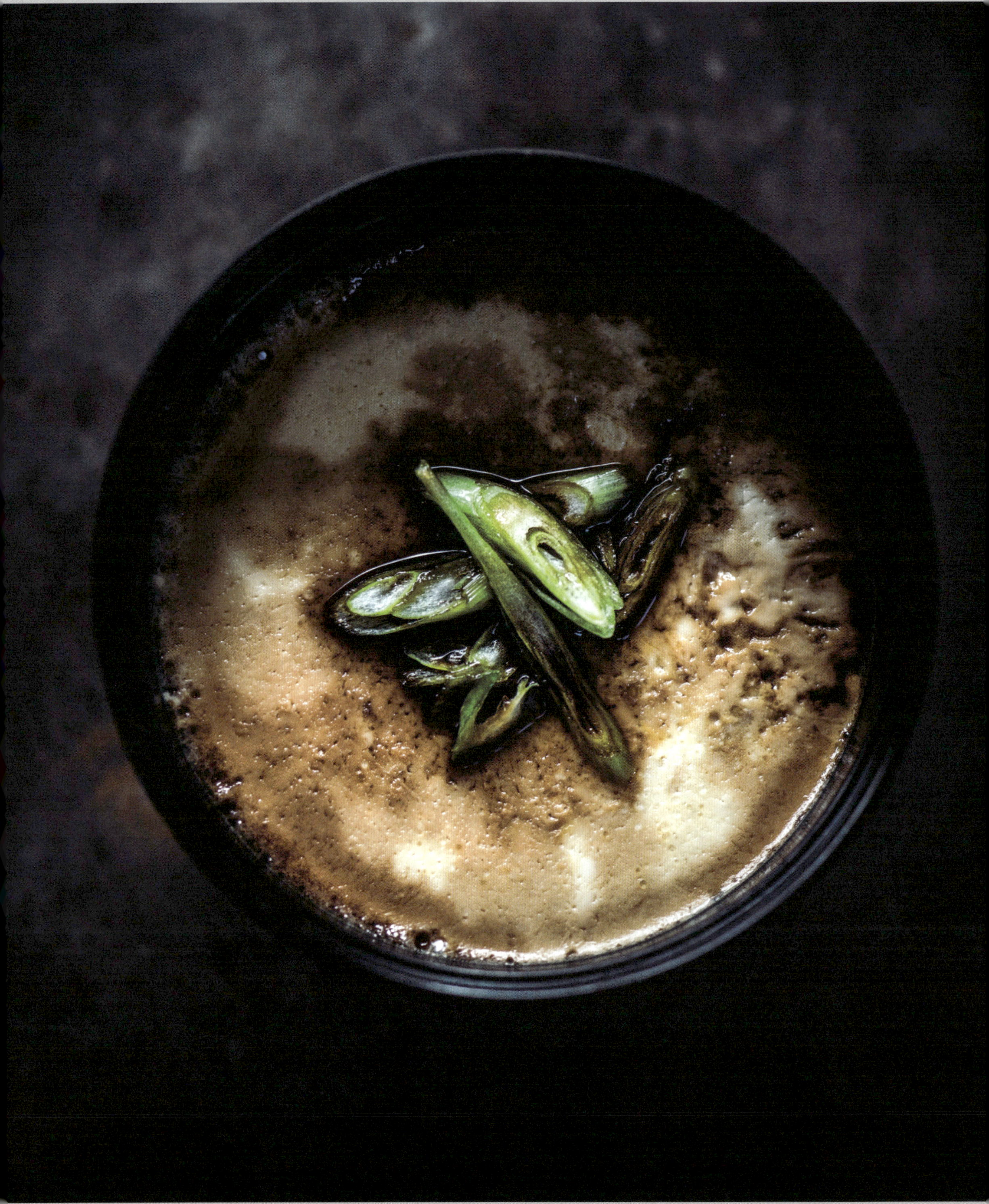

CHAWAN MUSHI

●●●●○○

INGREDIENTS

3 eggs ·
250 ml dashi stock ·
1 Tbsp. sake ·
1 Tbsp. soy sauce ·
100 g kamaboko ·
1 boneless chicken breast ·
shiitake ·

METHOD

Beat the eggs using two chopsticks.

Mix the cold dashi stock with the eggs, the sake and the soy sauce. Mix in the kamaboko. Push through a fine sieve. Cut the chicken breast into cubes and fry with the shiitake. Place some of this mixture into small bowls. Pour the egg mixture on top. Cover with cling film.

Steam in a steamer for about 15 minutes.

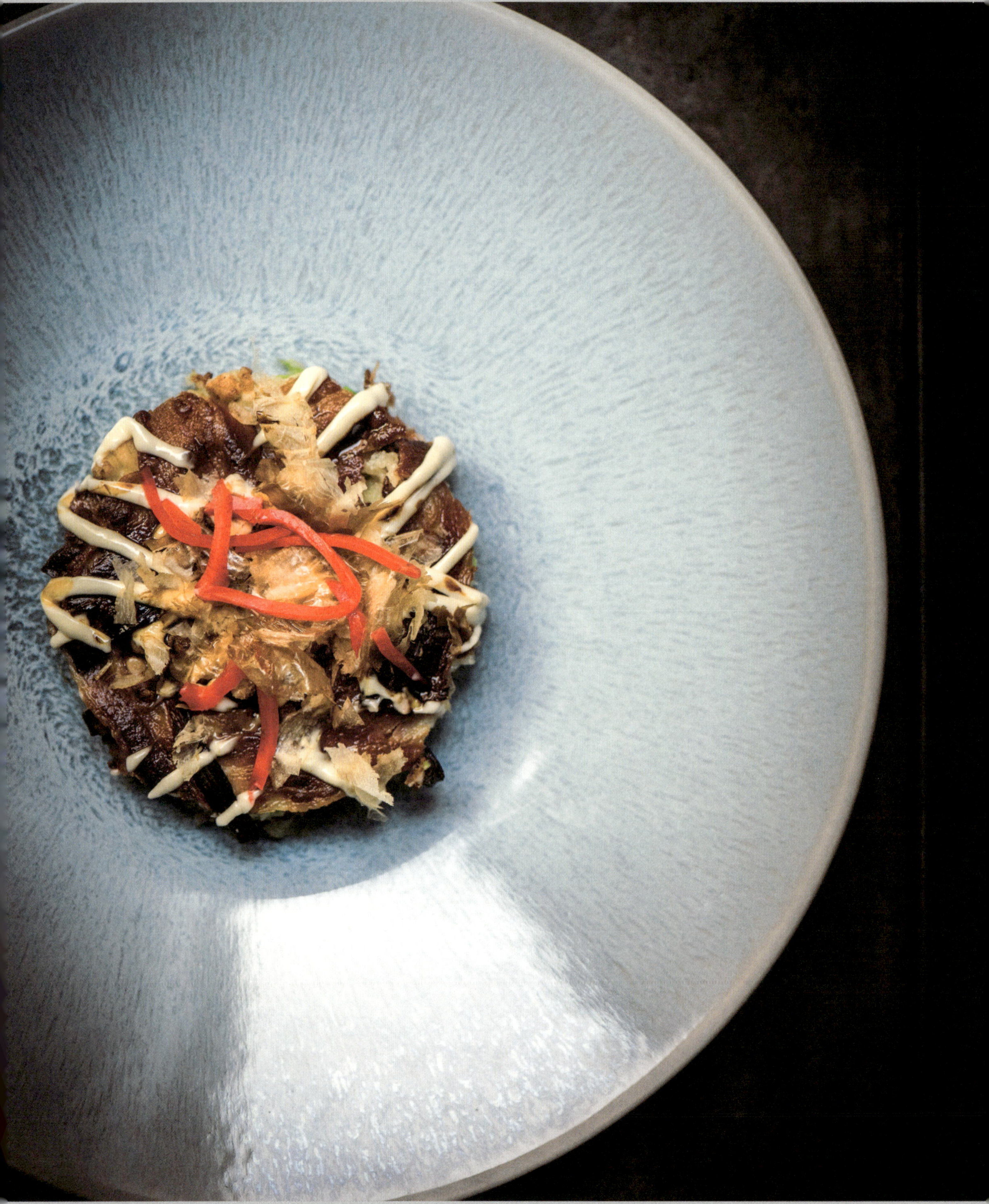

OKONOMIYAKI

●●●○○○

INGREDIENTS

150 g flour ·
2 tsp baking powder ·
140 ml cold dashi stock ·
4 Tbsp. sake ·
1 Tbsp. mirin ·
1 Tbsp. soy sauce ·
100 g grated yamaimo ·
500 g oxheart cabbage, ·
finely chopped
4 eggs ·
thin strips of smoky bacon ·

To finish
Japanese ketchup and mayonnaise ·
Bonito flakes ·

METHOD

Sieve the flour with the baking powder into a mixing bowl. Stir in the dashi stock, sake, mirin and soy sauce. Stir in the yamaimo. Leave in a cool place to rest for two hours.

Heat the teppanyaki grill or an ordinary pan. Grease a little with oil.

Mix some dough, cabbage and egg in four small bowls. Stir. Turn the bowls out onto the teppanyaki grill and flatten them a little. Cover the top with strips of bacon. Turn them over and grill the okonomiyaki on both sides until brown and cooked. Cook them a bit more in the oven if you wish.

Finish them off with okonomiyaki sauce and bonito flakes.

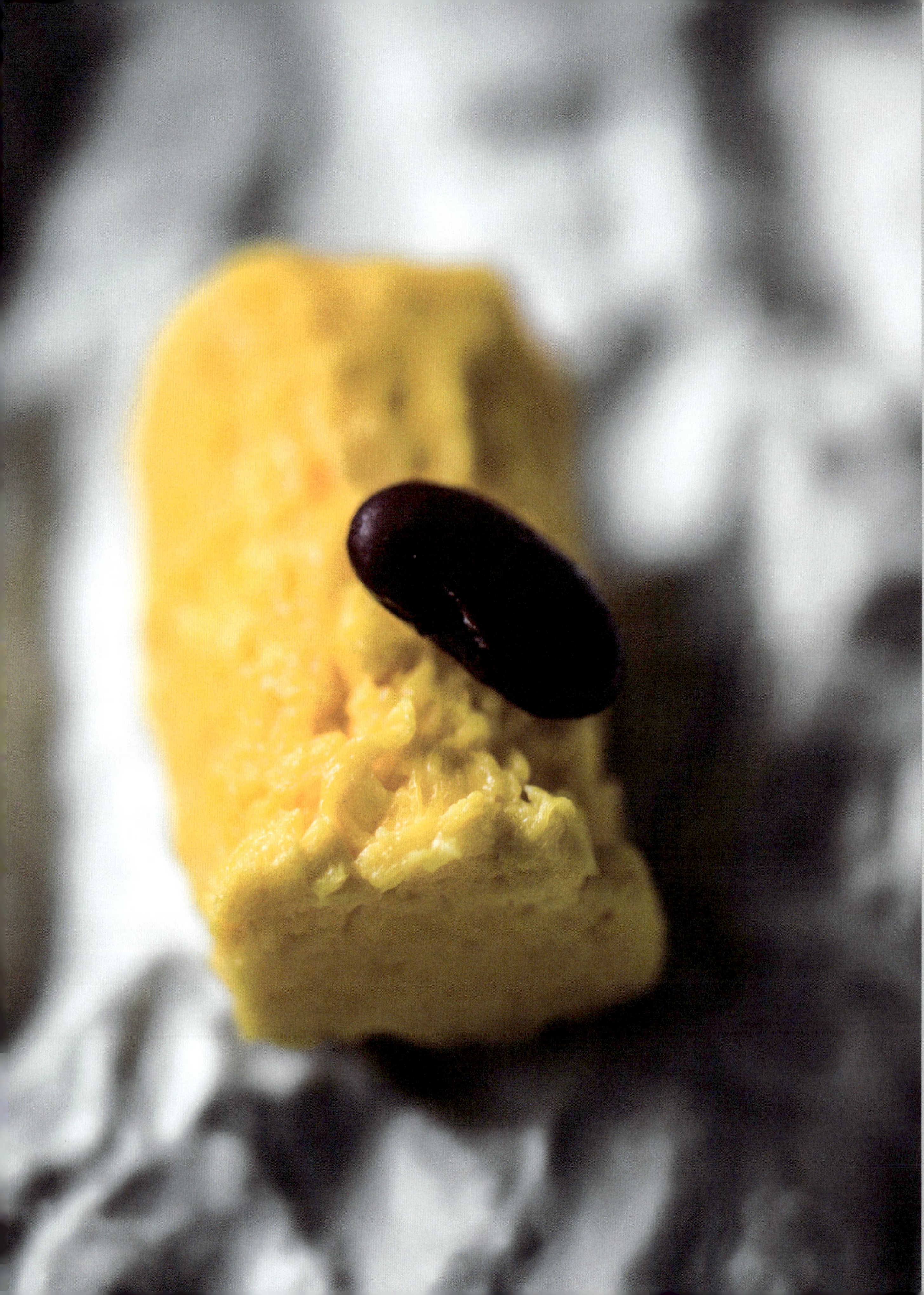

TAMAGO SOMEN

●●●○○○

INGREDIENTS

2 kg sugar ·
500 g mizuame ·
2 egg whites ·
2 litres of water ·
10 egg yolks ·

METHOD

Start by making the syrup by putting all the ingredients except the egg yolks in a pan and boiling them for about 30 minutes.

Push the egg yolks through a fine sieve and pour this mixture into a forcing bag. Using nice circular movements, squeeze the egg mixture into the syrup. Remove the egg mixture from the syrup using bamboo chopsticks and squeeze them into round shapes in a bamboo mat.

Finish off with azuki beans if you like.

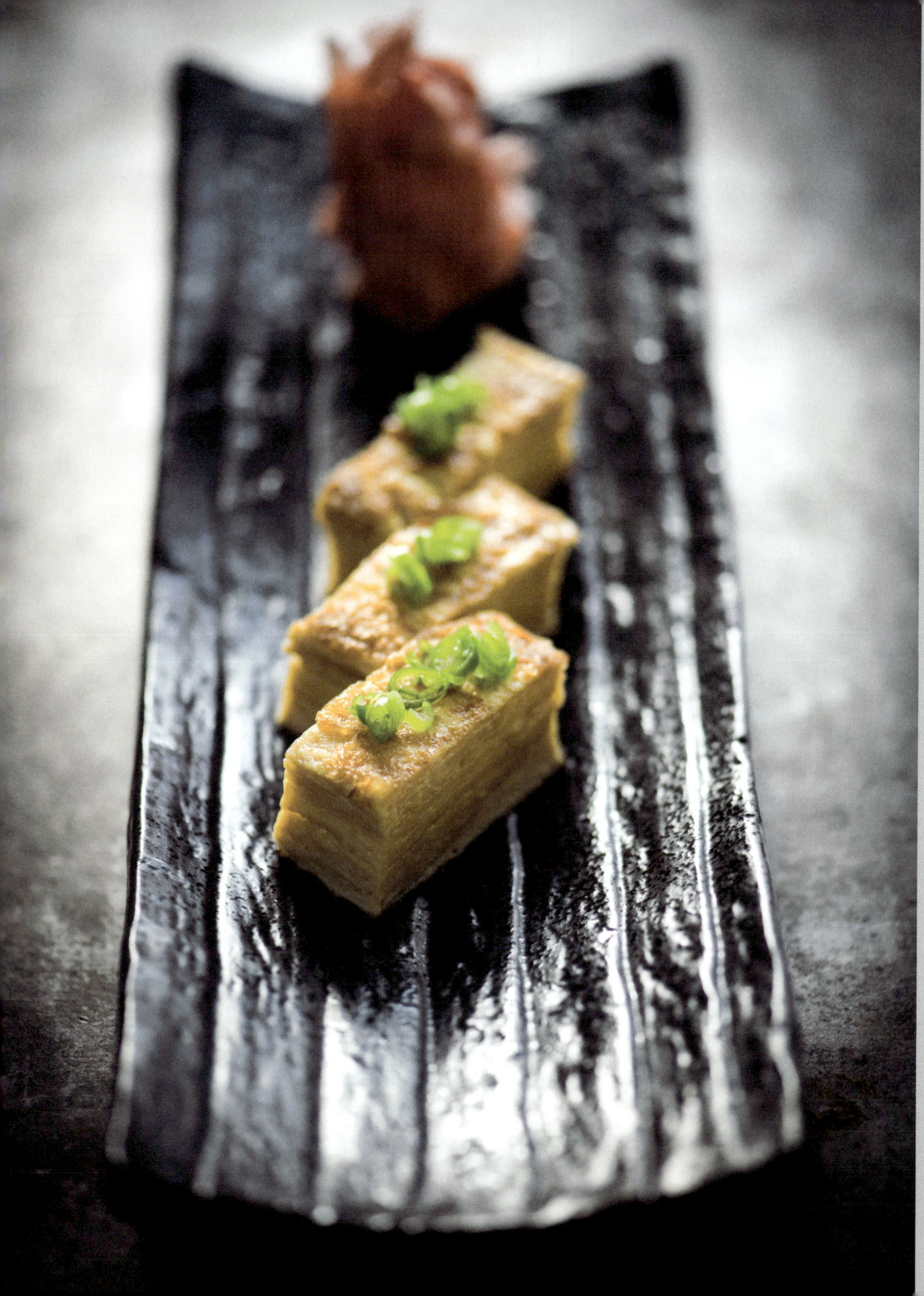

TAMAGO DASHI

INGREDIENTS

50 ml water ·
2.5 ml soy sauce ·
1 Tbsp. dashi powder ·
2 Tbsp. sugar ·
5 eggs ·

METHOD

Boil the water with the soy sauce, dashi powder and sugar. Leave to cool. Mix with the eggs.

Cook the egg mixture in a kotobuki pan, layer by layer, using a little oil. The inside mustn't brown, but the outside can.

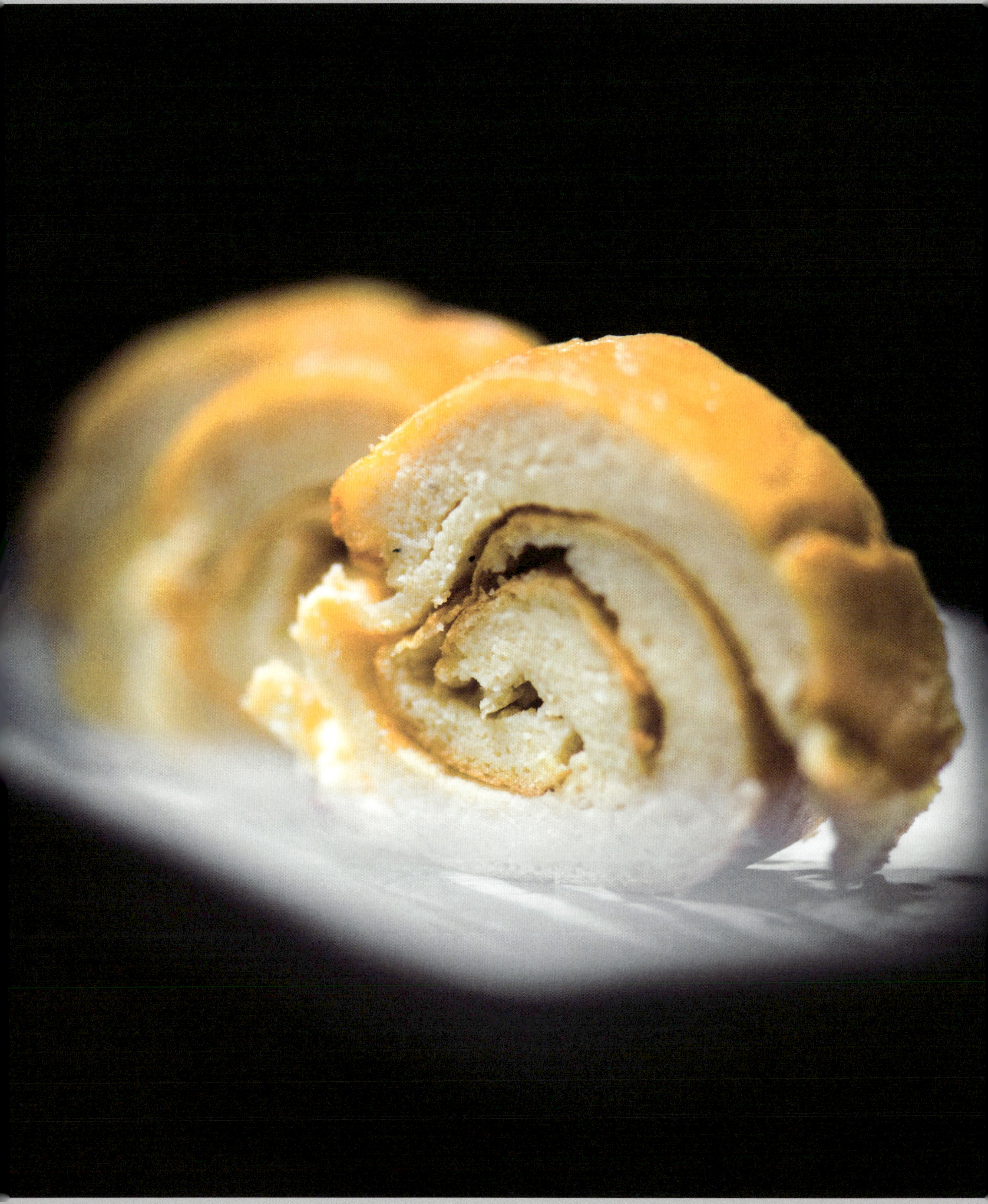

DATEMAKI

●●●○○○

INGREDIENTS

100 g hanpen ·
4 eggs ·
2 Tbsp. mirin ·
2 Tbsp. sake ·
1 tsp sugar ·
1 tsp soy sauce ·

METHOD

Mix all the ingredients in a blender. Bake in the oven in a square tin, roughly 20 x 20 cm, for about 20 minutes at 200 °C.

Roll the cake up while it is still warm using bamboo mats; press down firmly and allow to cool.

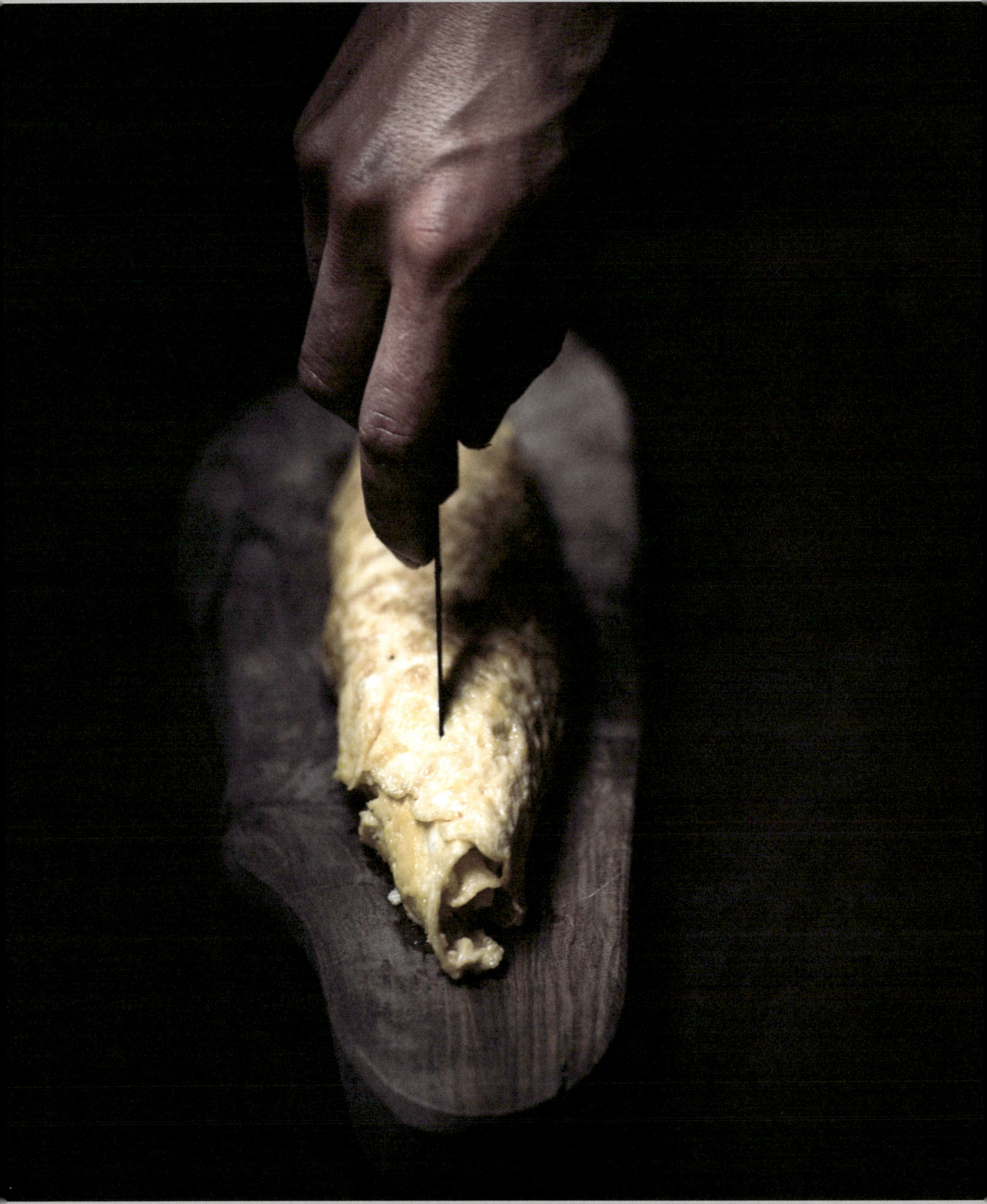

OMURICE

●●●●●○

INGREDIENTS

100 g boneless chicken thighs, diced ·
salt and pepper to taste ·
4 Tbsp. ketchup ·
1 tsp soy sauce ·
1 tsp sugar ·
1 Tbsp. finely chopped onion ·
2 Tbsp. finely chopped mushrooms ·
a few spoonfuls of cooked rice ·
4 eggs, lightly beaten ·
milk ·
1 tsp Japanese mayonnaise ·

METHOD

Season the chicken with salt and pepper.

Mix the ketchup, soy sauce and sugar in a bowl.

Fry the onion in some oil in a pan then add the mushrooms. Add the rice and the ketchup mixture. Mix. Stir everything well and remove from the heat.

Whisk the eggs, milk and mayonnaise in a bowl. Heat the oil in a pan and fry the omelette in several phases so that the inside remains 'baveuse': slightly runny. Roll the omelette over and over repeatedly to make a sort of cigar shape and keep turning it. Arrange the rice on a plate and place the omelette on top; slice it open so that the omelette unfolds completely.

KOREA

66

Kimchee, a typical Korean dish.

KOREA

Korea, or *Uri-nara* as it is called in Korea, is a country with a very rich gastronomic culture. Incidentally, the western name Korea is an exonym of *Goryeo*, the 10th-century dynasty. The Dutchman, Hendrick Hamel (1630-1692), a shipwrecked sailor who lived in Korea for 13 years, introduced the name and spelling of Korea. Koreans who live in the south call their country *Hanguk;* South Koreans use *Bukhan* when they are talking about North Korea, while North Koreans call their country *Joseon*. They both use *Uri Nara,* which means 'our country'.

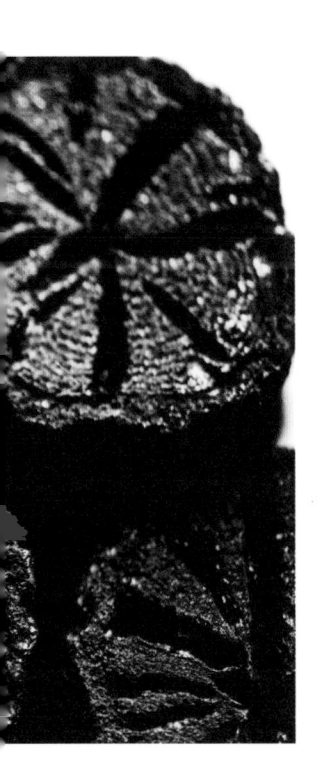

The *Samguk Yusa* tells us that King Suro, like Brahma, was born from a golden egg. Koreans and Indians are two completely different peoples, but there are a striking number of similarities in their earliest mythology and creation stories. Both the Kaya kings and Brahma were called into being by means of the golden egg metaphor. The *Karak Kukki* chapter is completely devoted to the miraculous birth of King Suro and five other Kaya kings from six golden eggs which were dangled down from the heavens in a golden basket attached to a purple rope. This detailed description makes the metaphor of the golden eggs even clearer. There is also a bull made of solid gold in the Pagoda of Miaco – in Japan in other words. The regally clothed animal is using its horns to push an egg that is floating on the water. The Japanese too believed that in times of chaos, before creation, the world was encased in an egg. Using the brute force of its horns, the bull broke open the egg and the rest is history.

Gastronomically, Korea is a country with a lot to offer, but there are still very few Korean restaurants worth their name in the west. If you do come across one, it's usually a bland, watered-down version of *gogigui,* or Korean barbecue. And that's a shame, because ignorance breeds contempt. That makes it all the more unusual for such a rich, ancient gastronomic culture to be conquering the world with a very simple chicken dish, *yangnyeom.* Korea's gastronomic culture reflects its philosophy of life. Pursuit of a balance between ying and yang: hot, cold, mild and spicy... An explosion of flavours, smells and textures: culinary sensations in which simplicity is the main ingredient.

KOREA

I love eggs

Koreans eat about two eggs a week, so they're not particularly popular at the moment. An amusing government promotional campaign is taking place through the website www.iloveegg.com. The website and obligatory merchandising are a big hit in Korea. The song that accompanies it rose to the top of the charts. The lyrics, not exactly Pulitzer Prize material in my opinion, say it all:

Eggs… get your eggs here!
Fresh and white eggs are here!
Wiggle jiggle, yellow middle thats the best of what you are
I love you egg
White and tender surround the center
Cozy sitting in the crackling shell
I love you
Vitamins and minerals in you
Oodles and their proteins too
Oodle doodle
Popular and perfect and so compelete every way
I love you egg, egg
Come into my tummy
Oh so very yummy
Crack, crack, crack, chip-a-chip away your shell and come to me
Get your eggs
I love you fresh eggs
I love you white eggs
Really really love you so
Fresh eggs
Eggs I love you, like the sky above
Eggs are the best
I love you fresh eggs
I love you
White eggs really really love you so
Eggs fresh fresh eggs
Three-hundred and sixty-five days I really love you so, I really love you so
Mmmm, Yummy

Ae Jin Huys

Ae Jin is a young lady of Korean descent who lives in Ghent in Belgium and is looking for her roots through Korean gastronomy. Her mission is to get people to taste Korean food and prove to them that the popular Korean barbecue is more than what they are usually served in the banal Belgo-Korean eateries.

Born in South Korea, but brought up in De Pinte in Belgium, she studied at art school and specialised in fashion design. The longing for her roots made her decide one morning to make her dormant idea that 'would never happen' a reality. Mokja was born and simply means: let's eat! The name is certainly not accidental because sharing food with others is very important in Korea.

She is completely uncompromising when it comes to food and is justifiably proud of her own home-made kimchee, Korea's national dish. Koreans even say kimchee instead of 'cheese' when they are having their photo taken. Her passion and enthusiasm for Korean gastronomy are truly infectious and her Mokja has rightfully become a household word and a success. Koreans couldn't wish for a better ambassador. If she is asked where she comes from, she answers in broad East Flemish dialect: Korea. One way or another, her only reference point for the Korean culture is food. She spoke the language as a child but she can hardly remember any more than ten words now. But she has never lost the flavours. She uses that while cooking too and she's starting to learn about Korean culture all over again through its cuisine.

DALGYAL JJIM
steamed egg with spring onion

●●○○○○

INGREDIENTS

4 eggs ·
250 ml yuksu (stock, see below) ·
1 spring onion ·

For the yuksu
6 large anchovies ·
1 piece of kelp (type of seaweed) (5 cm x 5 cm) ·
200 ml water ·
pinch of salt ·
½ Tbsp. fish sauce ·

METHOD

Yuksu

Remove the heads and entrails of the six large anchovies. Fry briefly in a hot pan. Add the kelp (5 cm x 5 cm) and 200 ml of water. Boil the stock for no more than 15 minutes.

Sieve the yuksu and season to taste with a pinch of salt and some fish sauce.

Dalgyal jjim

Beat the eggs and sieve into a heat-proof bowl. Stir in the cooled yuksu. Put a lid on the bowl and steam the egg mixture for 20 to 30 minutes (depending on the thickness and the shape of the bowl) in a steamer. Test the substance using a thin skewer; it should be the consistency of a silky-soft milk pudding.

In the meantime, chop the white part of the spring onion as finely as possible, in diagonal rings. Cut the green part into long thin strips. Use to decorate the dish.

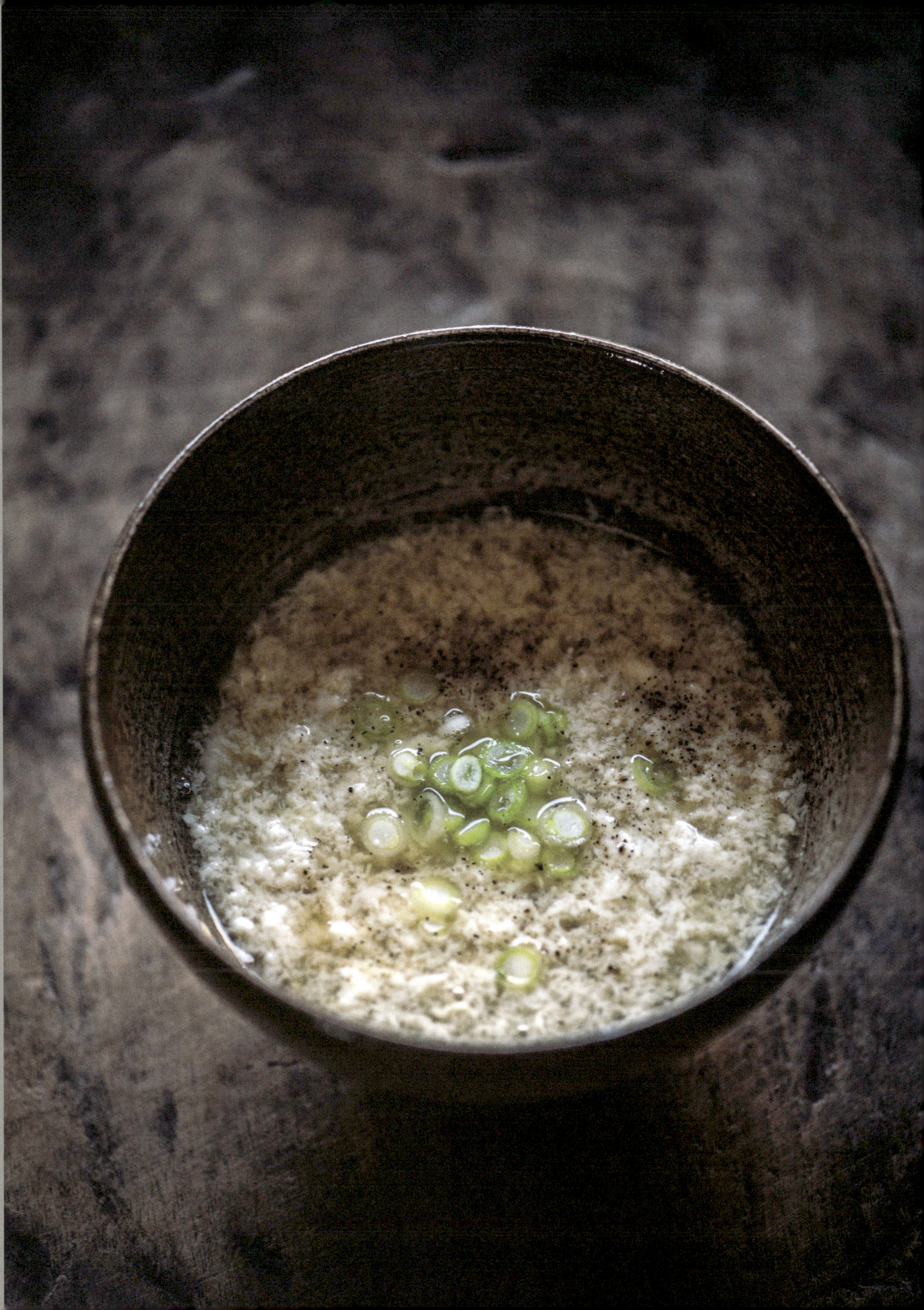

DALGYAL GUK

soup with egg clouds

🥚🥚🥚○○○

INGREDIENTS

400 ml yuksu (see the recipe under dalgyal jjim) ·
1 onion ·
1 slice of daikon (1 cm thick) ·
1 Tbsp. fish sauce ·
1 Tbsp. soy sauce ·
pinch of salt, pepper ·
2 eggs ·
1 spring onion, finely chopped ·
pinch of ground pepper ·

METHOD

Heat the yuksu with the onion, daikon, fish sauce, soy sauce and salt. Cook over a gentle heat until the vegetables are just tender. Remove the vegetables from the stock. Beat the eggs and sieve them into a bowl. Stir the egg mixture very gently into the soup to make wispy clouds.

Serve in a soup bowl and garnish with the spring onion and a pinch of ground pepper. Optionally, you can chop the daikon finely and serve it with the soup. There are many variations of this soup, depending on the season and on the region.

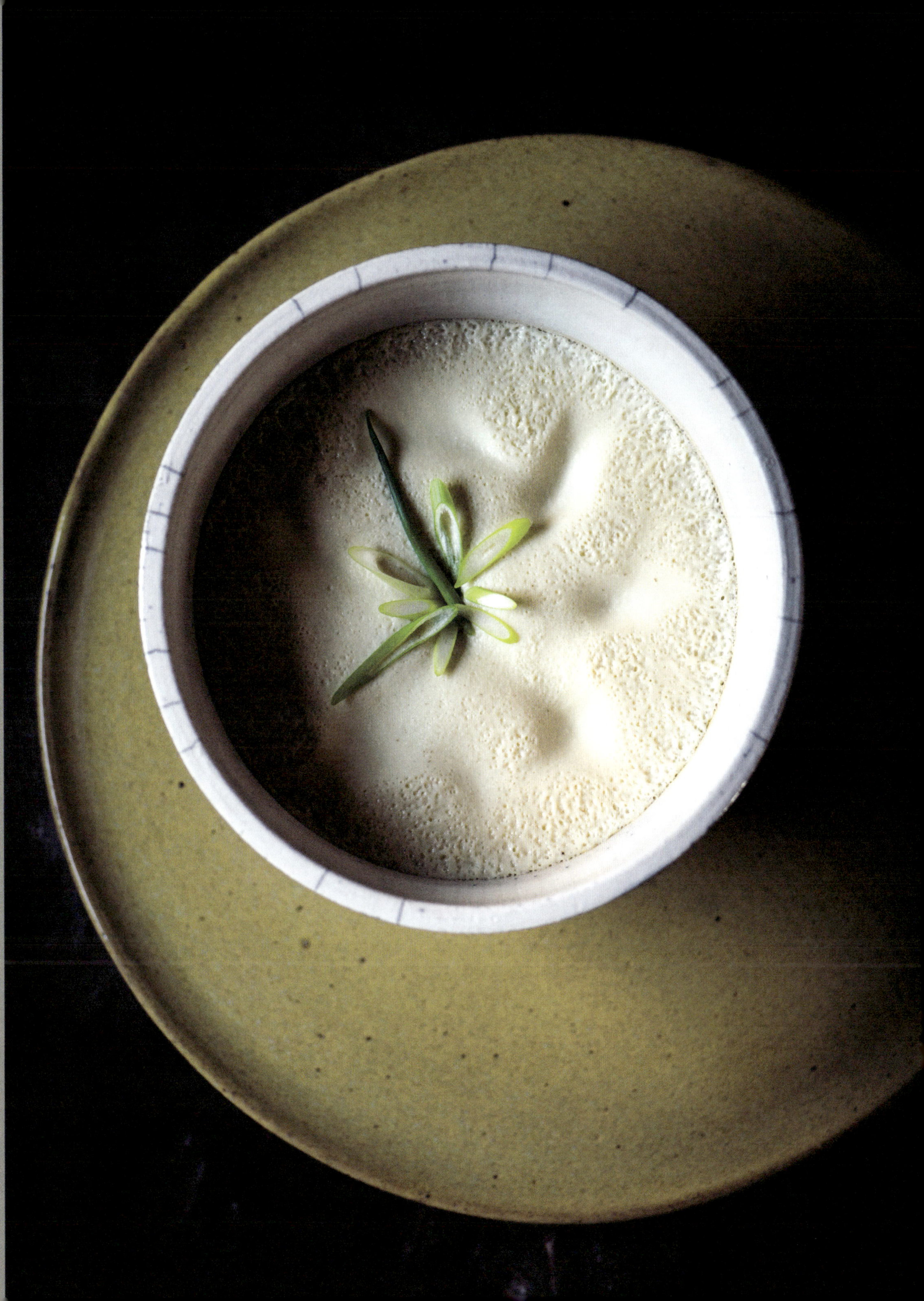

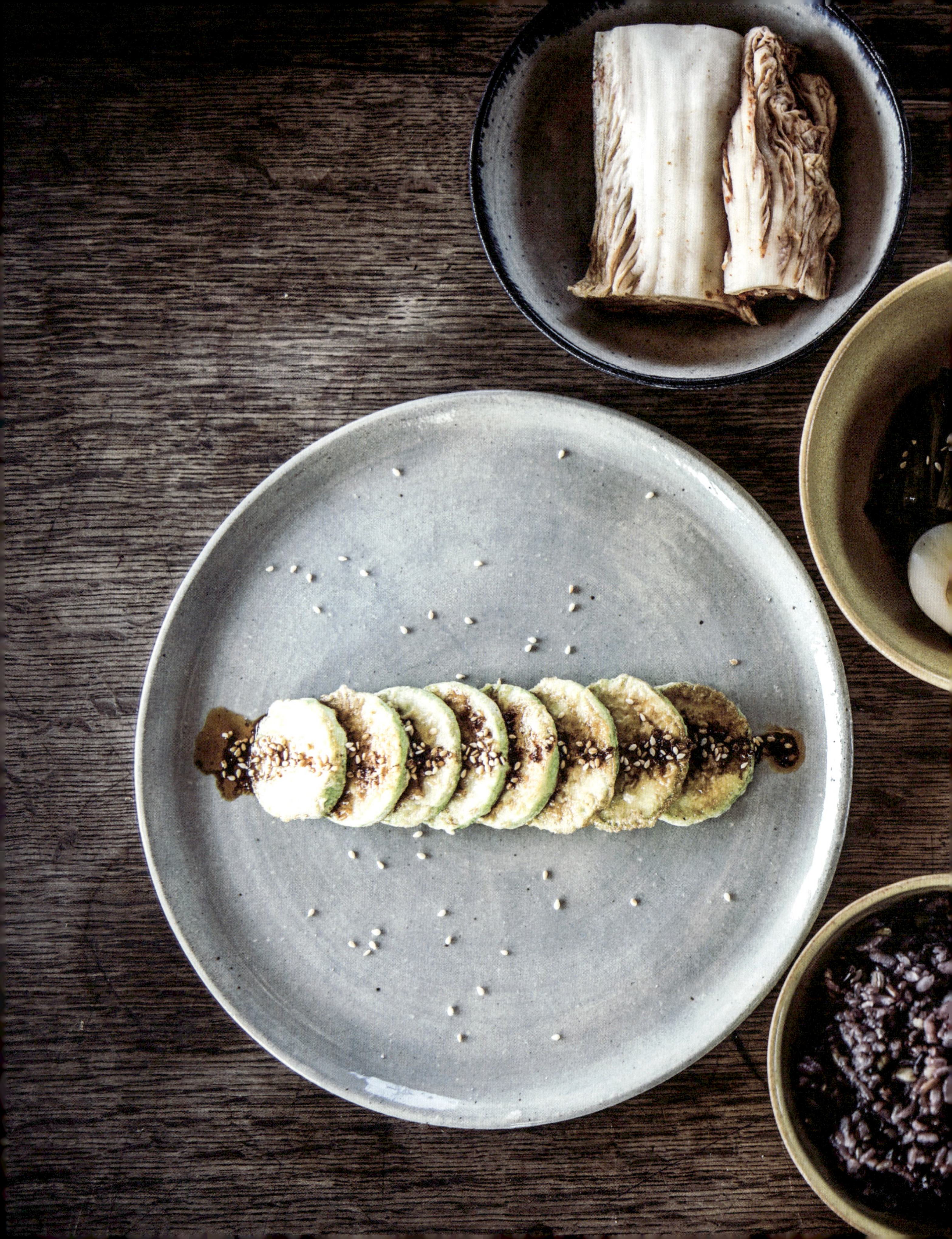

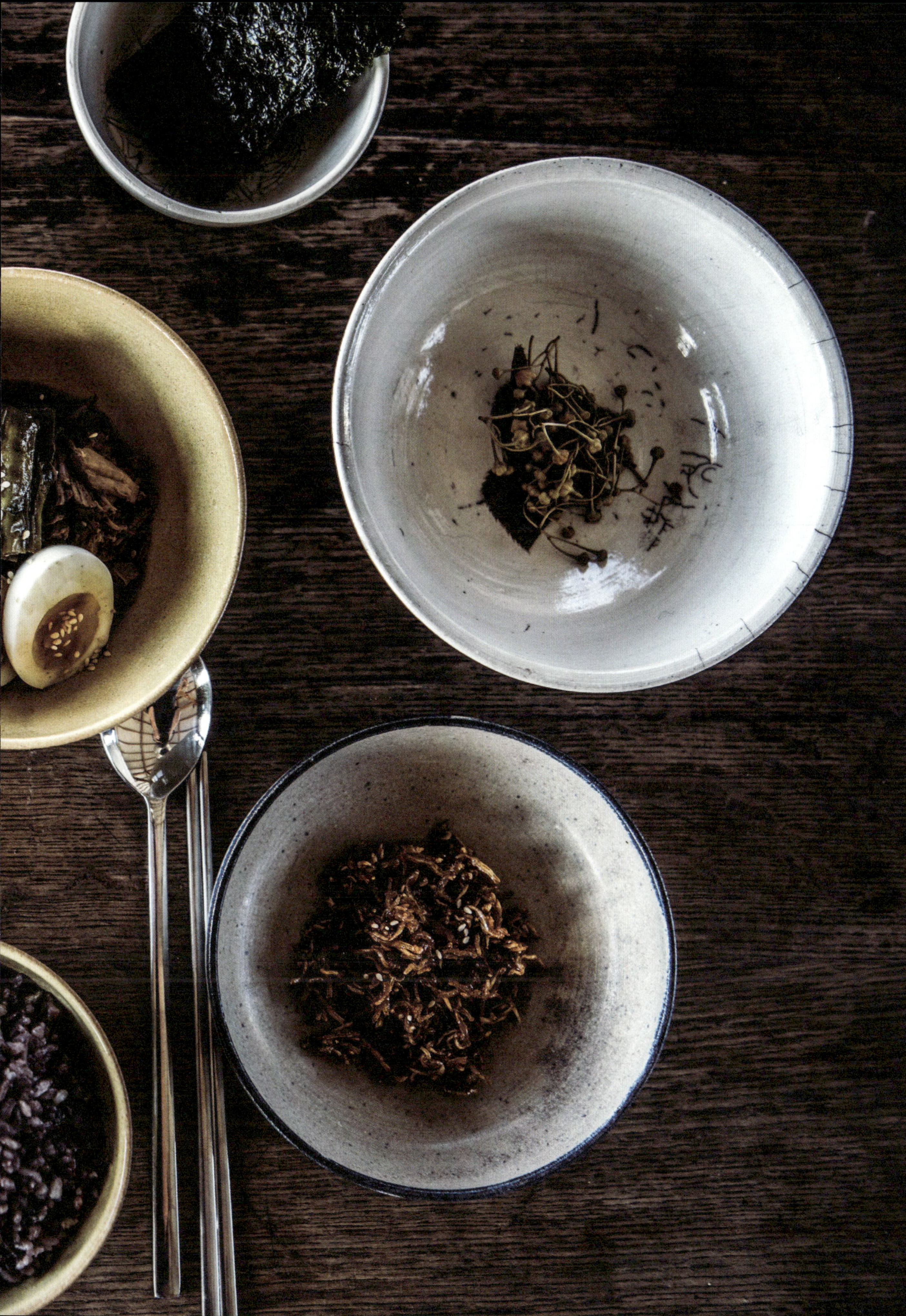

SOGOGI JANGJORIM
braised beef with quail's eggs

●●○○○○

INGREDIENTS

300 g stewing steak (large pieces 2 cm thick) ·
2 litres of water ·
2 pieces of kelp (type of seaweed) (5 cm x 5 cm) ·
100 ml soy sauce ·
½ garlic bulb, cut through the middle ·
1 slice of daikon (5 cm thick) ·
1 onion ·
1 leek (only the white part) ·
2 slices of ginger (0.5 cm thick) ·
20 black peppercorns ·
3 Tbsp. brown sugar ·
10 green, mild chili peppers ·
2 eggs ·

METHOD

Immerse the meat in water to get rid of any remnants of blood. At the same time, soak the kelp in two litres of water. Remove the kelp, retaining the water. Rinse the meat. Mix the soy sauce, garlic, daikon, onion, leek, ginger, peppercorns and sugar into the 'kelp water'. Bring to the boil on a medium heat, partially cover with a lid and cook for just under an hour, until the meat is cooked. Sieve the stock and leave the meat to cool on a plate. Tear the meat into strips.

In the meantime, boil the eggs for four minutes. Drain and remove the eggshells under cold running water.

Cut the green chili peppers into pieces about 5 cm long. Boil them in the stock until tender. Put the eggs in too so that they take on the colour of soy.

Arrange the meat, the peppers and the eggs in a deep plate and pour in a little stock to cover the bottom of the plate. Serve with rice.

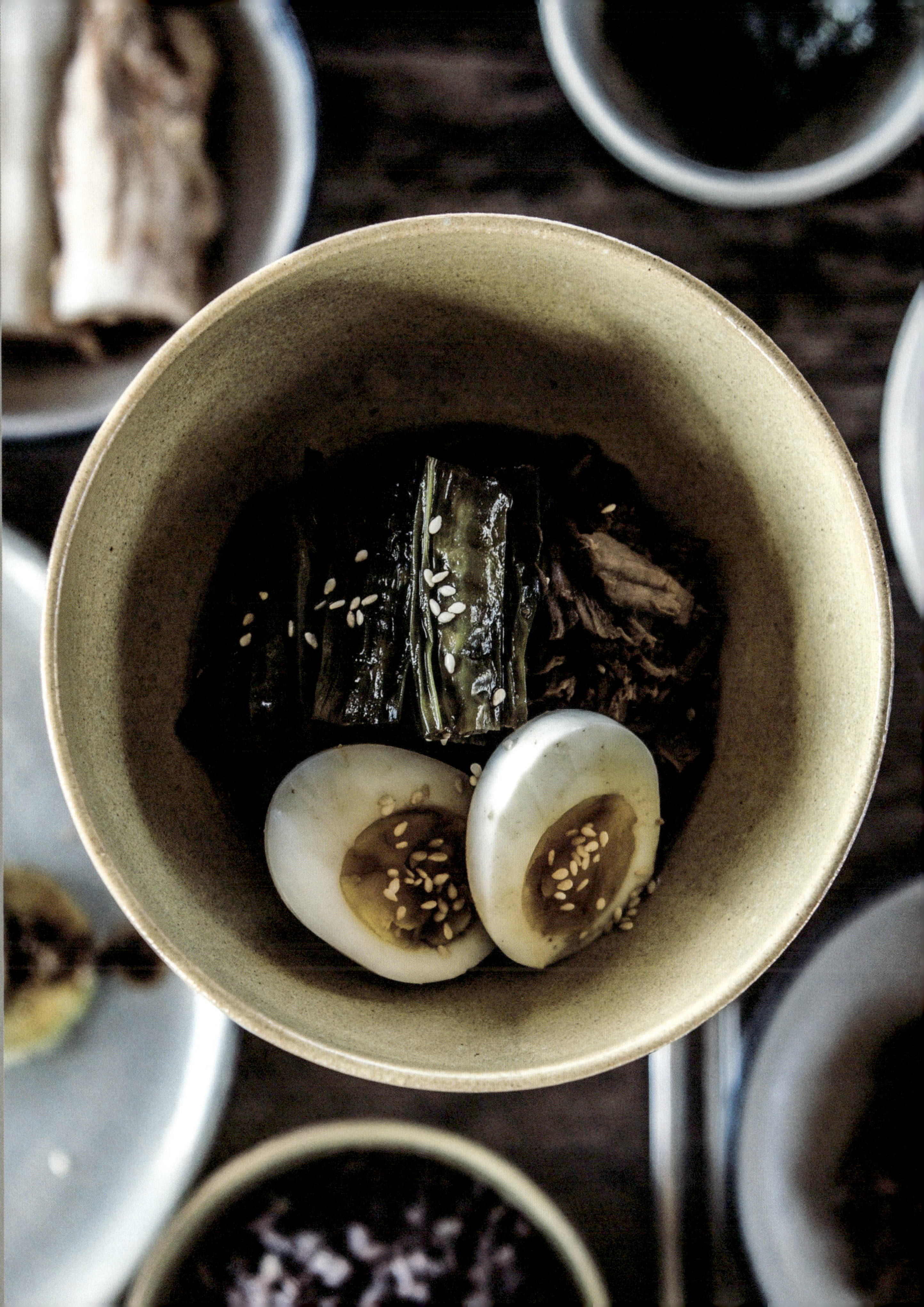

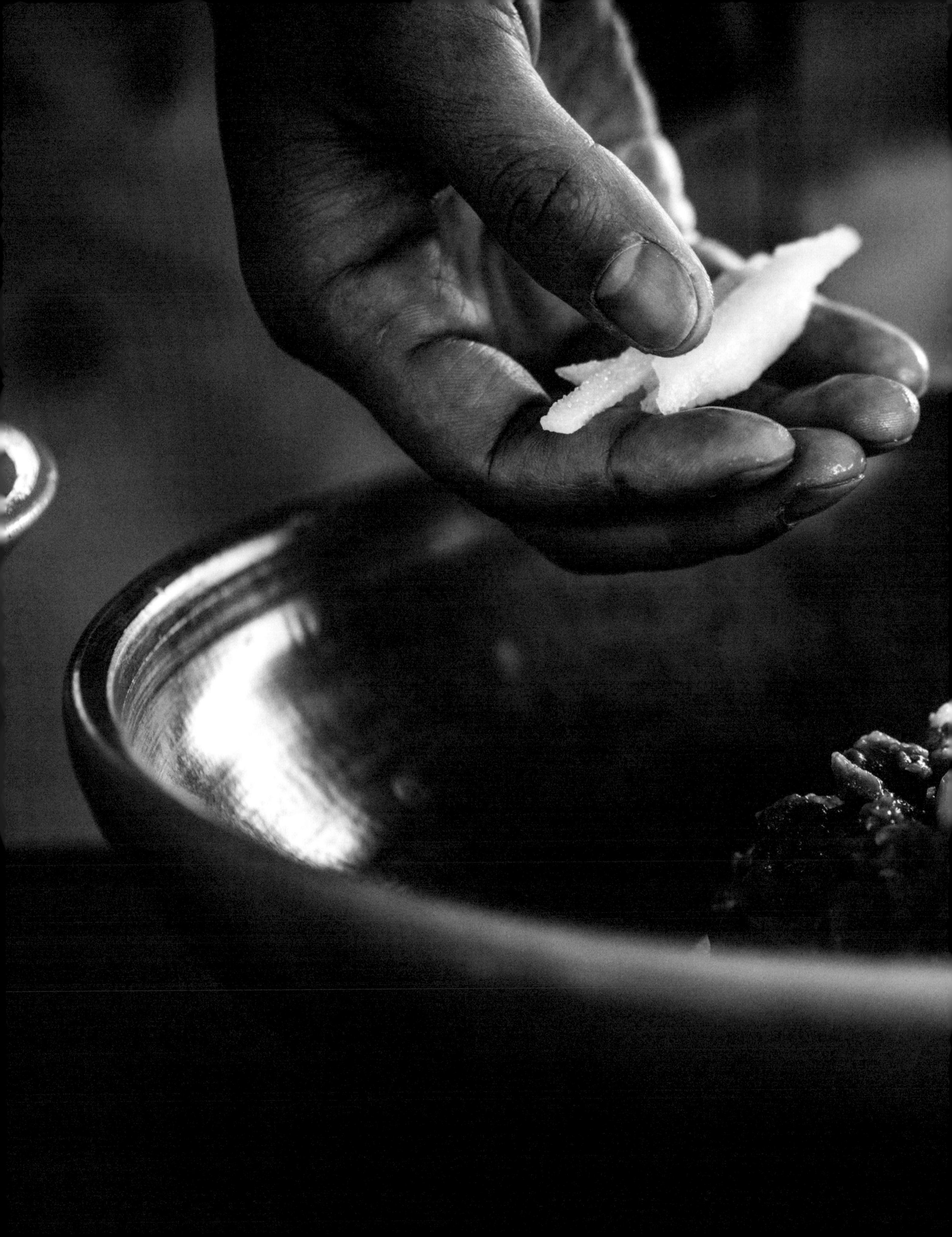

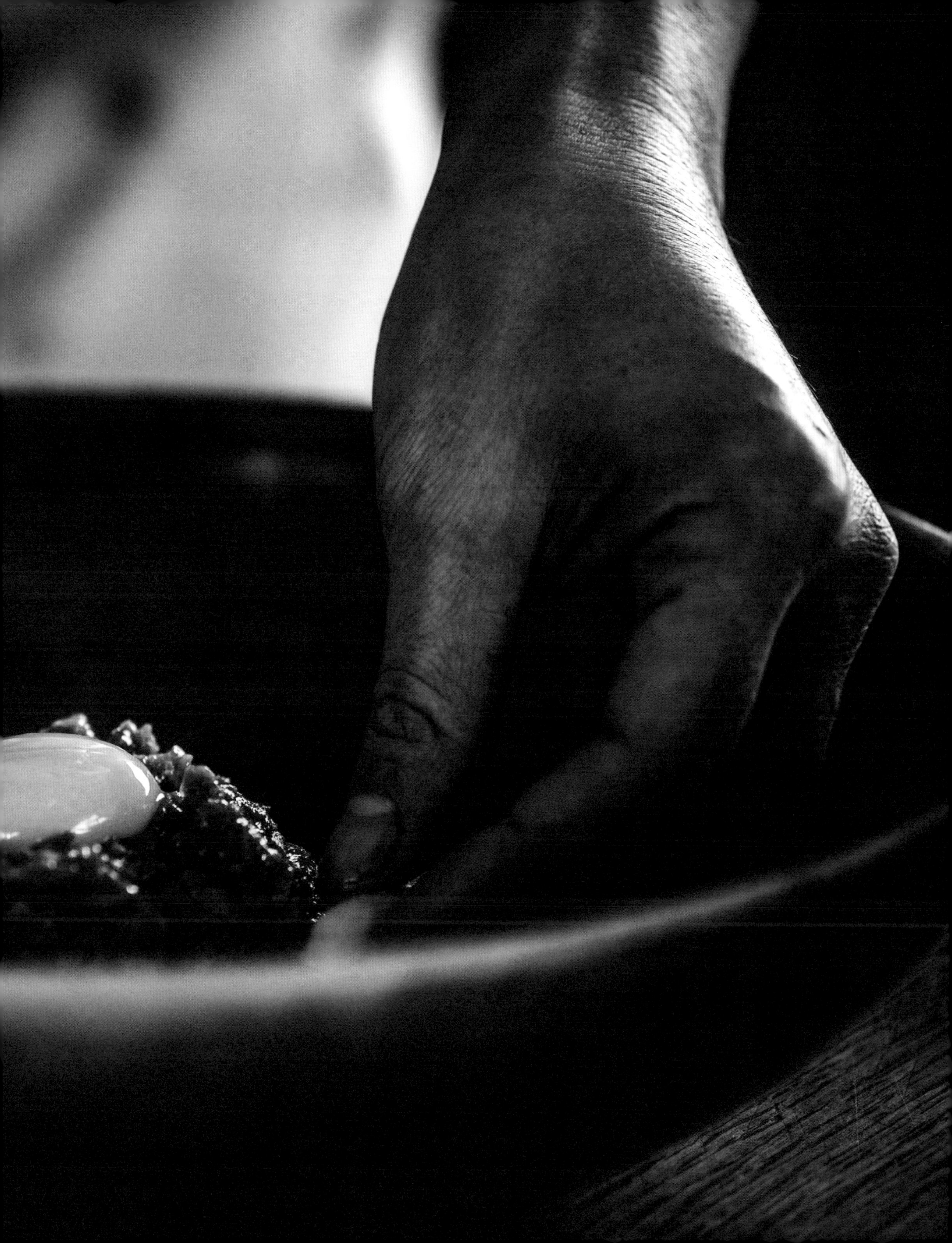

YUKHOE

steak tartar with egg yolk

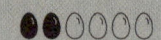

INGREDIENTS

400 g beef tenderloin ·
1 Korean pear (or similar ripe pear) ·
2 egg yolks ·
seasonal greens (e.g. mustard greens or frisée lettuce) ·

For the marinade
2 cloves of garlic, pureed ·
3 Tbsp. soy sauce ·
2 Tbsp. runny honey ·
4 Tbsp. roasted sesame seed oil ·
½ tsp black pepper ·
2 spring onions ·
2 Tbsp. freshly roasted sesame seeds ·

METHOD

Mix all the ingredients for the marinade: garlic, soy sauce, honey, sesame oil, black pepper, finely chopped spring onions and freshly roasted sesame seeds.

Peel the pear and remove the core. Cut the fruit into thin batons no more than 5 cm in length. Cover and set aside in the fridge.

Place the meat in the freezer for 10 to 15 minutes then slice thinly; cut the slices into strips and then dice of no more than 0.5 cm thick. Stir the marinade into the meat.

Arrange the pear batons in two deep plates and place the tartar on top. Make a dip in the middle for the egg yolk. Garnish the plates with seasonal greens and freshly ground black pepper.

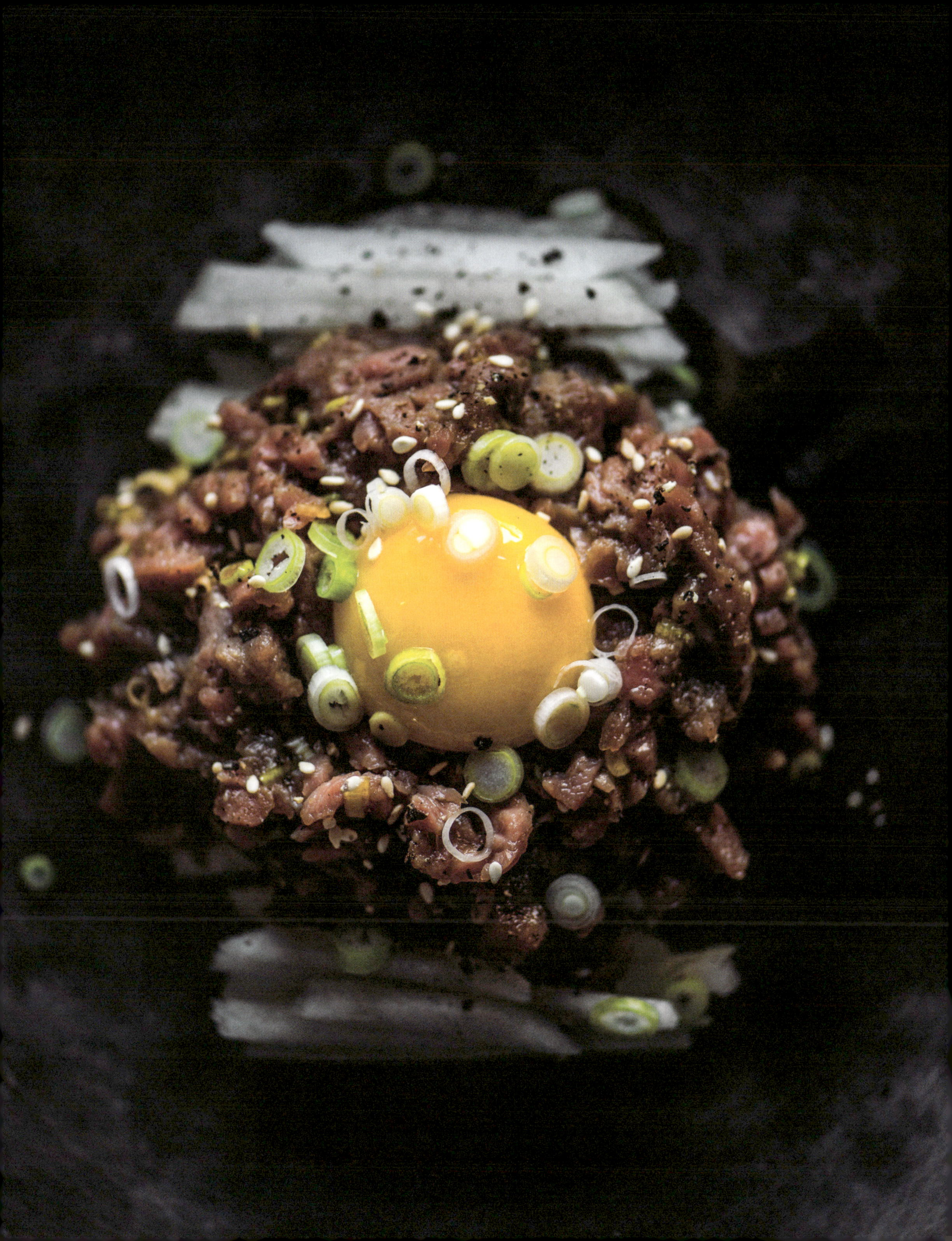

TURKEY

82

OTTOMANIA

There aren't that many Turkish restaurants where the glorious Turkish gastronomy is given the honour it deserves. The great diversity and variation that marks out Turkish cuisine is a direct result of the many invasions by foreign peoples all of whom left behind their own individuality and style of cooking. Furthermore, the Oghuz Turks integrated many other populations, partly through the expansion of the Ottoman Empire and the Seljuq dynasty, and in so doing also adopted their culinary arts.

Evidence of this is the gigantic kitchen in the Topkapi Palace, one of the main attractions in Instanbul. All the 'exotic' delicacies for the sultans and their entourage were made in this kitchen while the poorer rural districts of Turkey continued to perpetuate their local customs and cooking styles.

If you walk through Gaziantep's city park, which is incidentally one of the largest parks in the world, you soak up the rich history of the fifth largest city in Turkey. Some older people and locals still call the park Antep. The prefix Gazi was added in 1920 after the Turkish war of independence. *Gazi* means fighter, and *Antep* is derived from the Arabic word *Ayintab,* which means good spring. Together, the name means 'indestructible spring'. And that is what it is, an indestructible source of inspiration from a whole wealth of cultures: the Hittite Empire, the Hellenic Empire, the Persian Empire, the Byzantine Empire and of course the Ottoman Empire. All these aristocratic cultures ensure that the local food is a true experience.

The aristocratic culture of the Ottoman Empire began with the fall of Constantinople in 1453. At its height, it was a multinational empire led by Suleiman the magnificent, and it controlled South-Eastern Europe, Western Asia, the Caucasus, North Africa and the Horn of Africa. This melting pot with Istanbul as its epicentre therefore offers an amazing wealth of culinary influences.

Palace kitchen

Ingredients from all over the empire were gathered together in the enormous palace kitchen for the chefs to experiment with

TURKEY

84

Sinem Usta, whose cooking makes you realise that Turkish cuisine is very underrated.

them. The entrance exam to become one of the Palace brigade was simple: you had to be able to cook rice. Chefs were engaged from all corners of the empire to cook with exotic textures and ingredients and come up with new dishes incorporating them.

Each cook specialised in a particular task. Before a dish got to the sultan it had to travel a long road of refinement and experimentation. The last hurdle was the chesnidjibashi's palate; he was the emperor's taster. When the sultan then finally gave his blessing, the dish could gradually be introduced onto the market and become popular. Only the more extravagant dishes remained within the walls of the palace as a speciality.

The evolution into a major Turkish cuisine was therefore not just chance. Analogous to other great gastronomies in the world, several factors led to this result. There was the profusion and diversity of ingredients thanks to Turkey's rich fauna and flora. The legacy of the imperial kitchen in which for centuries a small army of top chefs did nothing other than create dishes to please the sultans' taste buds certainly also had an impact on the refinement of the cuisine as it is now in Turkey.

The palace kitchen was supported by a complex social organisation; the empire had total control of the Spice Route and as such, the kitchen reflected the culmination of wealth and the flourishing of culture in the capital city of this powerful empire. Time was also an essential factor – Anatolia for example, is 1000 years old and needless to say, so is its cuisine – and the transference of knowledge and dishes. Turkey's position at the border between Asia and the Mediterranean is an additional factor. It enjoys the best of both worlds.

The cultural transition from the Ottoman Empire to present-day Turkey led to the evolution of a major gastronomy through differentiation, refinement and perfection of dishes, and of the structure of meals.

Sinem Usta

Sinem was literally spoon-fed her passion for eating well. Her mother runs an excellent small restaurant in Istanbul and from a young age, Sinem was fascinated by the pots and pans. Her passion for Mediterranean cookery combined with her Turkish culinary roots makes her a very talented chef who can come up with some surprising dishes. Her cooking makes you realise that Turkish cuisine is very underrated. She works with precision and sensitivity. Although she was initially very attracted to Italian cuisine, she started to rediscover more and more of her own Turkish cuisine, which is almost used as a means of communication. I was lucky enough to witness Sinem and her mother in the kitchen and it was one of the most impressive gastronomic experiences I have had in recent years. I've been nagging her for ages to start her own restaurant and put Turkish cuisine on the map once and for all. I am certainly a huge fan …

MENEMEN

●●○○○○

INGREDIENTS

4 sivri biber ·
(long Turkish sweet peppers)
butter ·
4 good tomatoes ·
salt and pepper ·
4 eggs ·

METHOD

Cut the sivri into circles and fry them in butter. Add the tomatoes chopped into brunoise, add salt and pepper to taste and simmer for 15 minutes.

Break the eggs above the pan and carefully stir everything well for two to three minutes. Leave to rest for a moment before serving.

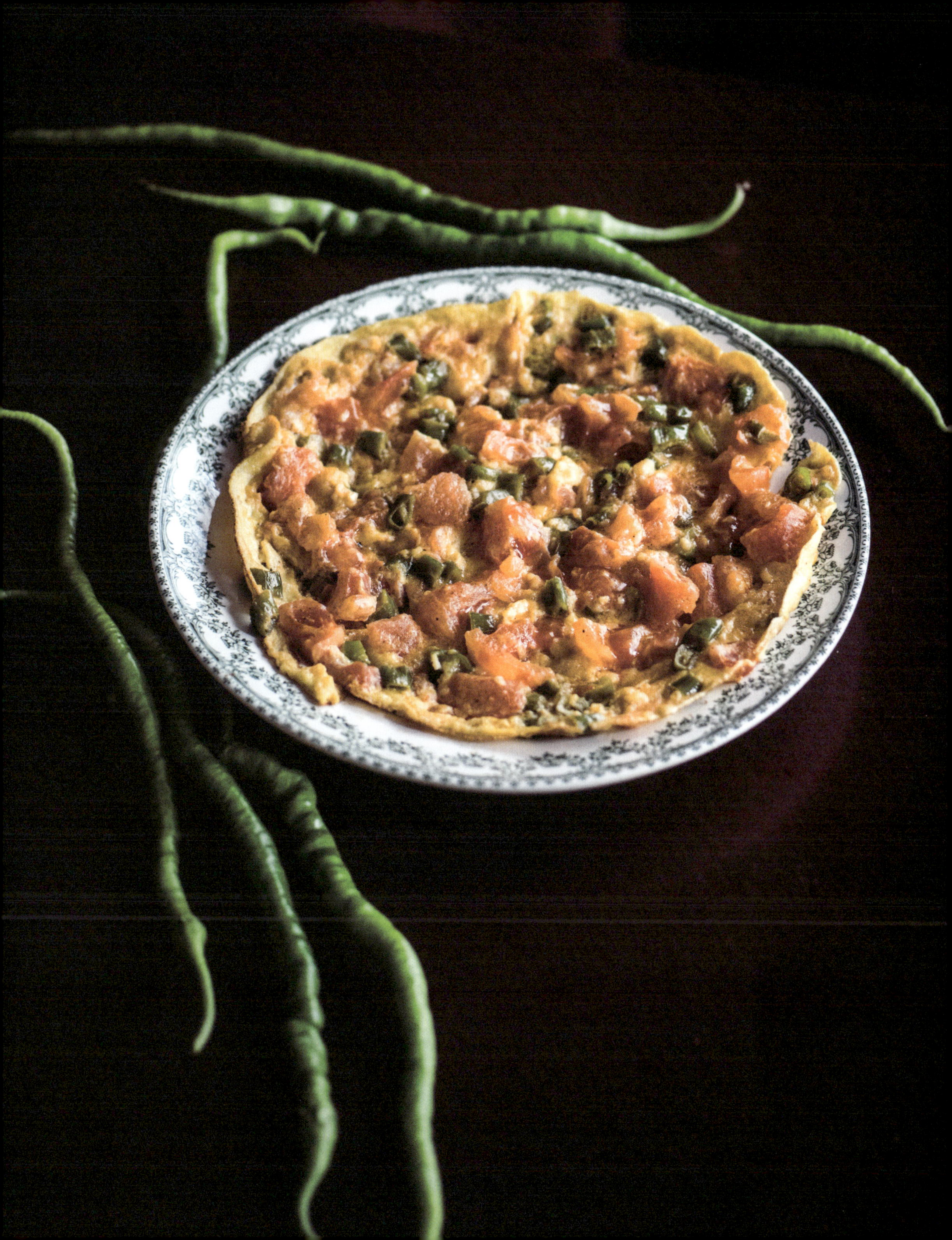

ELBASAN TAVA (WITH LAMB)

●●●○○○

INGREDIENTS

3 lambs' necks ·
a few onions ·
a few carrots ·
3 eggs ·
1 Tbsp. flour ·
2 Tbsp. yogurt ·

METHOD

Put the lambs' necks in a pan of cold water with the roughly chopped onions and carrots. Bring to the boil and then simmer on a low heat for an hour and a half. Pull the lamb apart until you have small pieces. Retain some of the cooking liquid. Pre-heat the oven to 180 °C.

Put the eggs, flour, yogurt and a little of the cooking liquid into a bowl and mix.

Place the meat in an oven dish and pour the egg mixture over it. Cook for 30 minutes in the oven.

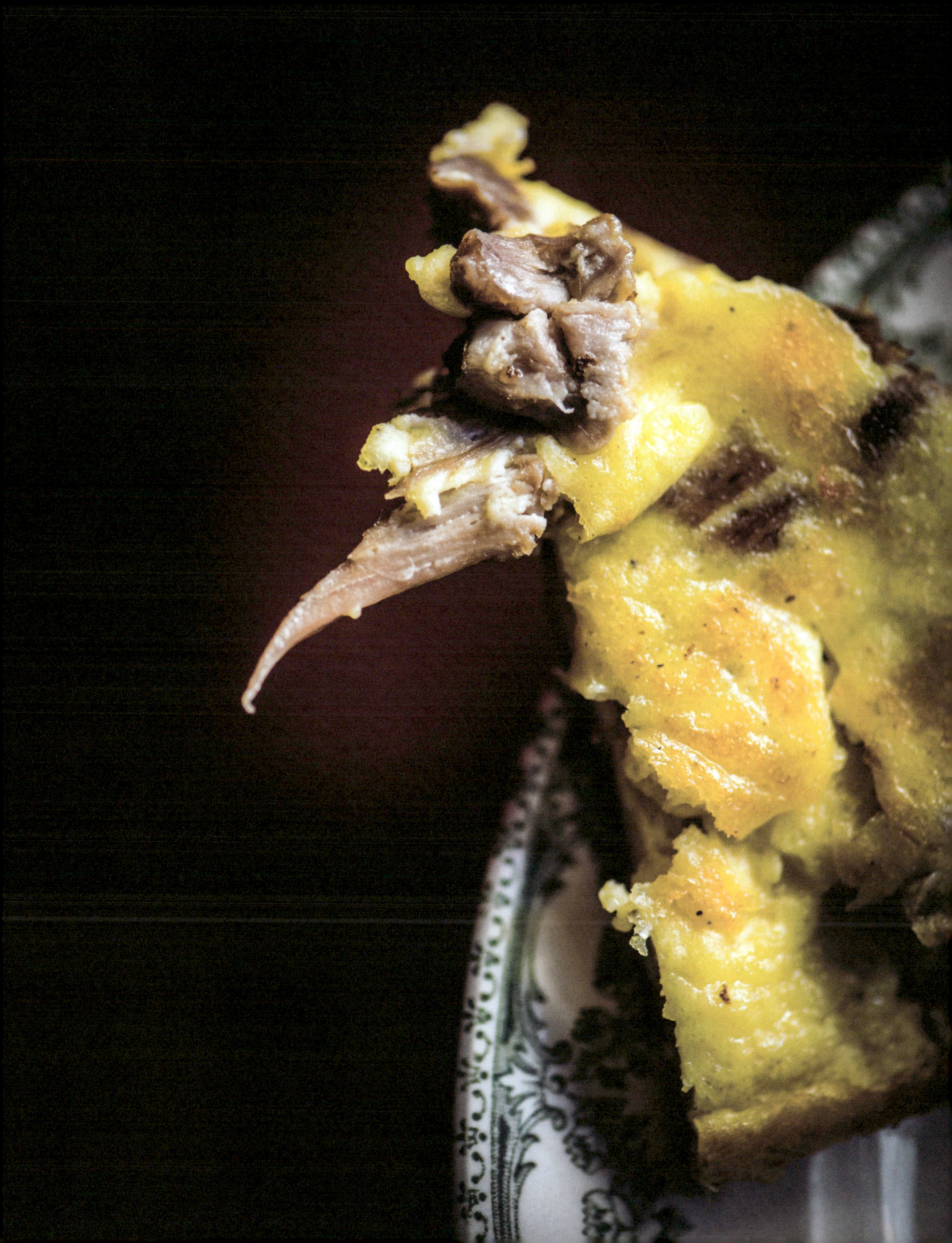

CILBIR

poached egg with yogurt

INGREDIENTS

1 clove of garlic per person ·
red Turkish chili peppers ·
3 Tbsp. yogurt per person ·
2 eggs per person ·
some olive oil ·

METHOD

Mix the finely chopped garlic and the finely chopped chili peppers into the yogurt and leave to infuse so that the flavours are well mixed.

Poach the eggs carefully then remove them from the pan; drain them on kitchen paper or a clean tea towel.

Pour the yogurt into a deep plate and place the poached eggs on top; garnish with some olive oil.

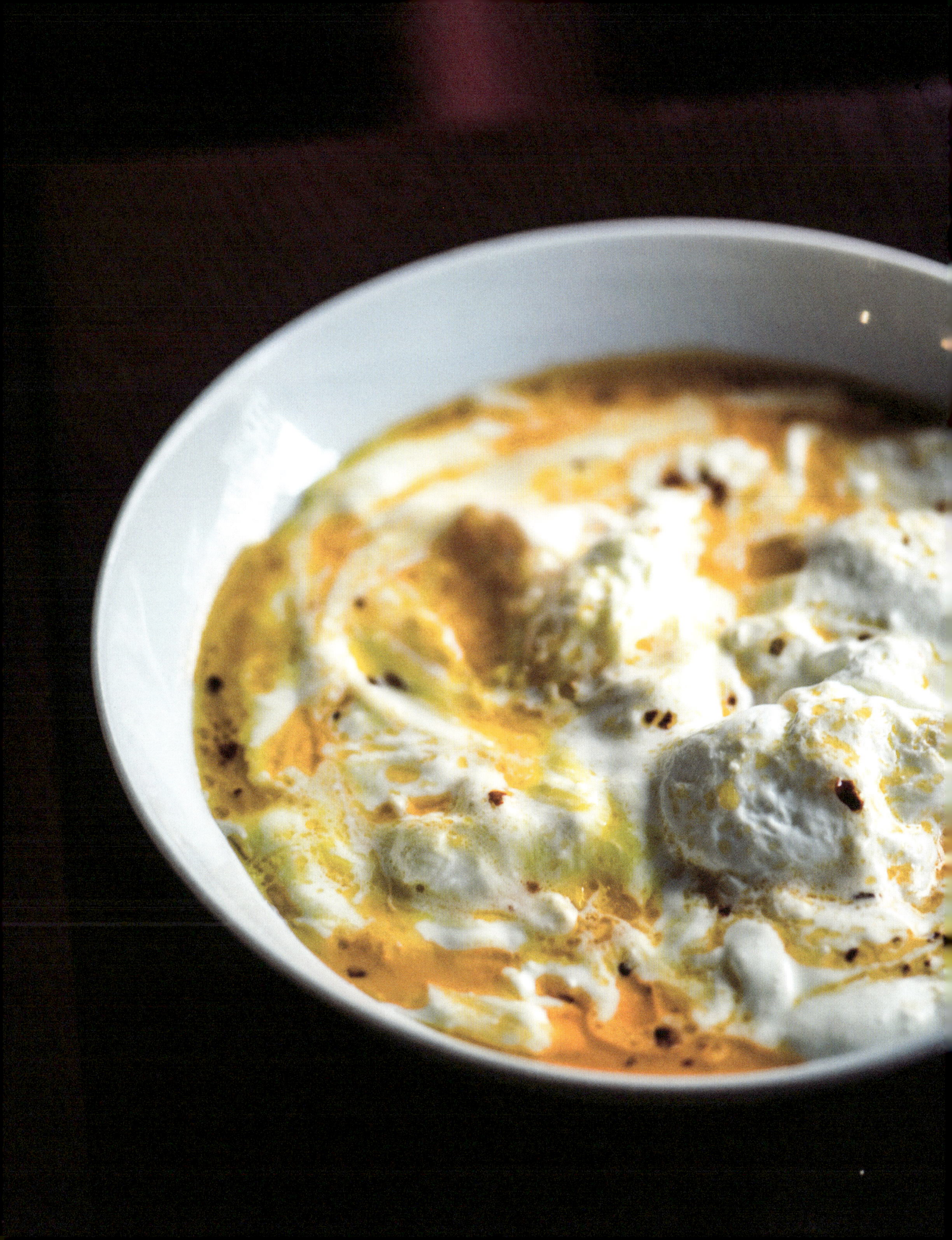

HAMSILI YUMURTA

●●○○○○

INGREDIENTS

100 g maize flour ·
500 g fresh anchovies ·
3 eggs ·

METHOD

Coat the anchovies in the flour and fry in a pan.

Beat the eggs well. Pour the eggs over the anchovies and cook gently.

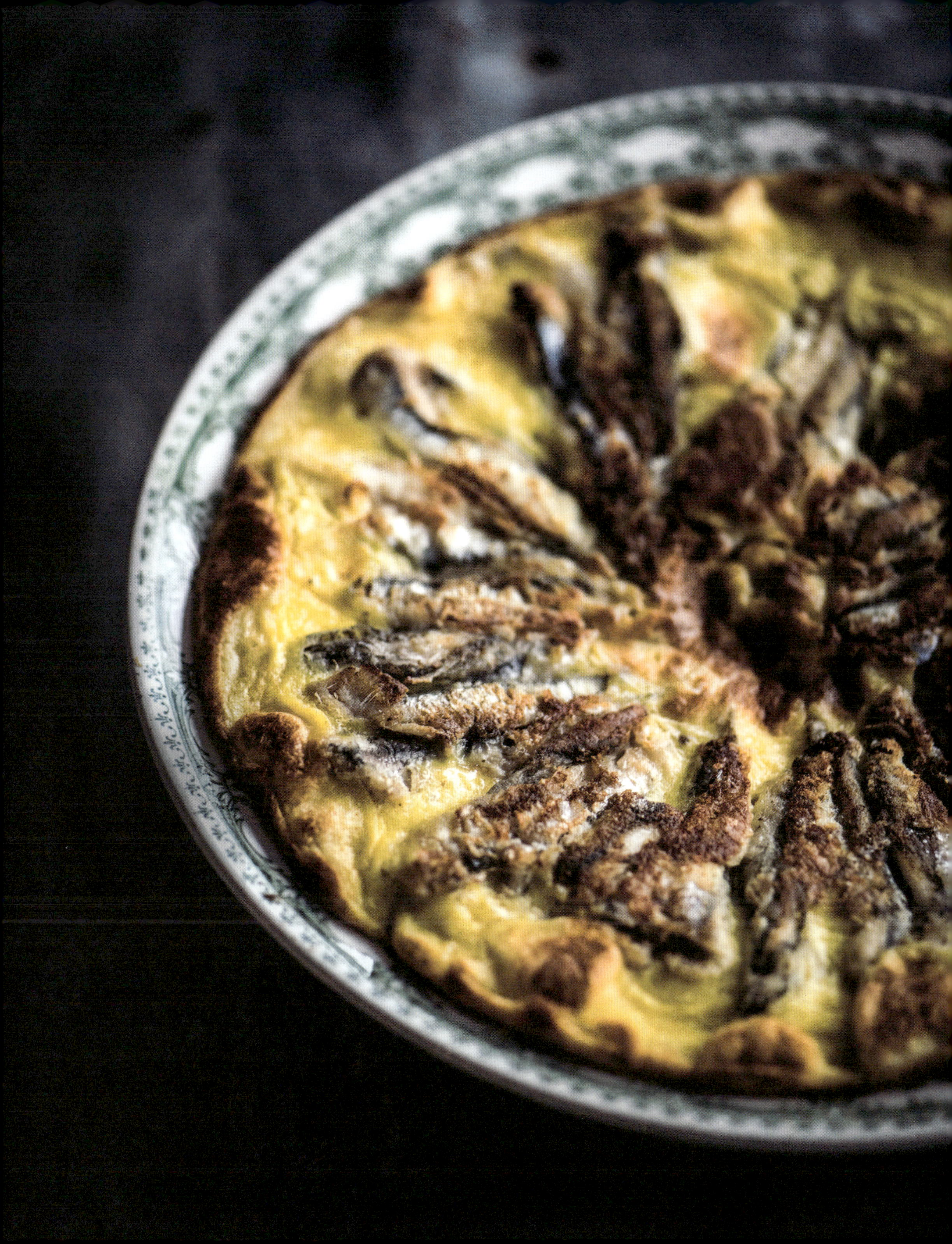

MUCVER

INGREDIENTS

3 courgettes ·
4 eggs ·
1 Tbsp. dill, finely chopped ·
salt and pepper ·
100 g flour ·
100 g feta ·

METHOD

Grate the courgettes, rinse them but dry them thoroughly.

Whisk the eggs in a large bowl and mix in the other ingredients.

Crumble the feta so that it can be evenly distributed over the dish.

Fry this mixture in the pan.

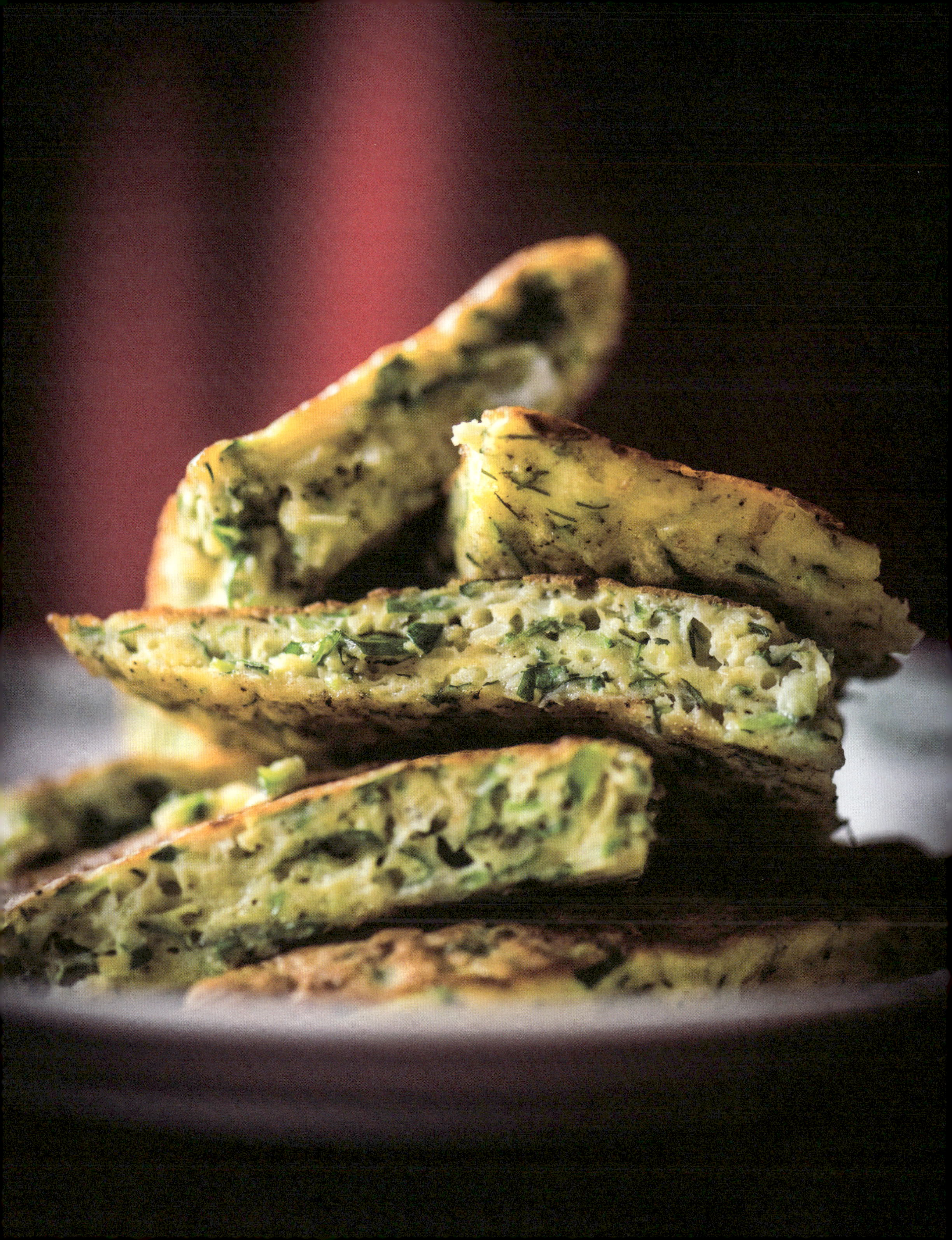

| IRAN

SEPIDEH SEDAGHATNIA

Sepideh (or Sepi to friends) is one of the best sommeliers in the country, a Belgian celebrity, restaurant owner, caviar distributor, author and self-confident woman... but few people know that she is also quite a dab hand with pots and pans in the kitchen.

There's no such thing as coincidence when you're born in a city called Shiraz. Many historians assert that the grape syrah effectively originated here and was brought to the West by the Greeks. What is certainly beyond doubt is that the city is a haven of culture, because Shiraz is famous for its poets, literature, wine and flowers.

Because she was born early in the morning, her parents called her 'sunrise' or Sepideh. Although born in Shiraz, she grew up in Isfahan, a large city with a very rich and long history. Iran does not have a particularly developed wine culture at present, but wine has always had a prominent place in art and literature. Wine, and especially the enjoyment it gives, is the topic of a huge number of poems and stories. Her father had a few vines on the border with Iraq; the young Sepi was allowed to pick them every year and stamp on them with her little feet. That was probably where her passion for wine comes from.

When she came to Belgium as a teenager, she was able to carry on studying maths and physics. She soon learned the language too and, as a result of her passion for wine, she took holiday jobs in a hotel, a restaurant and of course a wine bar. Wine won the day, and the University of Wine in Suze-la Rousse perfected the process and made her into the sommelier she is today. She often chooses surprisingly fascinating wines as a sommelier, probably due to her habit of dealing with the variety of flavours typical of Iran.

Incidentally, Iran cannot be captured in one flavour, and Sepi knows that only too well. Sepi is a busy bee; a woman with guts who knows what she wants. Respect!

IRAN

98

Is there life after kebabs?

It's enough to take a look at a map and learn a little about Iran's history to understand that there's no such thing as quintessential Iranian cuisine; apart from the various kebabs and the grilled lambs testicles there is much more than you might expect. There is caviar, pickled vegetables and smoked fish in the north, samosa, falafel and sweet and sour shrimps in the south, noodles, flatbread and rose-flavoured ice cream throughout the country. Once, Iran was the centre of the Persian Empire and its sphere of influence was as diverse as its neighbouring countries of the Soviet Union, Afghanistan, Pakistan, the Arab states and Turkey. Iran is part of the Middle East but maintains close relations with Europe, the Far East and even Africa.

Iranian gastronomy is on the up internationally thanks to the country's stability. More and more high quality Iranian restaurants are appearing in cities such as London, Los Angeles, Toronto, Vancouver and Washington where large numbers of Iranians live.

Alexander the Great conquered the Persian Empire in the 4th century. It was later overrun by Arabs, Turks, Mongols and Uzbeks. Prior to these invasions, the Iranians had a well-defined food identity, but they nonetheless succeeded in doing something with the new dishes introduced by the conquerors and made them their own. For example they have a type of borscht made with cumin and coriander.

Unlike other parts of the Middle East, Iran has well-defined seasons and the abundance of local pistachios, almonds, saffron, mint, oranges, pomegranates and grapes produces an exciting cuisine with lots of herbs, spices and fruit.

Hot and cold

The original Persian philosophy on food is one of hot and cold. This does not refer to spicy or mild, but to the ability of food to generate energy in the eater, or to help him cool off.

The cultural casserole is based on rice and noodles. The importance of these two ingredients can be traced back to India and China. For a long time, China was a trading partner along the Silk Road, while India, especially Northern India, exercised power over the pre-Islamic Persian states.

The West has the Persians to thank for such items as apples and aubergines. The Persians began importing potatoes around 1800, as well as tomatoes which are known in Farsi as 'European plums' or *gojeh farangi*. With a little imagination, *farangi* can be likened to 'foreign' and this word is used in Farsi to prefix everything that comes from Europe or the West; *tut farangi* are strawberries, for example, *tareh farangi* are leeks and *nukhud farangi* are peas. More recent foods have had their names amended; a kiwi is no longer known by its original Farsi name *tukhm-e-goril*, which translates to gorilla's testicle.

Iran in Brooklyn

The popularity of a cuisine like the Iranian cuisine is usually related to the quality of its culinary ambassadors. Sepi does more than excellent work in Belgium to defend the colours of her native country, and her colleague in NYC is Louisa Shafia. When

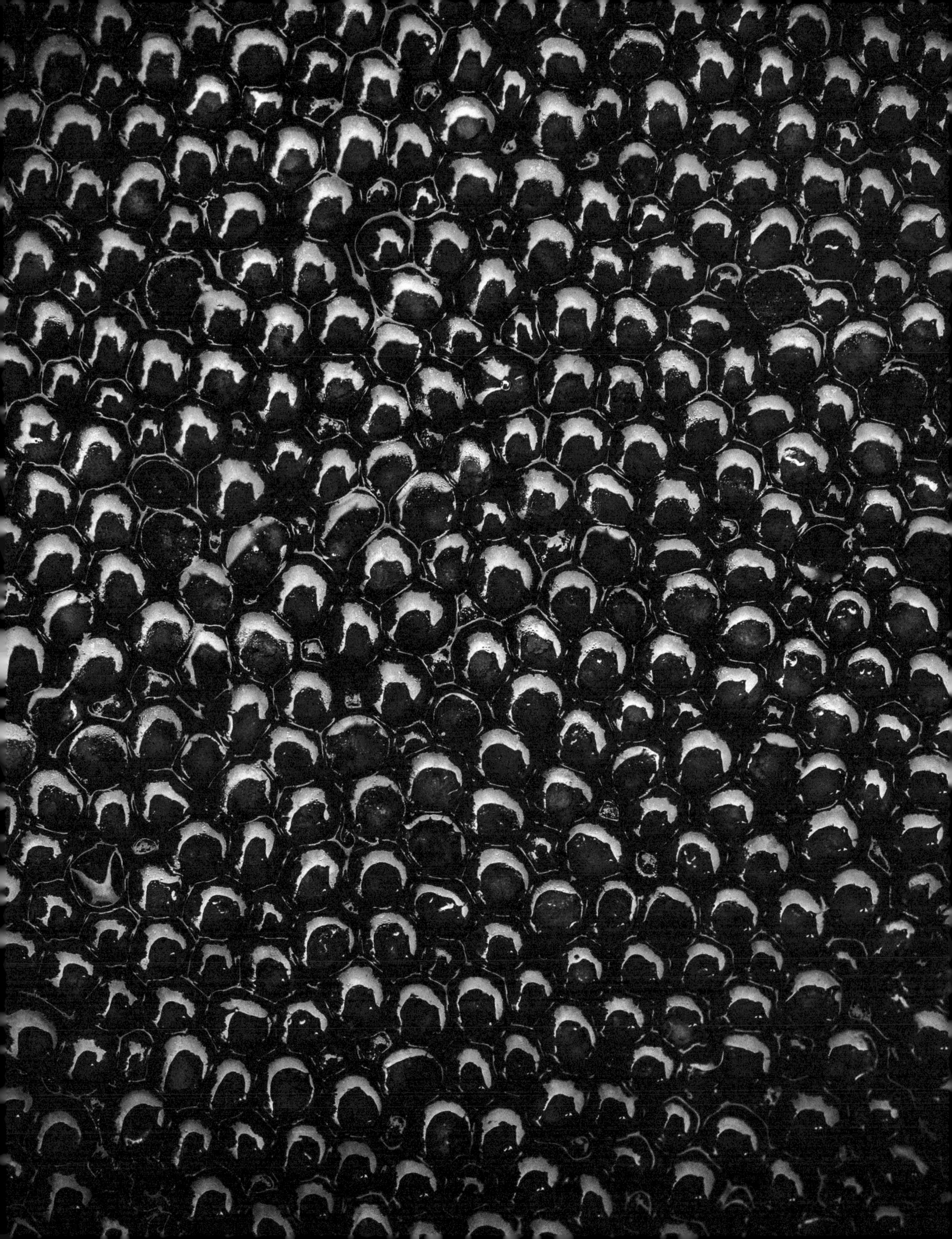

I met Louisa Shafia for the first time, she worked at Aquavit and there too, her enthusiasm for Iranian gastronomy was infectious. She wrote a book about it that became one of the best cookery books in the United States: *The New Persian Kitchen*, which provides an excellent introduction to Iran's complex cuisine. She now organises pop-ups every Monday to convince people of Iran's gastronomic values..

Iran's black gold...
is of course oil, but one of the country's other important export products is certainly the ultimate delicacy from the sea: caviar. For a long time, the Caspian Sea was the scene of battles between the Russians and the Iranians over caviar, but connoisseurs and lovers of caviar placed the Iranian caviar high above the Russian variant when it came to quality. The name caviar comes from the Persian word kaya-dar, which literally means 'laying eggs'.

This ultimate delicacy is simply the unfertilised eggs of the sturgeon. The first caviar eaters were incidentally the Persians who strongly believed that the consumption of caviar would improve their stamina (i.e. their potency). The ancient Egyptians are known to have eaten caviar and the Phoenicians regularly had caviar on the table.

In Russia, caviar was something only the rich could afford to eat. The Russian Orthodox Church permitted the eating of caviar on fast days when no meat could be eaten. Europe had not yet discovered caviar as a delicacy and dismissed it as a peasant dish. Louis XV's behaviour illustrates this well. He was the guest of honour at a reception hosted by Peter the Great. Louis XV was given a box of caviar as a gift. The custom was that the most eminent guests were presented with caviar, but the French taste buds were unaccustomed to it and spat the spoonful of caviar out again, causing a diplomatic incident.

Local caviar in the US and Europe was for peasants, for the masses. The immense caviar hauls from local rivers such as the Delaware meant that prices were so low that everyone was able to eat large quantities of the stuff. A clever Greek merchant began praising Russian caviar as a luxury item in 1780, and the idea caught on.

It took until after the Russian Revolution of 1917 before caviar was given a place on gourmet's tables in the rich West. Many Russian aristocrats fled to Paris where they introduced the Russian way of living. The clever, opportunistic Petrossian brothers signed an agreement with the Russian government and got their hands on the exclusive export rights for Russian caviar. They spared no expense at the World Exhibition in Paris in 1925. But there were a notable number of spittoons placed strategically around their stand just in case their audience were not enamoured of their offering.

In the end it was the billionaire, Charles Ritz, son of the famous César Ritz, who stimulated the eating of caviar among high society and the jet set and thus ensured that its fame endures today.

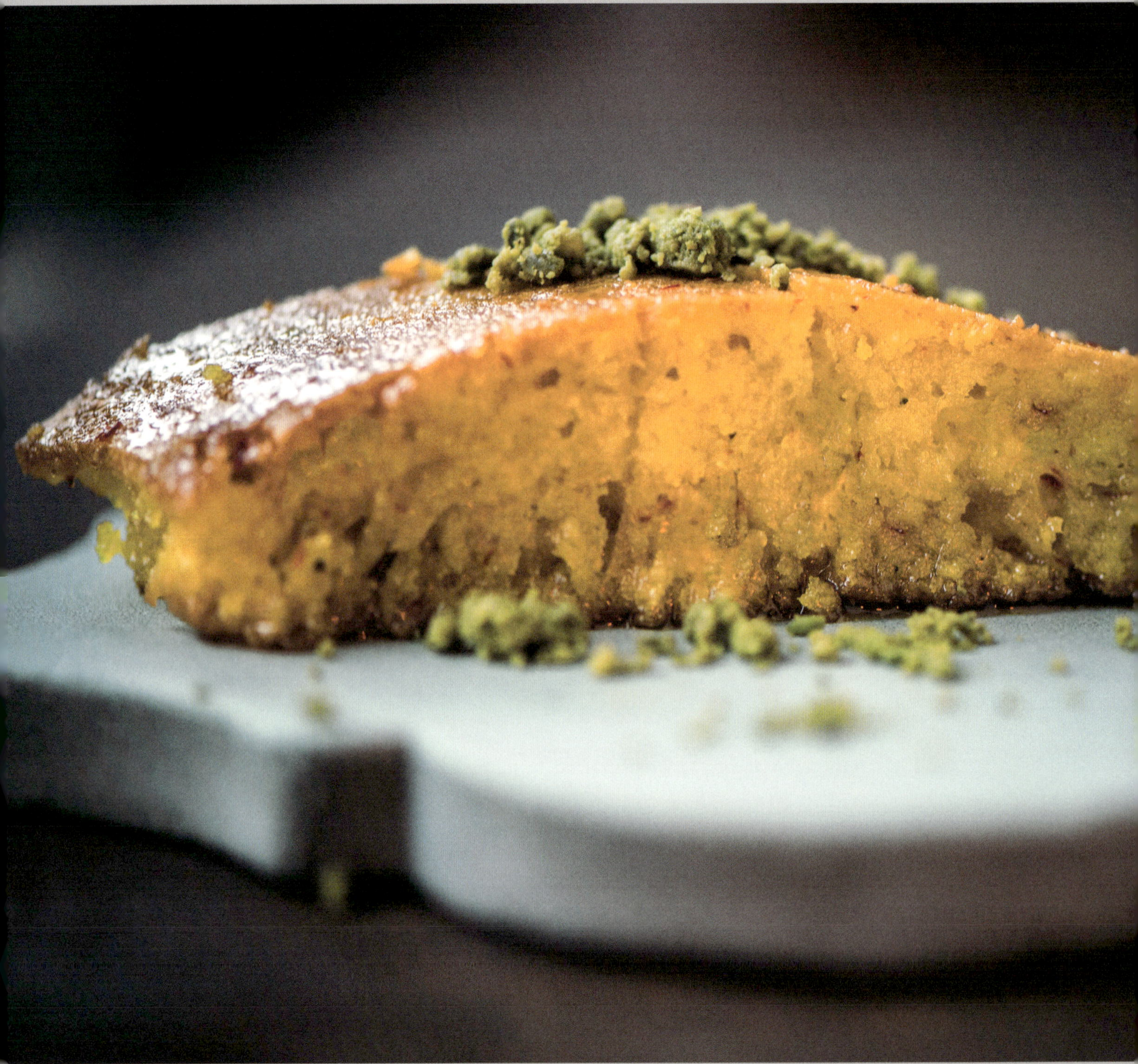

BAGHLAVA

●●●●○○

INGREDIENTS

For the dough
250 g butter ·
160 g sugar ·
6 eggs ·
120 g rosewater ·
260 g flour ·
20 g baking powder ·
4 g ground cardamom ·
260 g ground almonds ·
½ tsp saffron threads ·

For the syrup
200 g sugar ·
180 g water ·
a few saffron threads ·
60 g rosewater ·
2 tsp honey ·

METHOD

Beat the butter and sugar together. Add the eggs one by one. Add the rosewater. Sieve the flour with the baking powder into the same bowl. Add the ground cardamom and the ground almonds. Soak some saffron threads in hot water for half an hour. Add this saffron water to the mixture. Mix everything together, then spoon it into a loose-based cake tin or other cake tin and bake in a pre-heated oven (170 °C) for 35 minutes. Allow to cool slightly then cut into squares.

In the meantime, heat the ingredients for the syrup and keep it runny. Pour the syrup over the baghlava and serve.

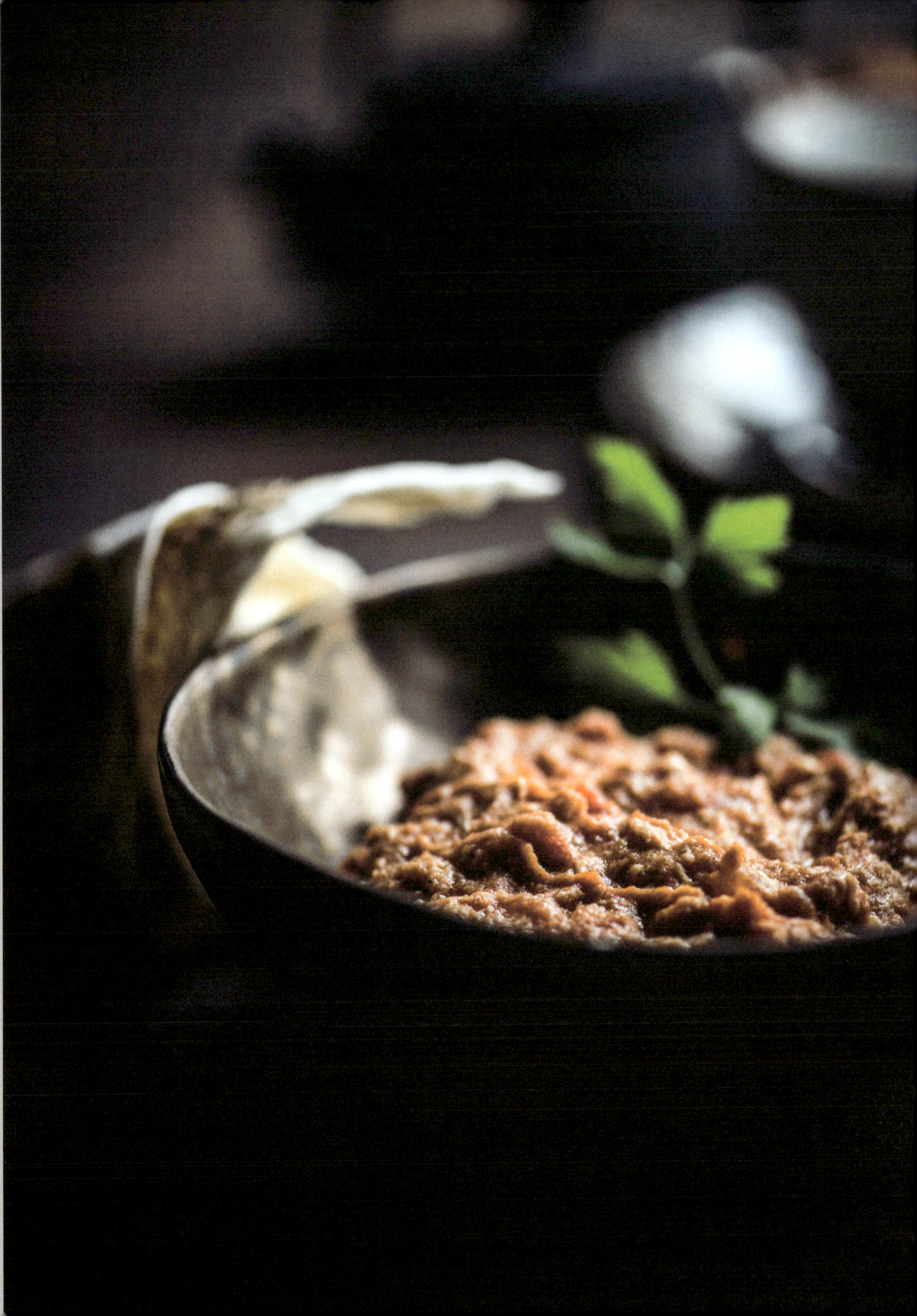

GOJEH FARANGI OMELETTE

INGREDIENTS

- 8 tomatoes, diced
- 1 Tbsp. olive oil
- salt and pepper
- 4 eggs

METHOD

Sauté the tomatoes in the olive oil, season with salt and pepper and then simmer for 5 to 10 minutes until you have tomato sauce.

Stir the eggs into the tomatoes over a gentle heat and keep stirring until you have a nice homogenous mass.

IRAN

106

SCRAMBLED EGG KHAVIAR DIVINITY

●●●○○○

INGREDIENTS

4 eggs ·
4 Tbsp. cream ·
some butter ·
30 g caviar ·

METHOD

Remove the top of the eggshells with a sharp knife.

Put the eggs, cream and butter in a saucepan over a gentle heat. Stir until smooth and season to taste with salt and pepper.

Scoop the egg mixture back into the clean eggshells and spoon the caviar on top.

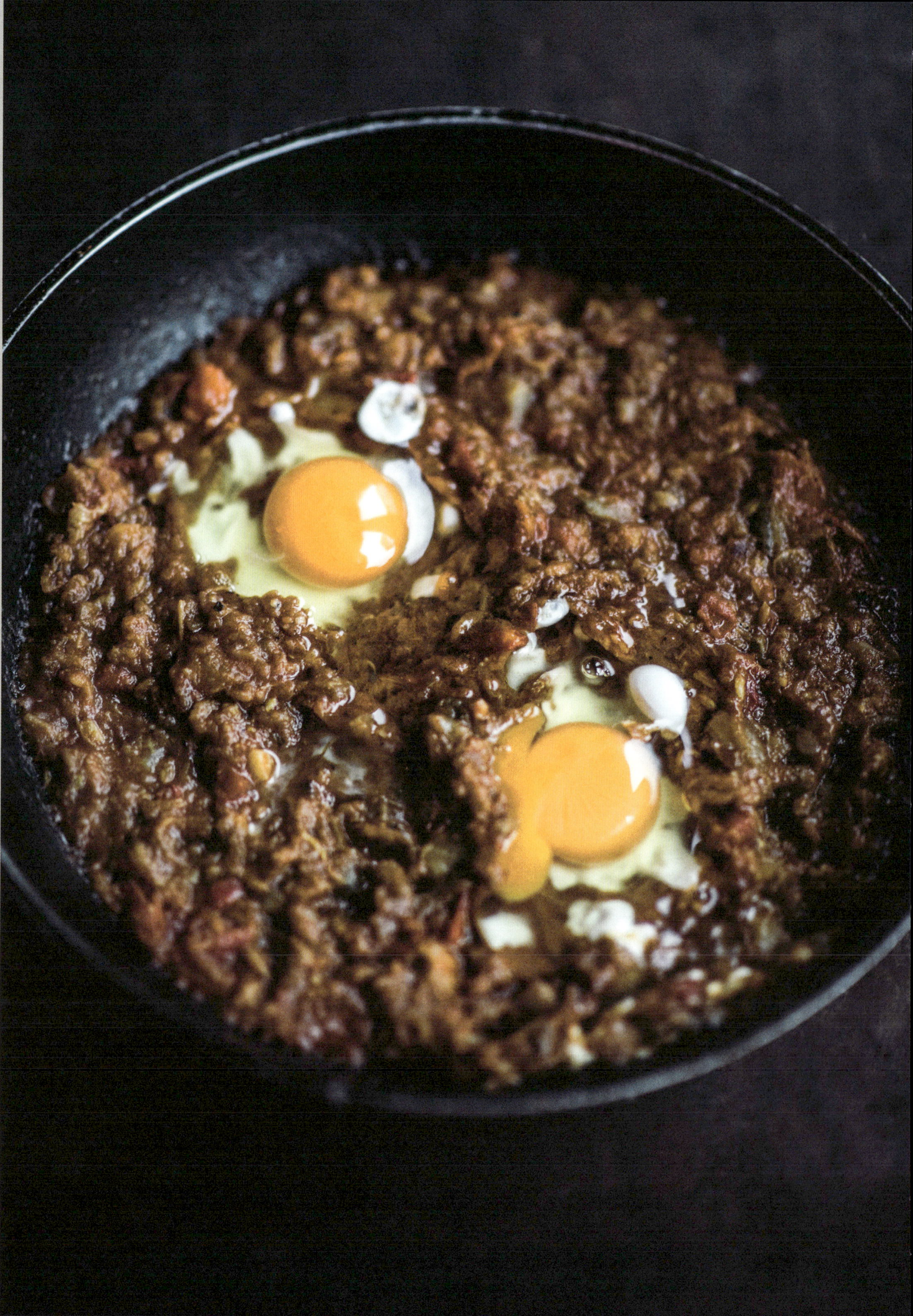

MIRZA GHASEMI

●●●○○○

INGREDIENTS

4 medium aubergines ·
coarse sea salt ·
8 cloves of garlic ·
olive oil ·
some butter ·
6 tomatoes ·
1 tsp turmeric ·
½ tsp cayenne pepper ·
4 eggs ·
pinch of oregano ·

METHOD

Grill the aubergines whole on a barbecue or in a grill pan until they are cooked and the skins have shrivelled. Remove the flesh, sprinkle with some coarse sea salt and place in the oven for five minutes to dry them out a bit and concentrate the flavour.

Crush the garlic and fry gently in olive oil and butter. Add the roughly chopped aubergine.

Peel the tomatoes, dice and add to the aubergines. Add the turmeric and cayenne pepper.

Once everything is smooth, make hollows in the mixture. Break the eggs into these hollows and cook them gently. Break the yolks with a fork as they start to set and spread them through the creamy mixture. Finish off with a sprinkling of oregano.

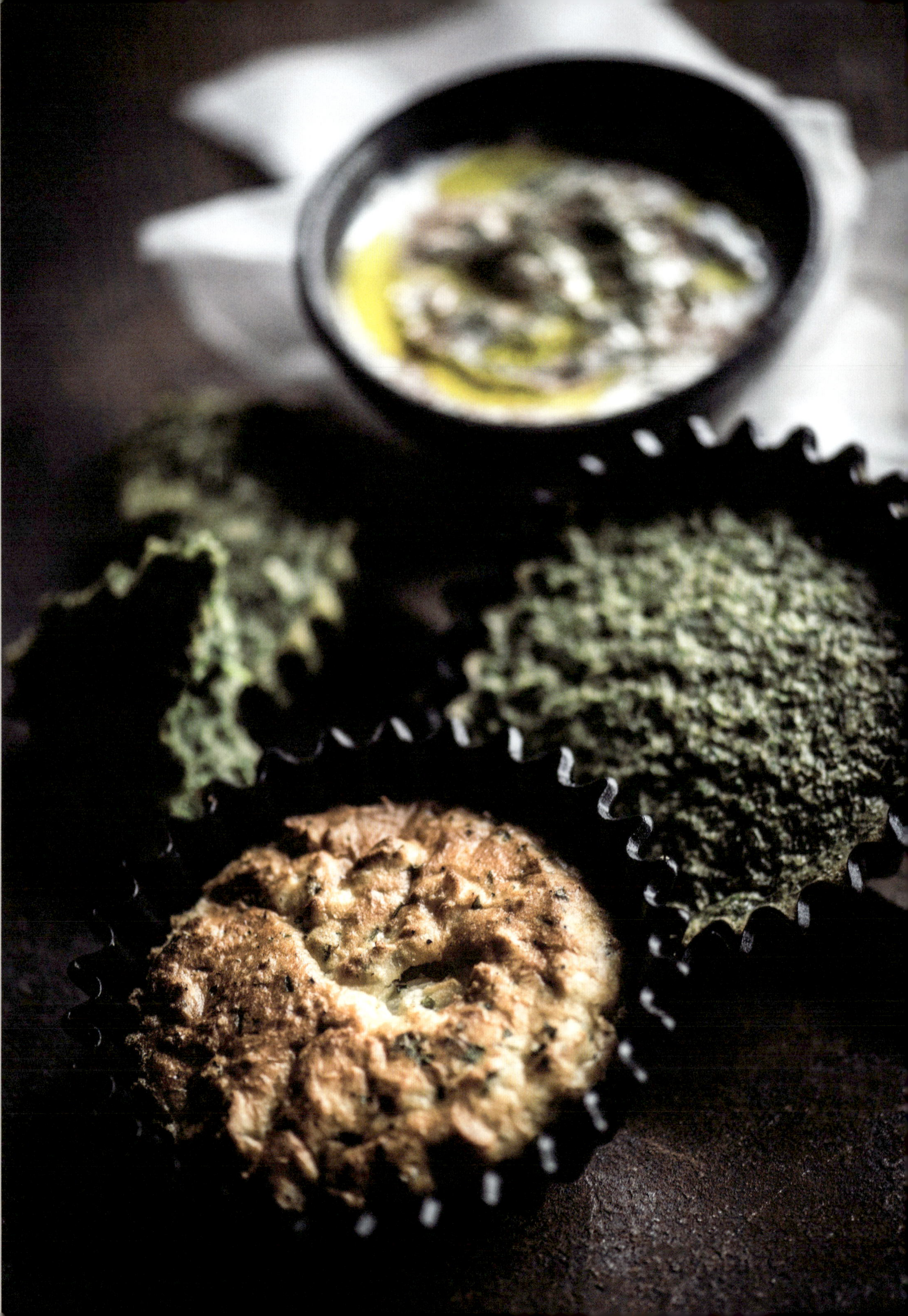

KUKU

INGREDIENTS

mashed potato (leftover potato is fine) ·
4 or 5 eggs ·
2 Tbsp. aromatic garden ·
herbs, including dill, coriander and tarragon
a few raisins ·
chopped walnuts ·

Kuku Sabzi
250 g garden herbs ·
4 eggs ·
1 Tbsp. flour ·
salt and pepper ·
½ tsp baking powder ·
a few sour berries ·
a few walnuts, chopped ·

METHOD

Mix the raw eggs and other ingredients into the mashed potato. Melt the butter in a pan and add the creamy mixture a spoonful at a time into the melted butter. Fry until the portions brown and then turn them over. Repeat this a few times until they are cooked. Serve with a dip made from yogurt, cucumber and garden herbs.

Kuku Sabzi
Mix all the ingredients together and fry in butter like a pancake. Turn over as soon as one side is crisp. Serve with a yogurt and dill dip.

RULES OF THE CAFÉ

NO SMOKING
NO FIGHTING
NO CREDIT
NO FOOD FROM OUTSIDE
NO TALKING LOUD
NO SPITTING
NO BARGAINING
NO CHEATING
NO WATER TO OUTSIDERS
NO MATCHES
NO GAMBLING
NO COMBING HAIR
ALL CASTES WELCOME

THUS SPOKE ZARATHUSTRA

Almost all the old Iranian cafés have now disappeared from Mumbai. At the beginning of the 20th century, an enormous number of Iranian immigrants arrived in what was then known as Bombay. There are now only a handful left of the over 400 cafés that were there in the 1960s, set up by the followers of the prophet Zarathustra.

→ Kerjiwal and qeema per eedu.

The number of followers of Zoroastrianism, an important religion in ancient Iran, is visibly shrinking. There are probably only about 100,000 left. One of the oldest cafés is the Merwan that dates from 1914.

These characteristic cafés were meeting places for rich businessmen, sweaty *taxi walla* and couples in love. Students had breakfast here, families dined, lawyers read their letters and writers invented their main characters. Everything happened there under a slowly revolving ceiling fan, where the Bentwood chairs were reflected in the spotted mirrors and where sepia family portraits hung on the wall. All Bombay cafés had photos of muscly Iranian wrestlers who thought that their bundles of muscles were due to eating a substantial breakfast. A classic dish in these old Iranian cafés in Bombay is a *kejriwal,* not to be confused with the famous Indian politician, Arvind Kejriwal.

Kejriwal is a classic breakfast dish in the prestigious Willingdon Sports Club in Mumbai. That institution, founded in 1918 by Lord Willingdon, is undoubtedly the most prestigious golf club in Mumbai. It was incidentally the first club in India that locals could join. There have been no new members from outside at all in the last thirty years and only blood relatives of people who are already members can join. *Kerjriwal* is a hit in this club. The dish is supposed to have been invented here after a man kept ordering a strange breakfast of toast with cheese, spring onion, chili and fried eggs. That man's name was Kejriwal and he was a Marwari, an ethnic group that is strictly vegetarian, sometimes even vegan. But his love of eggs was greater than his conviction and, since these delicacies were irrevocably a completely no-go area at home, he asked the staff in his favourite club to mix cheese with chili and spring onion, cook this on top of toast and then top it with two delicious fried eggs.

Although I'm not an Iranian wrestler, I like combining the *kejriwal* with the almost equally delicious *qeema per eedu,* in which nicely spiced minced chicken and chicken livers are fried with a fried egg and crispy chips.

DESSERTS

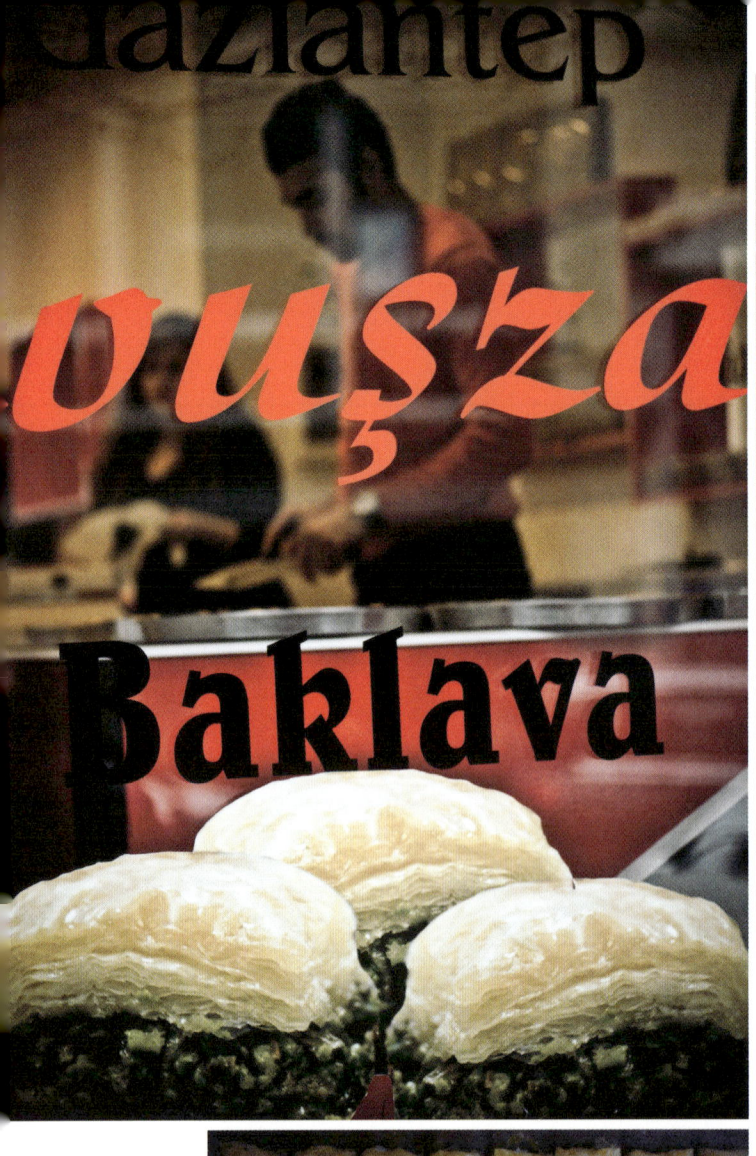

114

THE MAGIC OF BAKLAVA

People who know me, are aware that I don't really have a sweet tooth. I'm more likely to order an extra starter or a portion of cheese than a dessert. But there are one or two exceptions. I adore baklava.

It's a shame there are so few places you can really enjoy it. If you talk about sweet dishes from the Middle East, people generally think of sickly sweet, honey-drenched pallid stuff that may have lain somewhere near to a few pistachios or other nuts. But real baklava immediately gives you that thousand-and-one-nights sensation. There are few desserts more sensual than a perfect baklava.

Baklava only arrived in Gaziantep from Damascus in 1871, but it was such a success that a protected designation of origin was created for it in 2008. It's a good example of fusion in Iranian cuisine.

A pastry that has wine to thank for its existence

A *canelé* is an irresistible pastry from Bordeaux. It originated in the time that wine was still cleared with well beaten egg white. Because so much wine was produced in Bordeaux that needed to be cleared, there was a gigantic surplus of egg yolks. One way they were used creatively was the canelé. It went out of fashion for a long time, but it's back: hot and trendy.

The idea probably originated in Limoges where bread was made on the basis of flour and egg yolk, and called a *canole*. This bread was sold in Bordeaux as *canaule* or *canaulé*. In 1663, a bakers' guild was formed to unite all the *canaule* bakers. But the *canauliers* were not members of the Guild of Pastry Chefs, so milk and sugar were forbidden to them. The Guild of Pastry Chefs had a statutory monopoly on those items. But after the *canauliers* challenged this monopoly, the Council of State in Versailles agreed with them in 1755. An edict to lay this down in law, as well as the number of *canauliers* allowed in each town, appeared in 1767. There were already 39 in

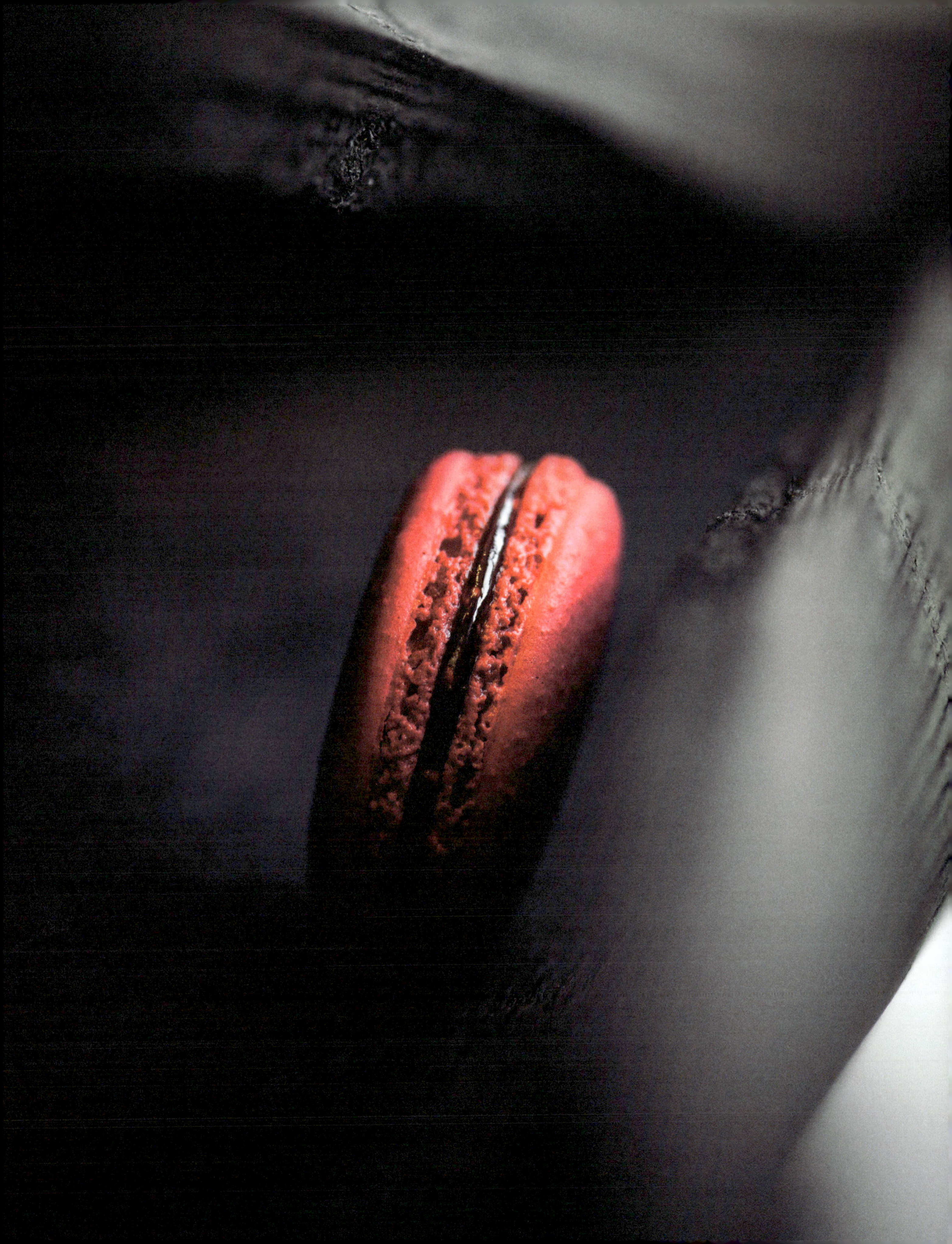

Bordeaux in 1785. The French Revolution of 1789 put an end to guilds in France, but not to the profession of *canaulier*.

Into the groove

A pastry chef from Saint-Emilion dug out an old *canaule* recipe at the beginning of the 20th century and added rum and vanilla to it. He gave the pastry its current form because the association between *canaule* and *cannelure* (groove or notch) was pretty obvious. No one knows when exactly the name changed to *cannelé*, but we do know that the spelling with two 'n's was changed to *canelé* in 1985. The very traditional pâtissiers Ladurée or Pierre Hermé tended to retain the old traditional spelling for this perfectly caramelised pastry with its unique fluffy heart.

Macarons

Why are these tiny meringue sandwiches in all sorts of colours and flavours so popular? In Paris especially they are still a symbol of refinement and class, and the French have a sort of chauvinistic relationship with them. But did they originate in France?

The macaron has been around in France since the Middle Ages. Then as now, they were made from almonds, egg whites and sugar: crunchy on the outside, soft on the inside. In Rabelais' time it was only a single layer, not a sandwich as it is now.

The assumption is that Catherine de Medici brought the maccheroni to France from Italy in 1533, when she became a member of the French royal family. Others assert that maccheroni were produced as early as 791 in the Abbey of Cormery and were given the name 'monk's navel' because of their shape.

Nostradamus does not mention the macaron in his *Traité des Fardements et des Confitures*, written in 1552. Later that year however, Rabelais published the recipe for macarons in his *Quart livre*. In the Basque country, more precisely St.-Jean de Luz, the macaron appeared at the wedding of Louis XIV in 1660. A pastry chef named Adam apparently had the recipe lying around in a drawer somewhere.

The secret remained in the Venetian monasteries, however, until the first recipe for macarons appeared in France where it soon became immensely popular.

Two nuns from the Carmelite Order in Nancy are known to have baked macarons and sold them to stay alive during the French Revolution in 1792. They became known as 'the Macaron sisters'. The city of Nancy honoured them in 1952 and the place where they used to bake their macarons was named after them. It is and remains incredibly difficult to make the perfect macaron; that's probably why there is no definitive recipe. Through time, the recipes were altered a little in the various regions, but the sisters' recipe was considered to be the basis.

The Dalloyau brothers had been making macarons at the court of Versailles since 1682. They were served to all the sovereigns up to Louis XVI and Marie-Antoinette. In 1802, the descendants of the Dalloyau brothers founded the world-fa-

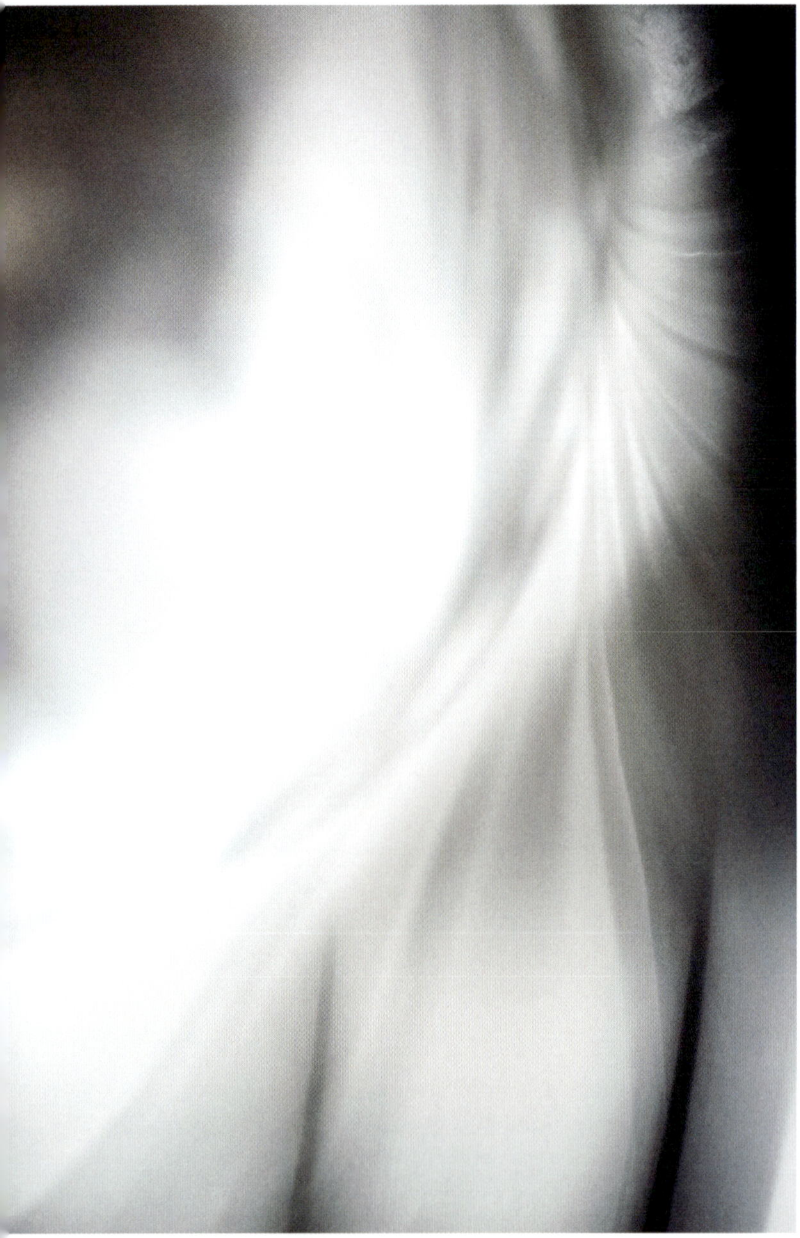
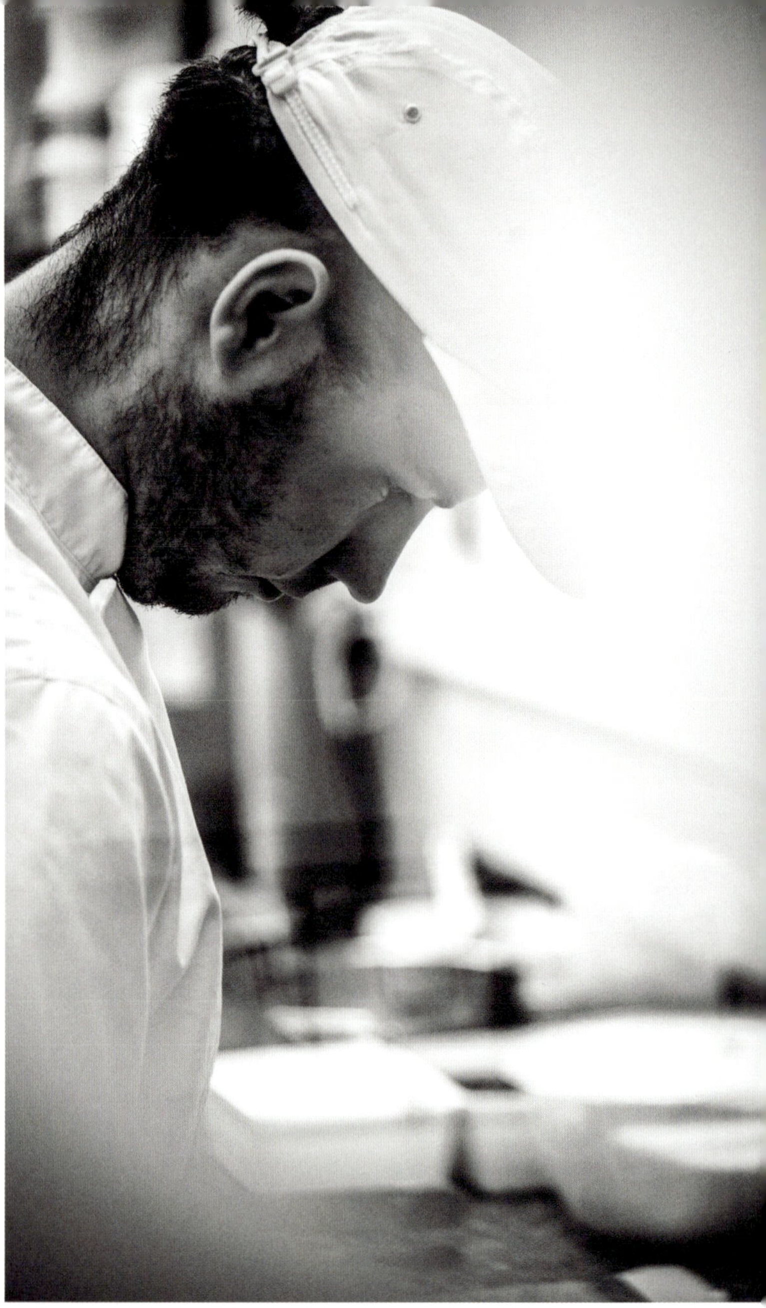
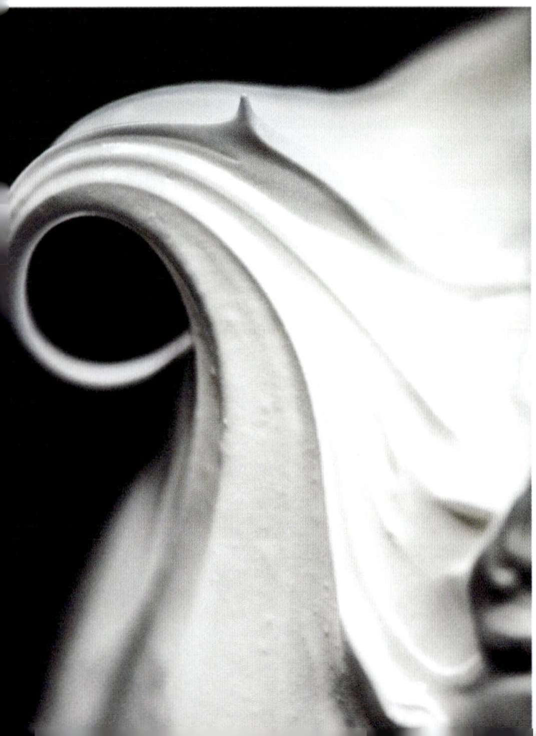
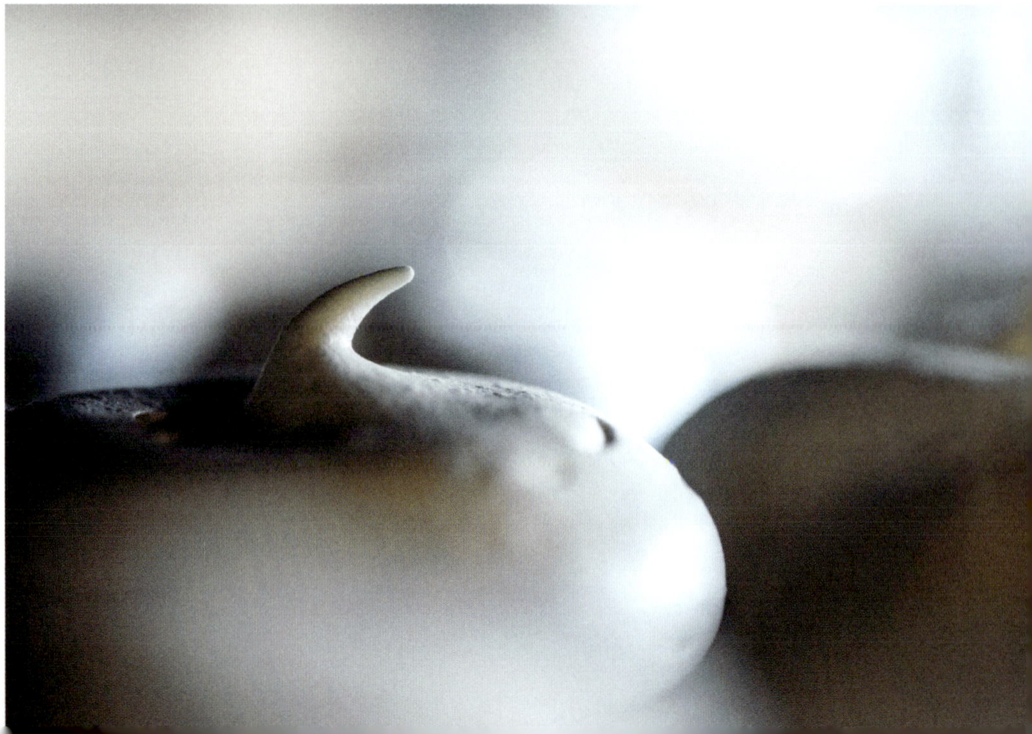

→ Joost Arijs

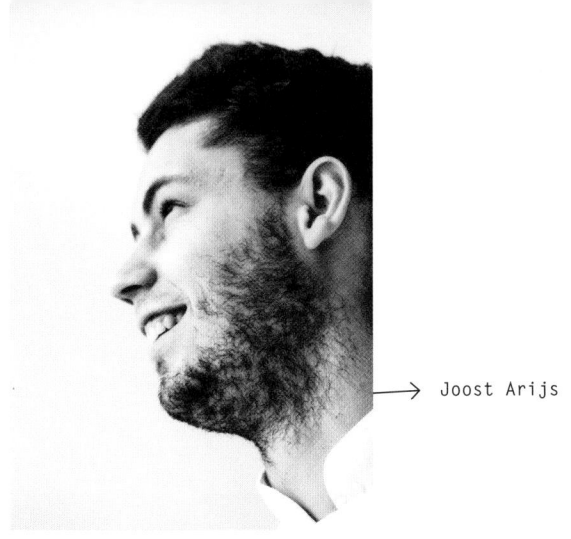

mous house of the same name.

The shape, a sort of meringue sandwich held together with a soft, sweet filling, was an idea that came from Paris. The *macaron Parisien* appeared in 1830, later made popular by the company owned by a certain Louis-Ernest Ladurée.

The macaron was on the march and would not be stopped. I think that Marie-Antoinette had something to do with it too. The eponymous film by Sofia Coppola made in 2006 depicts the queen literally surrounded by decadent pyramids of multi-coloured macarons (all from Ladurée's workshops of course). Since then we have seen the macaron popping up in America, China, Japan and South Korea. If you are tempted to buy macarons, buy them on 20 March. Pierre Hermé proclaimed that date as Macaron Day in 2005. The better shops then often give away free samples of their craft...

Fast as lightning

Around 1850 something fantastic turned up in the patisserie world in Lyon, something so delicious that you eat it as fast as lightning, which is why it is called éclair. It is a large finger-shaped pastry made from choux pastry, filled with *crème patissière* and covered with a layer of chocolate icing. Choux pastry was already known in the Middle Ages. Crème patissière was invented by François Massialot in 1691 and Gillet of the Lemoine bakery gave us the fondant technique in 1824.

The choux pastry master in the 18th century was of course Antonin Carême, without doubt the biggest name in the history of patisserie. He perfected choux pastry and used it in a few of his legendary inventions such as the *croquembouche*, the *profiterole* or the *duchesse*, the old name for the éclair. No one dared to change the name of the *duchesse* until 20 years after Carême's death.

Joost Arijs

Perfection and nothing less: that is what Joost Arijs aims for. In contrast to many of his colleagues, he makes truly no-nonsense patisserie. No circus tents of Louis Vuitton handbags, but a purified style that reveals enormous precision. He went to college in Bruges and learned from the grand masters of patisserie. Before he started out on his own, he was chef pâtissier at the best restaurant in Belgium, Hof van Cleve. This native of Kluisberg stayed there two years, perfecting his philosophy. He continued to believe in the purity of ingredients, flavours and textures.

Taking a peek at the display counter in his shop in Ghent or Antwerp tells you enough: you won't see any twiddly bits or over-ornate creations; instead, his work reflects an almost Japanese calm. The flavours are exceptionally balanced; they show clearly that Arijs has mastered the classic dishes perfectly and that they form the basis for his evolution into a great master, because let's not be too discreet about this, it can't get much better than this.

DESSERTS

120

OPÉRA

Coffee biscuit base, chocolate ganache, crème au beurre with coffee, coffee syrup and ganache icing – recipe for a cake measuring 12 cm by 12 cm.

INGREDIENTS

Coffee biscuit base
- 210 g egg white
- 112 g granulated sugar
- 162 g egg yolks
- 25 g coffee extract
- 62 g ground almonds
- 62 g icing sugar

Chocolate ganache
- 10 g cream (35%)
- 50 g whole milk
- 80 g dark chocolate (70%), broken into pieces
- 25 g butter (soft)

Crème au beurre with coffee
- 72 g granulated sugar
- 5 g glucose
- 10 g water
- ½ egg yolk
- ½ egg
- 112 g butter (soft)
- ¼ vanilla pod
- 2 g coffee extract

Coffee syrup
- 80 g coffee syrup*
- 80 g cream (35%)
- 80 g water
- 12.5 g condensced milk
- 6 g instant coffee
- 27 g coffee extract

Ganache icing
- 250 g cream (35%)
- 90 g glucose
- 90 g granulated sugar
- 90 g butter
- 250 g fondant chocolate, broken into pieces

Building up and decorating
- 100 g fondant chocolate, melted

METHOD

Coffee biscuit base
Pre-heat the oven to 180 °C. Whisk the egg whites with the granulated sugar. Add the sugar a third at a time (see tip). Fold the whisked egg yolks and the coffee extract into this mixture and then add the ground almonds and icing sugar. Divide the batter over three baking trays and bake in the oven for 17 minutes. Set aside to cool.

Tip:
If you are whisking egg whites with granulated sugar, add the sugar in three batches instead of all at once. This prevents the sugar from dissolving and making the egg white limp.

Chocolate ganache
Bring the cream and the whole milk to the boil. Pour the boiling cream and milk over the pieces of chocolate. Cool to 35 °C and mix in the soft butter. Set aside.

Crème au beurre with coffee
Bring the sugar and the glucose to the boil with the water (to 121 °C). In the meantime, whisk the egg yolks and the egg and pour on the boiling sugar water in a constant stream. Beat until cold. Finally add the butter, vanilla and the coffee extract and mix well.

Coffee syrup
Bring all the ingedients to the boil then divide the syrup into three equal portions.

Ganache icing
Bring the cream, glucose, sugar and butter to the boil then pour the boiling liquid over the pieces of chocolate. Beat until smooth, cover with cling film and place in the fridge.

Building up and decorating
Take one flat biscuit base and spread a wafer-thin layer of dark chocolate over it (so that the syrup doesn't make the biscuit mushy). Turn the biscuit base over so that the layer of chocolate is on the bottom. Now spread one portion of the coffee syrup on the biscuit base. Pour the chocolate ganache over the top and spread it evenly. Place a second biscuit layer on top and spread the second portion of coffee syup over it. Pour half of the crème au beurre over it and spread it evenly.
Place the third biscuit base on top and again spread it with coffee syrup. Finish off with the rest of the crème au beurre and again spread it evenly. Put the cake in the fridge overnight to set. Heat the ganache icing, pour it over the cake and spread it evenly. Let the cake harden and the cut a square out of it measuring 12 by 12 cm.

DESSERTS

122

CHOCOLATE MACARONS

Recipe for 50 macarons

●●●●●

INGREDIENTS

200 g ground almonds (100%) ·
200 g icing sugar ·
75 g egg whites at room temperature ·
40 g dark chocolate (70%), melted ·
200 g granulated sugar ·
50 g water ·
another 75 g egg whites at room temperature ·
some cocoa powder ·

Filling: chocolate ganache
250 g cream (35%) ·
25 g inverted sugar syrup ·
225 g dark chocolate (70%), broken into pieces ·
25 g cocoa mass ·
85 g butter (soft) ·

METHOD

Sieve the ground almonds and the icing sugar finely and mix with the first lot of egg white. Add the chocolate. Bring the granulated sugar and the water to the boil (to 118 °C). In the meantime, whisk the second lot of egg white. Once the sugar water reaches 118 °C, pour it onto the whisked egg white in a continuous stream. Cool the mixture to 50 °C. Now mix it into the ground almonds and icing sugar mixture until the batter becomes softer; spoon into a piping bag.

Pre-heat the oven to 160 °C.

Pipe little blobs (max. 4 cm) onto a baking tray lined with greaseproof paper or a silicone baking mat. Sieve a little cocoa powder over the top. Leave the macarons to rest for 15 to 30 minutes until they form a crust before putting them in the oven. Give them 14 minutes at 160 °C and they will be ready. Remove them from the oven and allow to cool.

Filling: chocolate ganache
Bring the cream to the boil with the inverted sugar syrup. Pour this mixture through a fine pointed sieve over the pieces of chocolate and the cocoa mass. Mix well and cool to 35 °C. Finally, mix the butter into it and leave the ganache to set.

Fill the macarons with a thin layer of ganache.

DESSERTS

124

MATCHA CAKE

Matcha biscuit base, citrus coulis, matcha cremeux, white chocolate mousse

🥚🥚🥚🥚🥚◯

INGREDIENTS

Matcha biscuit base
- 40 g egg yolks
- 280 g eggs
- 180 g sugar
- 136 g flour
- 16 g matcha powder
- 55 g milk
- 30 g oil

Matcha cremeux
- 5 g powdered gelatine
- 25 g water
- 22 g milk
- 365 g cream
- 12 g matcha powder
- 88 g egg yolks
- 65 g sugar

Citrus coulis
- 4 g powdered gelatine
- 20 g water
- 130 g passion fruit, pureed
- 52 g bergamot, pureed
- 40 g calamansi, pureed
- 15 g orange juice
- 1 vanilla pod
- 5 g fresh mint leaves
- 0.5 g cloves
- 8 g calamansi vinegar
- 2 drops of bergamot extract
- 40 g sugar

White chocolate mousse
- 20 g gelatine powder
- 100 g water
- 530 g whole milk
- 107 g egg yolks
- 50 g sugar
- 1190 g white chocolate
- 1040 g cream (35%)

METHOD

Matcha biscuit base
Beat the egg yolks with the whole eggs and the sugar. Sieve the flour and the matcha powder. Warm the milk gently with the oil and mix everything carefully. Spread the batter out on a baking tray in a circle with a diameter of 16 cm (use a baking ring) and bake in a pre-heated oven at 180 °C for about 15 minutes.

Matcha cremeux
First sprinkle the powdered gelatine into the water and leave to soak. Boil the milk with the cream and the matcha powder. Mix the egg yolks into the sugar and make a custard with the boiled cream. Add the dissolved gelatine and mix. Leave to cool.

Citrus coulis
Sprinkle the powdered gelatine into the water and leave to soak. Add all the other ingredients together, heat gently and allow the flavours to infuse for five minutes. Sieve the mixture and put in the fridge to set.

White chocolate mousse
Sprinkle the powdered gelatine into the water and leave to soak. Whip the cream to form soft peaks. Make a custard with the whole milk, egg yolks and the sugar. Pour the custard onto the white chocolate and mix in the soaked gelatine. Cool to 27 °C and then fold in the whipped cream.

Assembling the cake
Use a 4-cm-high baking ring with a diameter of 16 cm. Place the matcha biscuit base inside it and build the cake up in the same order as the recipes. Put the cake in the fridge for 60 minutes before serving. Decorate as you wish.

DESSERTS

126

LEMON MERINGUE PIE

Pâte sablée, lemon crème, Italian meringue

INGREDIENTS

Pâte sablée
- 480 g butter ·
- 240 g icing sugar ·
- 8 g salt ·
- 3 eggs ·
- 100 g ground almonds (100%) ·
- 800 g flour ·
- vanilla ·

Lemon crème
- 150 g eggs ·
- 300 g sugar ·
- 4 g lemon zest ·
- 260 g lemon juice ·
- 400 g butter ·

Italian meringue
- 50 g water ·
- 200 g sugar ·
- 100 g egg white ·

METHOD

Pâte sablée
Mix all the ingedients together to make the pastry. Roll out and cut out rings 2 cm deep and 6 cm in diameter. Bake in a pre-heated oven at 170 °C for 15 minutes.

Lemon crème
Mix the eggs, sugar, lemon zest and lemon juice together. Heat to 85 °C and pour through a sieve. Allow to cool to 40 °C. Mix the softened butter into the mixture.

Italian meringue
Boil the water with the sugar to 115 °C. Whisk the egg yolk. Bring the sugar water to a fast boil until it reaches 121 °C. Pour the boiling sugar mass onto the beaten egg yolk and whisk the mixture until it cools.

Constructing the pie
Fill the pastry cases with lemon crème and then pipe spiralsof Italian meringue on top.

DESSERTS

CANELÉS DE BORDEAUX

●●●●●●

INGREDIENTS

300 g flour ·
1300 g sugar ·
180 g egg yolks ·
200 g eggs ·
2500 g milk ·
1 vanilla pod ·
300 g dark rum ·

METHOD

Mix all the ingredients together and bake in cannelé moulds for 60 minutes at 180 °C.

DESSERTS

CARAMEL CHOUX

●●●●○○

INGREDIENTS

Choux pastry
200 g milk ·
200 g water ·
176 g butter ·
8 g salt ·
8 g sugar ·
224 g flour ·
120 g egg whites and 80 g egg yolks ·

Hazelnut crumble
180 g butter ·
200 g powdered hazelnuts ·
200 g caster sugar ·
240 g flour ·
6 g salt ·

Caramel
1000 g cream ·
1000 g sugar ·
1 vanilla pod ·

Caramel crème
375 g cream ·
375 g crème patissière ·
6 g powdered gelatine ·
30 g water ·
225 g caramel ·

Constructing the choux
puff pastry ·
icing sugar ·

METHOD

Choux pastry
Heat the milk, water, butter, salt and sugar together. Stir in the flour. Keep stirring until the batter leaves the sides of the pan clean. Transfer to a food mixer and mix in the eggs. Pipe little profiteroles of equal-sizes.

Hazelnut crumble
Mix all the ingredients together then roll out between two sheets of greaseproof paper until wafer thin. Press out small circles and place them on top of the piped profiteroles. Ensure that the profiteroles are covered completely. Bake the profiteroles with the crumble topping in a pre-heated oven at 200 °C for 20 minutes.

Caramel
Boil the cream with the vanilla pod. Caramelise the sugar and pour on the boiled cream. Leave to cool.

Caramel crème
Whip the cream. Sprinkle the powdered gelatine into the water and leave to soak. Heat the crème patissière gently and stir in the caramel and the dissolved gelatine. Fill the baked profiteroles with the caramel crème.

Assembling the cake
Bake a square of puff pastry and cut out a ring from it measuring 6 cm in diameter. Pipe a blob of caramel crème on top and stick three filled profiteroles onto it. Decorate with a little icing sugar.

CLASSIC DISHES

132

Peter van Goossens from the Hof van Cleve restaurant.

PETER GOOSSENS

The hen that laid golden eggs
The age-old story warning the listener against greed was first found in the fourth section of the Buddhist book Vinya, in the Suvannahamsa Jataka, and is about a swan with golden feathers. This swan allows the poor man to pluck a golden feather every day in order to sell them. But the greedy mother plucks all the feathers at once, causing them to turn immediately into ordinary white feathers. To make matters worse, when the swan starts to grow new feathers they are also ordinary white ones.

A Greek version of this moral tale circulated in the formerly Persian territory of Sogdiana. A succession of panels in a mural in Panjakent, in the Western province of Sugdh in Tajikistan, depicts a man who finds a golden egg and then kills the goose that laid it in order to get more of the gold faster. And in Mahabharata there is a story about wild birds that spat gold and were strangled in an attempt to get more.

The versions by Avianus and Caxton are the best known in the West: a poor farmer sees a goose that lays a golden egg every day. After a few days, one egg a day is no longer enough. The man thinks that there must be a large lump of gold inside the animal and so kills it, with the resulting consequences. It took until Jean de la Fontaine`s fable *La Poule aux oeufs d'or* for the goose to become a hen.

Peter Goossens puts a lovely interpretation of it in one of his dishes.

Kruishouten, the egg capital of the world
World fame sometimes comes without being sought. In September 1670, Louis XIV promoted Aaishove from a Seigniory to a County. One of the perks this brought was that an annual fair could now be arranged. That was usually a reason for festivities lasting for days and income for everyone. But no one expected that this annual fair would give the municipality such a flying start that the consequences would still be apparent today.

The most notable local product was eggs, and Kruishoutem acquired a reputation for trade in eggs that extended far beyond the national borders. Kruishoutem has been at the pinnacle of the European egg trade since the 1950s. The export of eggs was an extremely important source of income for this pretty rural village. That was a good enough reason to bring the theme up to date and focus attention on this folklore heritage and reinstate it. Two giants were built in 1952 to symbolise the vitality of the local people, and were named Pier de Eierboer and Mie de Boterboerin [Pete the Egg Farmer and Mie the Farmer's Wife]. The crowning glory was the first edition of the Golden Egg Festivals in 1955. Since then Kruishoutem has been welcoming

CLASSIC DISHES

134

many thousands of visitors every year throughout the Easter weekend who want to witness the election of the Egg King and Egg Queen and of course the spectacle of eggs being thrown from the church tower. Chance will have it that this municipality has another national treasure who rules over Belgium's culinary scene. We asked the maestro, Peter Goossens, whose world-famous culinary temple, Hof van Cleve, is situated in Kruishoutem, to share some egg dishes with us.

Simply the Best

Hof van Cleve will celebrate its 30th anniversary in 2017 and it has become a permanent fixture at the top of the world's very best restaurants in recent years. Being able to eat here is like making an appointment with history every time. There are still a few certainties in this world and one of them is that Hof van Cleve is a benchmark for your palate, a benchmark for people who enjoy verifying the very highest scores in the most renowned guides, and a benchmark for teamwork, a perfectly oiled machine in which a Champions League match is played twice a day by the entire team. This old farmhouse at the top of a hill in the Kruishoutem landscape is a factory, a factory where they smile and produce happy people.

Peter Goossens – bigger than Jesus

I have immense respect and admiration for Peter Goossens and I make no attempt to disguise it. I get to visit a great many culinary celebrities, but I will always have a soft spot for this kitchen, purely because I have such immense respect for this child of the gods whose food tastes as if it has been touched by an angel.

Goossens' cuisine has it all: flavour, depth, creativity, respect for tradition, simplicity,... His cuisine is a craft and you can see and taste exactly that. Goossens is a chef who is bigger than his restaurant. The Godfather of Belgian gastronomy is probably the greatest chef Belgium has ever known. Now, more than ever, he serves as an example to all the young pups in the kitchen. Goossens is there for his guests; the entire process revolves around them. Their experience is crucial. Their expectations are sky-high and failure isn't an option. Goossens' professional honour is something many colleagues could learn from.

Goossens understands the art of placing oneself in the service of a product, playing second fiddle to trends and fashion fads, and not being guilty of taking an ego trip – by putting his guest's happiness first. A great chef and above all, a great man.

CLASSIC DISHES

GOLDEN EGG

●●●●○○

INGREDIENTS

Crème Comté
- 125 g milk
- 25 g cream
- 50 g chicken stock
- 75 g Comté cheese
- 2.5 g agar agar
- salt and pepper

Egg yolk crème
- 125 g egg yolk
- 75 g cream
- 75 g milk
- 3 g agar agar
- nutmeg
- salt and pepper

Jellied ham
- 100 g cooked ham
- 100 g dried ham
- 1 medium onion, chopped finely
- 5 button mushrooms, chopped finely
- 3 cloves of garlic, chopped finely
- 100 ml sherry
- thyme and bay leaf
- chicken stock
- 3.5 g vegetarian gelatine
- 2 sheets of gelatine

Chorizo powder
- 100 g chorizo

METHOD

Crème Comté
Bring the milk, cream, chicken fond and cheese to the boil with the agar agar. Put in the fridge to set. Mix in a Thermomix until smooth. Push through a fine sieve.

Egg yolk crème
Bring all the ingredients to the boil. Put in the fridge to set. Blend until smooth. Add the seasoning. Push through a fine sieve.

Jellied ham
Cut the ham into chunks and fry. Add the onion, mushrooms and garlic. Fry until golden. Moisten with sherry. Add the thyme and bay leaf and cover with chicken stock. Simmer on a low heat for 60 minutes. Pass through a fine sieve and leave to cool in the fridge. Remove the layer of fat. Boil down until you have the flavour you want. Bring 200 g ham stock to the boil with 3.5 g vegetarian gelatin. Add the sheets of gelatine to it and leave to set in a mould of your choice.

Chorizo powder
Slice the chorizo thinly and leave for 24 hours in an Easy Dry food dehydrator. Chop finely in a blender.

Now fill the golden egg. First put in the egg yolk crème, then the jellied ham and finally the crème Comté. Garnish with chorizo powder.

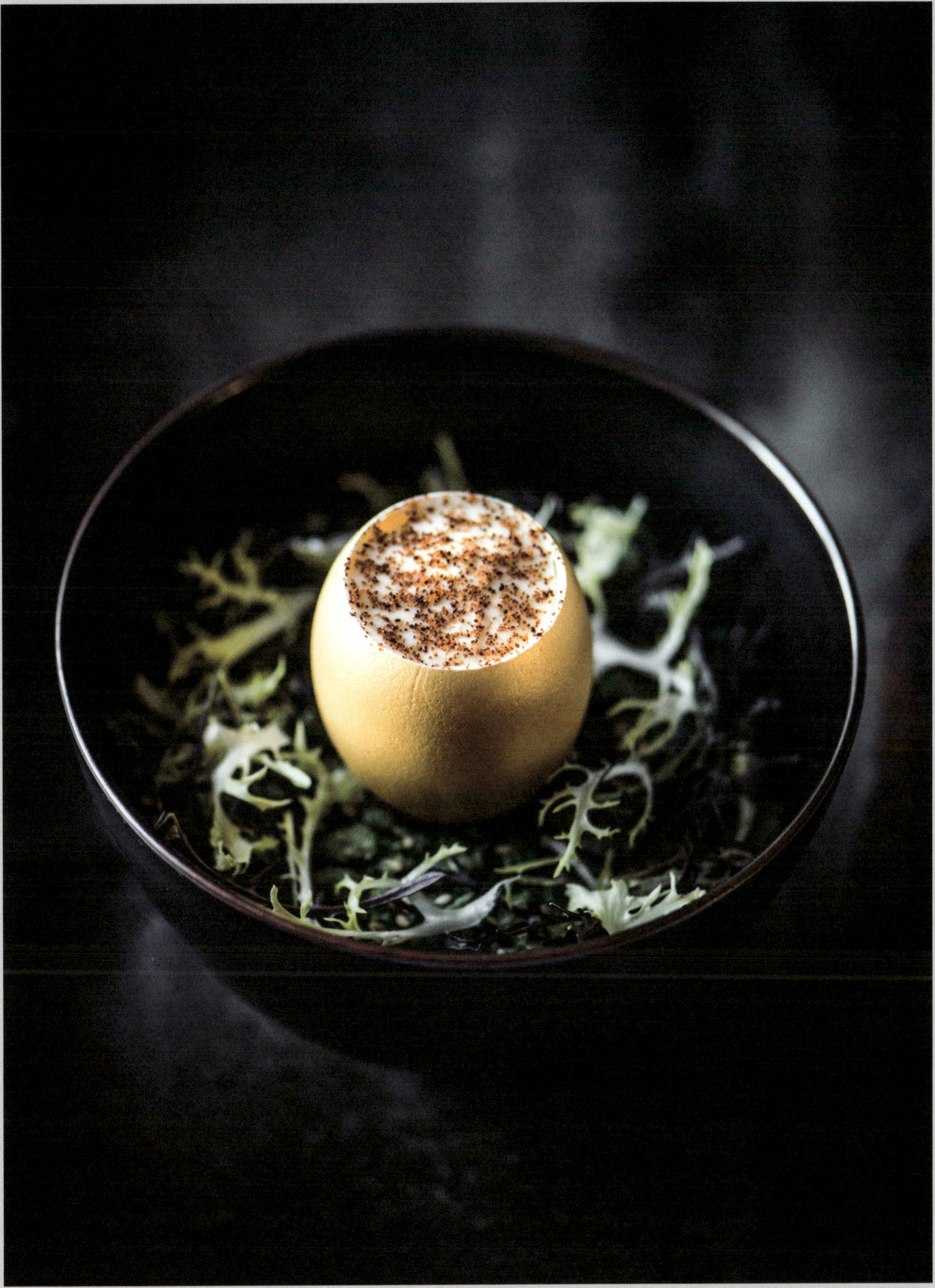

CLASSIC DISHES

WHITE TRUFFLE OMELETTE

●●●○○

INGREDIENTS

Egg batter
- 2 eggs
- 2 Tbsp. cream
- nutmeg
- salt and pepper

Garnish for omelette
- 3 slices of leek, cooked
- compote of Cevennes onions
- Stracchino cheese

Compote of Cevennes onions
- 4 Cevennes onions
- butter
- 1 sprig of thyme
- 1 bay leaf
- 1 cube of dried ham
- salt and pepper

Corsé chicken
- 6 chicken wings
- 2 shallots
- 4 cloves of garlic
- 10 button mushrooms
- thyme and bay leaf
- 3 litres of chicken stock
- 4 dessertspoonfuls of clarified butter
- 50 g white truffle

METHOD

Egg batter
Beat the eggs with the cream. Add the seasoning and then pass through a fine sieve. Pour into a whipped cream dispenser and add two gas cartridges. Place in the fridge. Heat a non-stick pan. Carefully squirt the mixture into the pan and add the garnish.

Compote of Cevennes onions
Thinly slice the onions. Cook in butter with the thyme and bay leaf and a cube of dried ham. Leave to simmer for one hour on a gentle heat. Remove the herbs and season with salt and pepper.

Corsé chicken
Roast the chicken wings in the oven at 180 °C until dark brown. Fry the shallot, garlic and mushrooms until brown. Add a sprig of thyme and a bay leaf. Add the chicken wings and moisten with chicken stock. Simmer on a low heat for 2 hours. Push through a fine sieve. Put in the fridge to set. Remove the fat from the fond and boil down until you have the flavour you want. Season and add the clarified butter.

Omelette
Heat a non-stick frying pan. Carefully squirt the batter into the pan and add the garnish. Roll up. Place the omelette on a plate and scatter slices of white truffle on top. Finish the dish by drizzling the Corsé Chicken sauce around the plate.

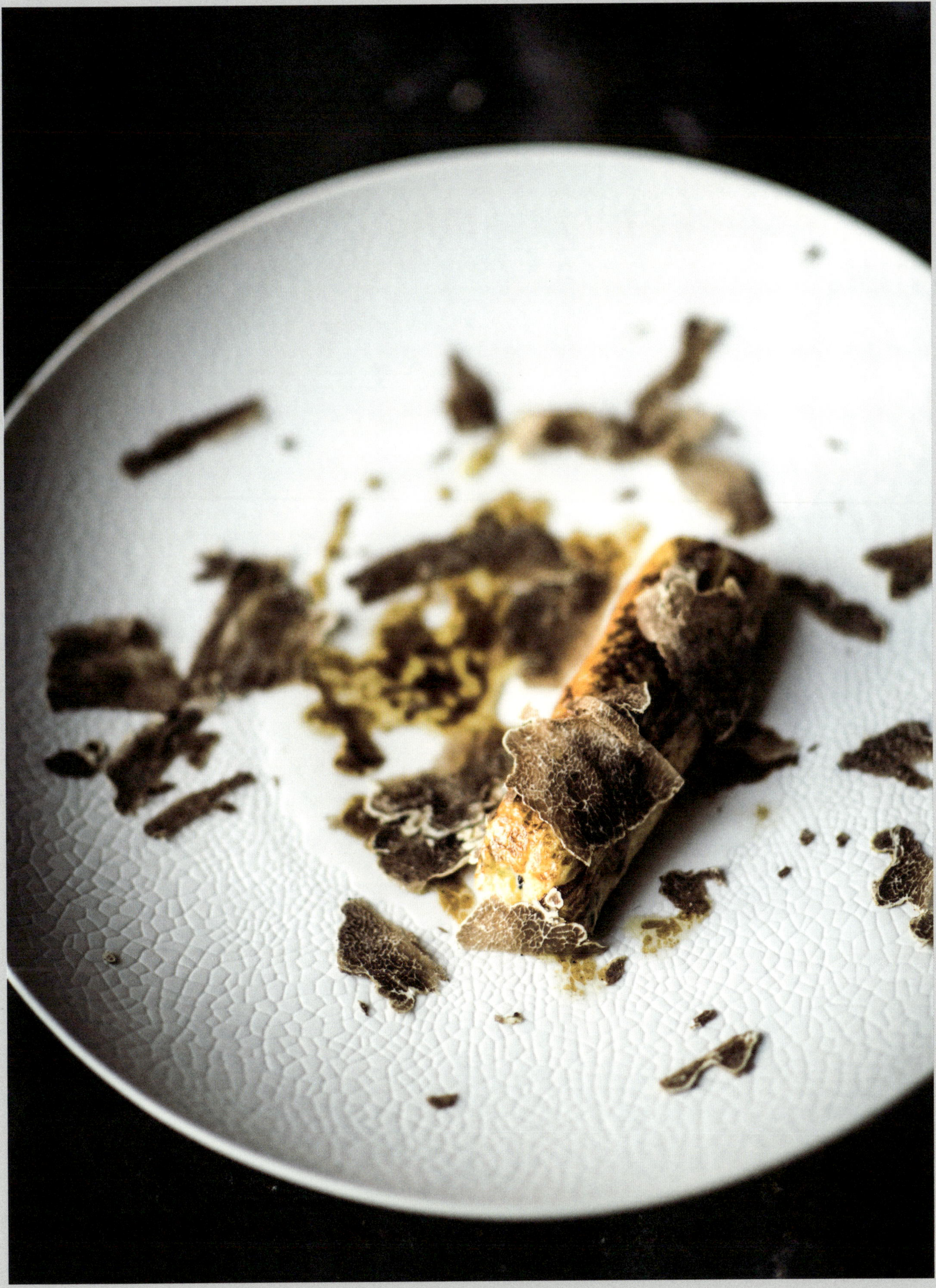

CLASSIC DISHES

LANGOUSTINE EGG YOLK

●●●●●●

INGREDIENTS

Raw egg yolk emulsion
2 egg yolks ·
2 drops of Tabasco ·
1 g Worcester sauce ·
1 tsp mayonnaise ·
4 g white miso paste ·
2 g soy sauce ·

Black garlic crème
120 g milk ·
80 g chicken stock ·
3 g agar agar ·
100 g black garlic ·
50 g dark miso paste ·
50 g squid ink ·
1 tsp soy sauce ·
1 tsp lime juice ·
salt and pepper ·

Leek oil
30 g leeks, green part only ·
20 g parsley ·
30 g spinach ·
250 g olive oil ·

Hijiki marinade
20 g fine hijiki ·
40 g water ·
40 g soy sauce ·

Langoustine tartare
200 g langoustine tartare ·
1 tsp white soy sauce ·
1 tsp olive oil ·
5 coriander leaves ·
salt and pepper ·
1 tsp sushi vinegar ·
2 drops of sesame oil ·
40 g water ·

Garnish
grated Cecina (Spanish smoked beef) ·
coriander cress ·

METHOD

Raw egg yolk emulsion
Whisk everything together to form a homogenous mass.

Black garlic crème
Bring the milk, chicken fond and agar agar to the boil then leave to set in the fridge. After that, mix all the ingredients to form a smooth emulsion and season to taste. Push through a fine sieve.

Leek oil
Mix everything together in a Thermomix for seven minutes at setting 7 at 70 °C. Push through a fine sieve.

Hijiki marinade
Leave to marinate for 24 hours in the fridge.

Langoustine tartare
Remove the langoustines (size 18-24 per kilo) from their shells. Cut them in two and remove the intestinal tract. Chop the flesh into 1 cm x 1 cm cubes. Chop all the ingredients as finely as possible and mix with the chopped langoustines; season well. Form the langoustines into the shape of a quenelle. Finish off with the egg yolk, black garlic crème, leek oil, cecina and coriander cress as shown in the photo.

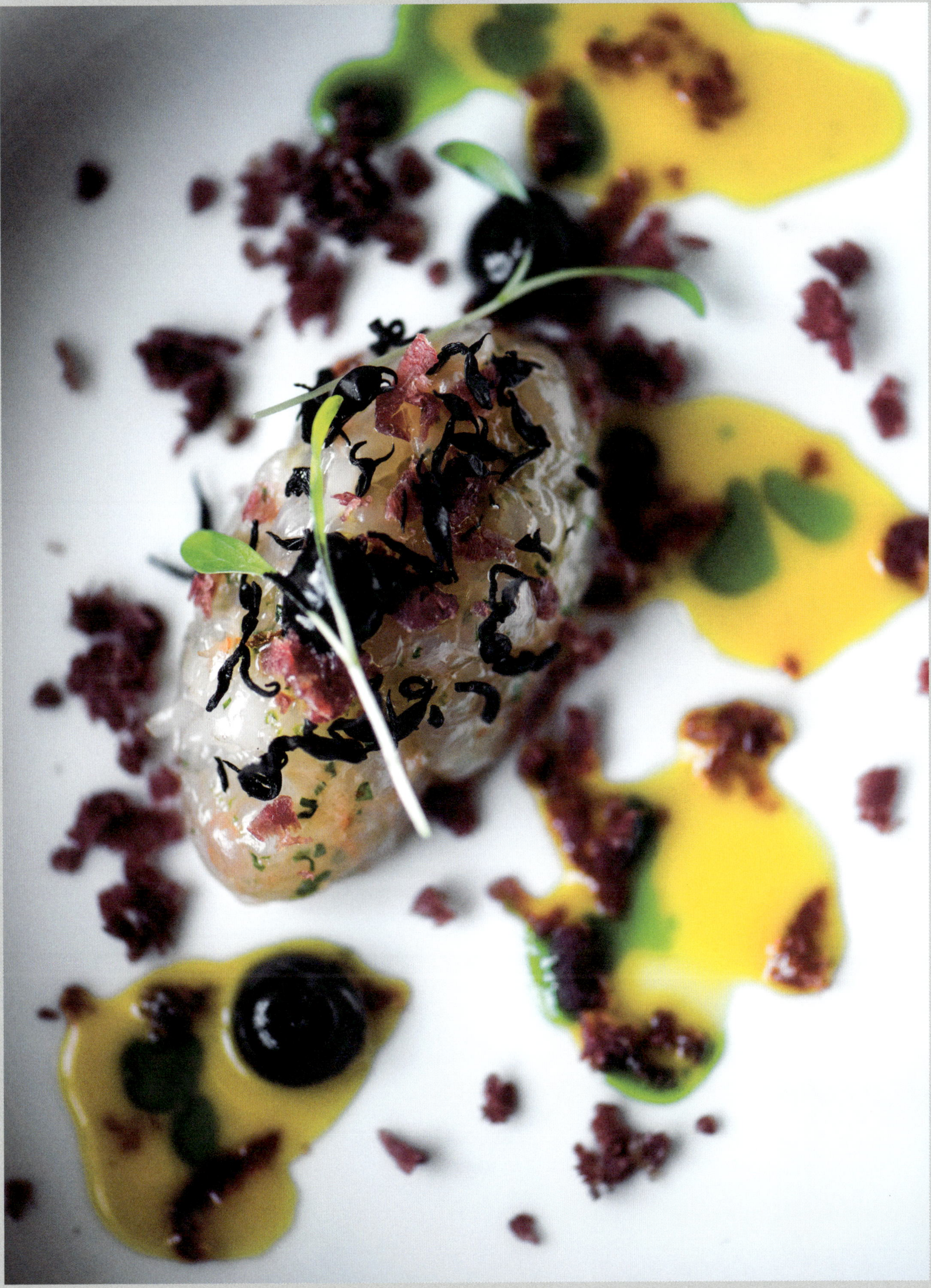

CLASSIC DISHES

62 °C EGG

●●●●●○

INGREDIENTS

2 oxtails ·
1 onion ·
½ bulb of garlic ·
2 carrots ·
2 litres of chicken stock ·
2 litres of brown stock ·
5 tomatoes ·
2 leeks ·
3 sticks of celery ·
thyme and bay leaf ·
200 g pure beef, minced ·
200 g egg white ·

Celeriac crème
1 celeriac ·
cream ·
milk ·
chicken stock ·
salt and pepper ·

Juniper berry oil
30 g juniper berries ·
250 g grape seed oil ·

4 eggs ·
50 g woodland mushrooms (Trompette de la Mort) ·
100 g Parmesan cheese ·
purslane leaves ·
1 shallot, chopped finely ·

METHOD

Brown the oxtails in a roasting tin. Remove the tails and add the onion, garlic and one carrot to the roasting tin. Brown them in the oxtail fat. Pour in the chicken stock and brown stock. Add the tomatoes, one leek, two sticks of celery, thyme, bay leaf and the pieces of oxtail. Simmer on a low heat for six hours. Sieve and remove the meat from the bone. Put the gravy in the fridge to set and then remove the fat.

Mix one stick of celery, one carrot, one leek and the minced beef briefly in a food processor. Stir the egg white into the mixture. Bring the gravy to the boil and pour onto the mixture. Put everything back into a pan and clarify gently. When the gravy is clear, push it through a cheesecloth. Boil the clarified gravy down until you have the flavour you want.

Celeriac crème
Peel the celeriac. Cut into large pieces. Pour the cream, milk and chicken fond in three equal measures over the celeriac to cover it completely. Simmer on a gentle heat until the celeriac is cooked. Strain the liquid from the celeriac but retain it. Put the pieces of celeriac in a Thermomix. Add the cooking liquid very gradually until you get the right consistency. Push through a fine sieve and season to taste with salt and pepper.

Juniper berry oil
Mix everything together in a Thermomix for seven minutes at setting 7 at 70 °C. Push through a fine sieve.

Cook 4 eggs for 35 minutes at 62 °C and keep warm. Fry the mushrooms briefly in butter and season to taste with salt and pepper. Heat up the meat from the oxtail in butter and some of the consommé. Season to taste with salt and pepper and the chopped raw shallot. Very carefully, break the eggs.

Arrange in a deep plate: the celeriac on the bottom, followed by the oxtail, then the egg and the mushrooms. Garnish with grated Parmesan cheese and purslane leaves.

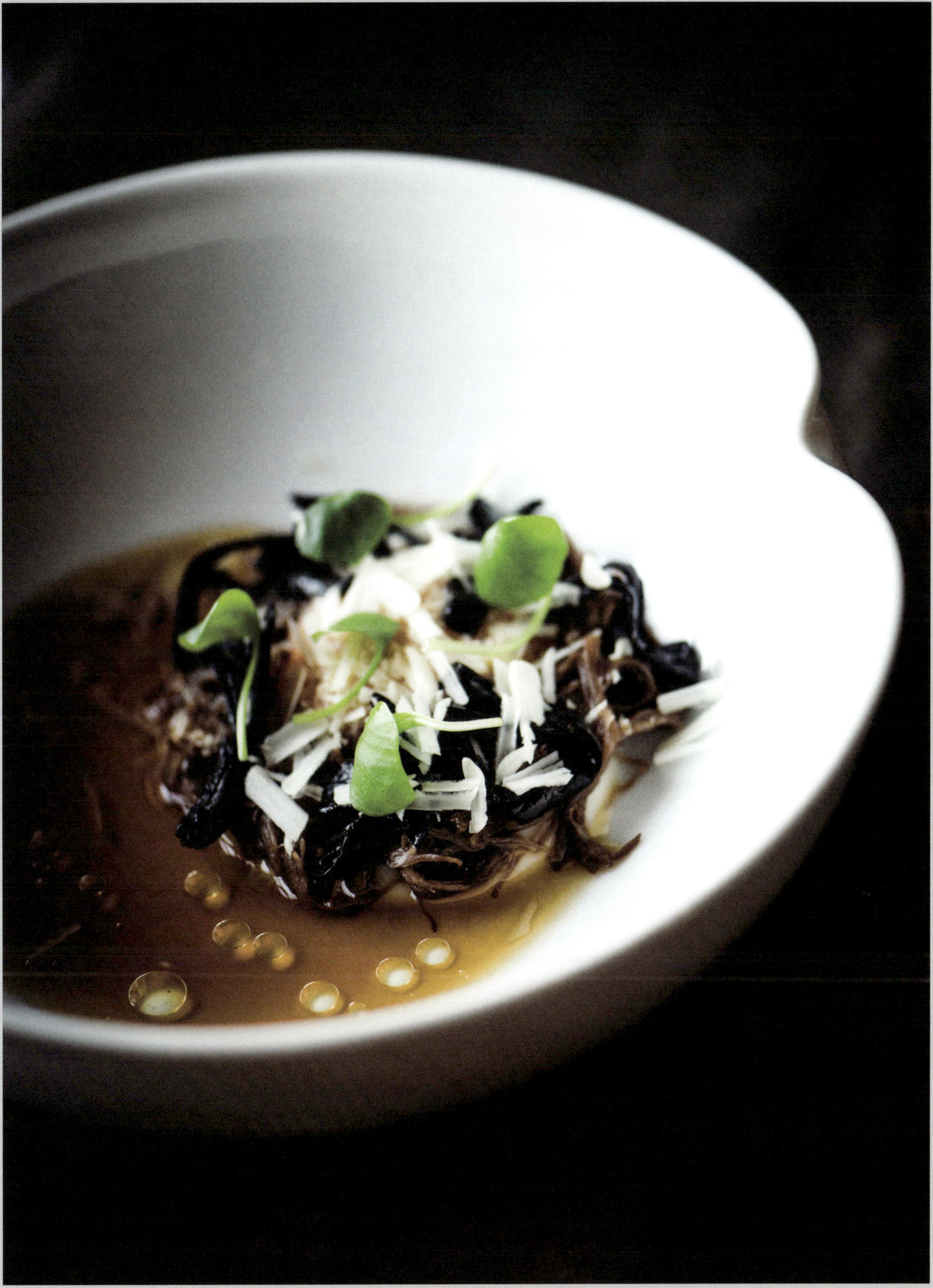

CLASSIC DISHES

MANDARIN SABAYON

●●●●●○

INGREDIENTS

Iced hammam tea
800g sugar water 50/50 ·
50 g palatinose ·
50 g maltodextrine ·
1 litre of water ·
30 g hammam tea ·
1 sheet of gelatine ·
juice of 1 lemon ·

Tangerine oil
10 g dried tangerine peel ·
Easy Dry food dehydrator ·
50 g grape seed oil ·

Yogurt crème
160 g Greek yogurt ·
1 sheet of gelatine ·
2 g tangerine zest ·
20 g icing sugar ·
5 g tangerine juice ·

Sabayon Grand Marnier
2 egg yolks ·
20 g sugar ·
30 g Grand Marnier ·
20 g tangerine juice ·

Campari with orange zest
1 orange ·
150 g sugar water ·
50 ml Campari ·
1 drop of red food colouring ·

METHOD

Iced hammam tea
Bring the sugar water, palatinose, maltodextrin and water to the boil. Add the hamman tea and infuse for 15 minutes. Push through a fine sieve and add the gelatin. Cool completely. Add the lemon juice.

Tangerine oil
Put the tangerine peel in water and bring up to the boil three times. Place in an Easy Dry food dehydrator for 24 hours then mix to a powder. Add the grape seed oil and heat once to a temperature of 80 °C. Leave to soak at room temperature for six hours. Push through a fine sieve.

Yogurt crème
Gently heat the yogurt. Soak the gelatine and add it to the lukewarm yogurt. Add the tangerine zest, icing sugar and tangerine juice to the yogurt. Put in the fridge to set.

Sabayon Grand Marnier
Mix everything together in a saucepan and whisk over a gentle heat until it forms a smooth sabayon.

Campari with orange zest
Peel the orange. Cut the peel into fine julienne strips. Bring to the boil three times in 300 g sugar water. Add 100 ml Campari. Leave to cool in the liquid. Add a drop of red food colouring.

Peel the tangerines, divide into segments and remove the pith. Arrange the tangerine segments randomly on the plate. Squirt on two dots of yogurt crème and place a quenelle of ice cream on top. Garnish with the zest, powder, oil and sabayon.

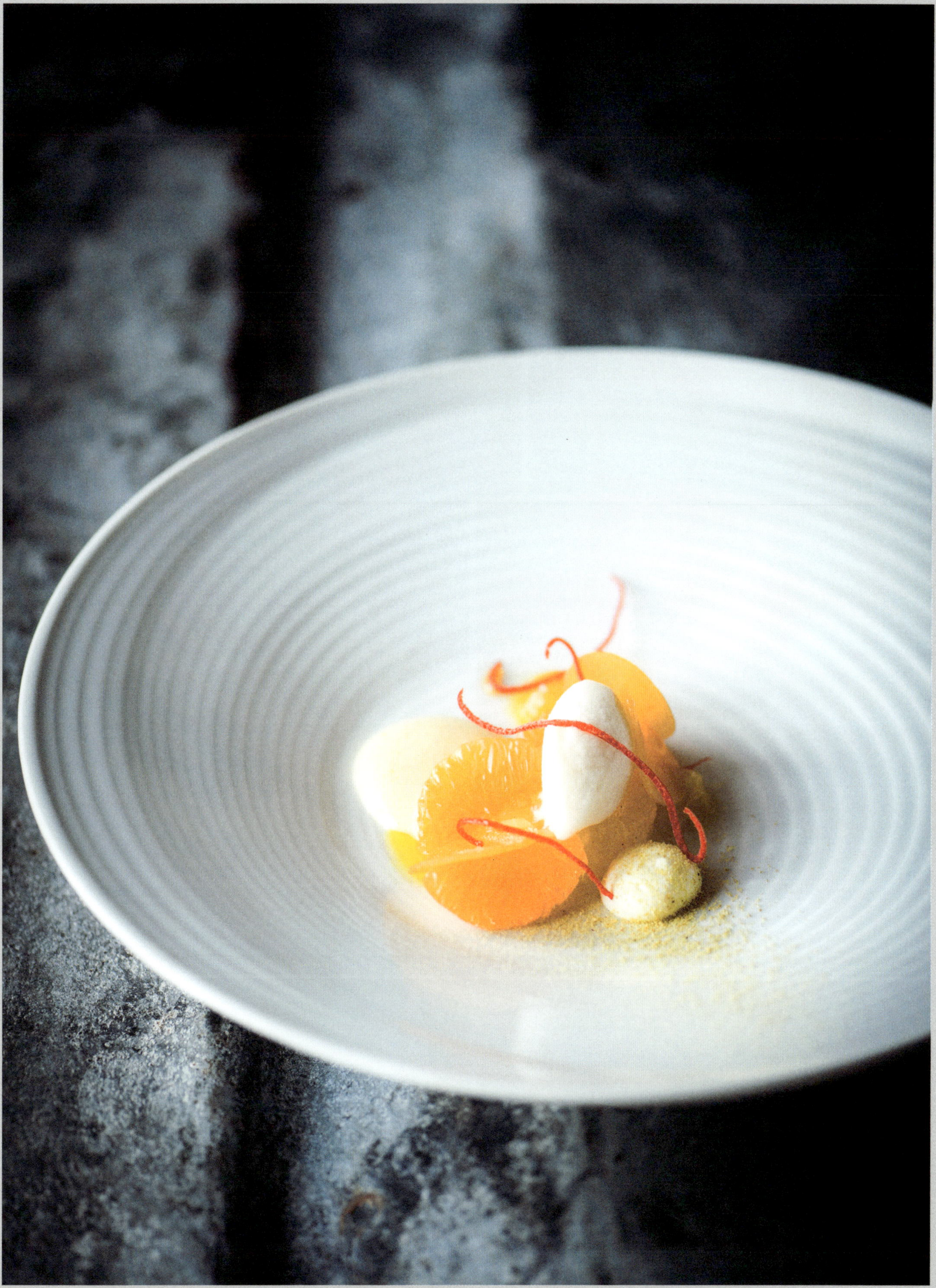

Teamwork in the kitchen at the Bon Bon restaurant.

CLASSIC DISHES

146

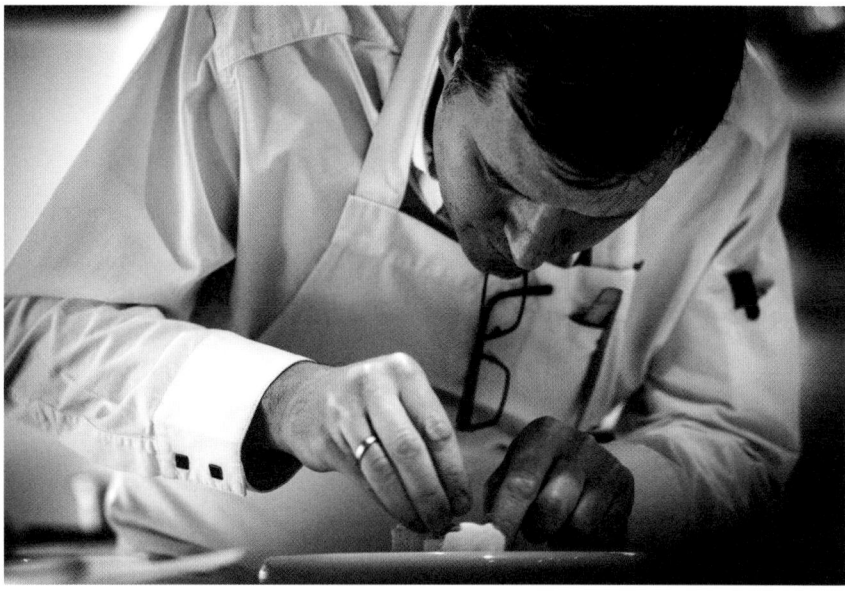

Christophe Hardiquest knows better than anyone that creating top dishes is a matter of teamwork that demands precision, dedication and exceptional focus.

Christophe Hardiquest

When I met Christophe for the first time, he was cooking lunches in a showroom of a well-known brand of kitchens, where he had taken over a model kitchen and was making a few people very happy every day. Even then, his talent oozed from every pore. He had a look about him that showed how determined he was. If you imagine a cooking competition, Christophe's expression is enough to tell you that he would be in the winning team.

Now, years later, he's made it, I reckon. He doesn't think so though, because things can always be done better. Christophe is charismatic and tries to surround himself with exceptional people. He is a chef who is reactive and empathic.

His primary heroes are Passard, Roellinger, Gagnaire, Alléno and Japan, but he derives inspiration from everyday things. A kitchen for him is a way of bringing spiritual riches, a philosophy of life and balance into his life and existence. He clearly regards gastronomy as cultural heritage. He tries to reinvent some dishes, not just because he can, but because he wants to prepare them for eternity so that this valuable cultural heritage will not be lost. His art of cooking involves explosive flavours and it challenges your senses to go to the limit.

Hardiquest knows better than anyone that creating top dishes at his level and with his frequency is a question of teamwork that demands precision, dedication and exceptional focus. He is prepared to give that to his guests, as his team is for him. He is a great leader whose team would go through fire and water for him. I take my hat off to him.

CLASSIC DISHES

EGGS AND BACON

●●●●●○

INGREDIENTS

8 egg yolks ·
8 thin slices of Alsatian belly pork ·
1 onion ·
30 g green pistachios ·

For the bread
100 g bread ·
100 g chicken stock ·
3 egg whites ·
1 bay leaf ·
salt and pepper to taste ·

METHOD

Season the egg yolks, form them into a sausage shape and put them in the freezer. Leave them there until they are firm. Once they are frozen, vacuum-seal the sausage shape. Cook them for 20 to 21 minutes sous-vide at 70 °C and then cool them immediately in ice-cold water.

Lay the slices of belly pork flat and place the sausage-shaped egg on top. Roll the egg in the belly pork so that you get a cylinder surrounded with bacon. Trim the ends neatly.

Slice the onions into rings, dry them and grind to a powder.

Roast the pistachios in a dry pan over a medium heat.

Bread

Mix the bread into the chicken stock and the egg yolk to make a smooth paste. Season to taste. Roll the paste out on a baking sheet and bake at 165 °C for 8 minutes.

Fry the egg-yolk-and-bacon 'sausages' briefly on a high heat and serve with the other ingredients.

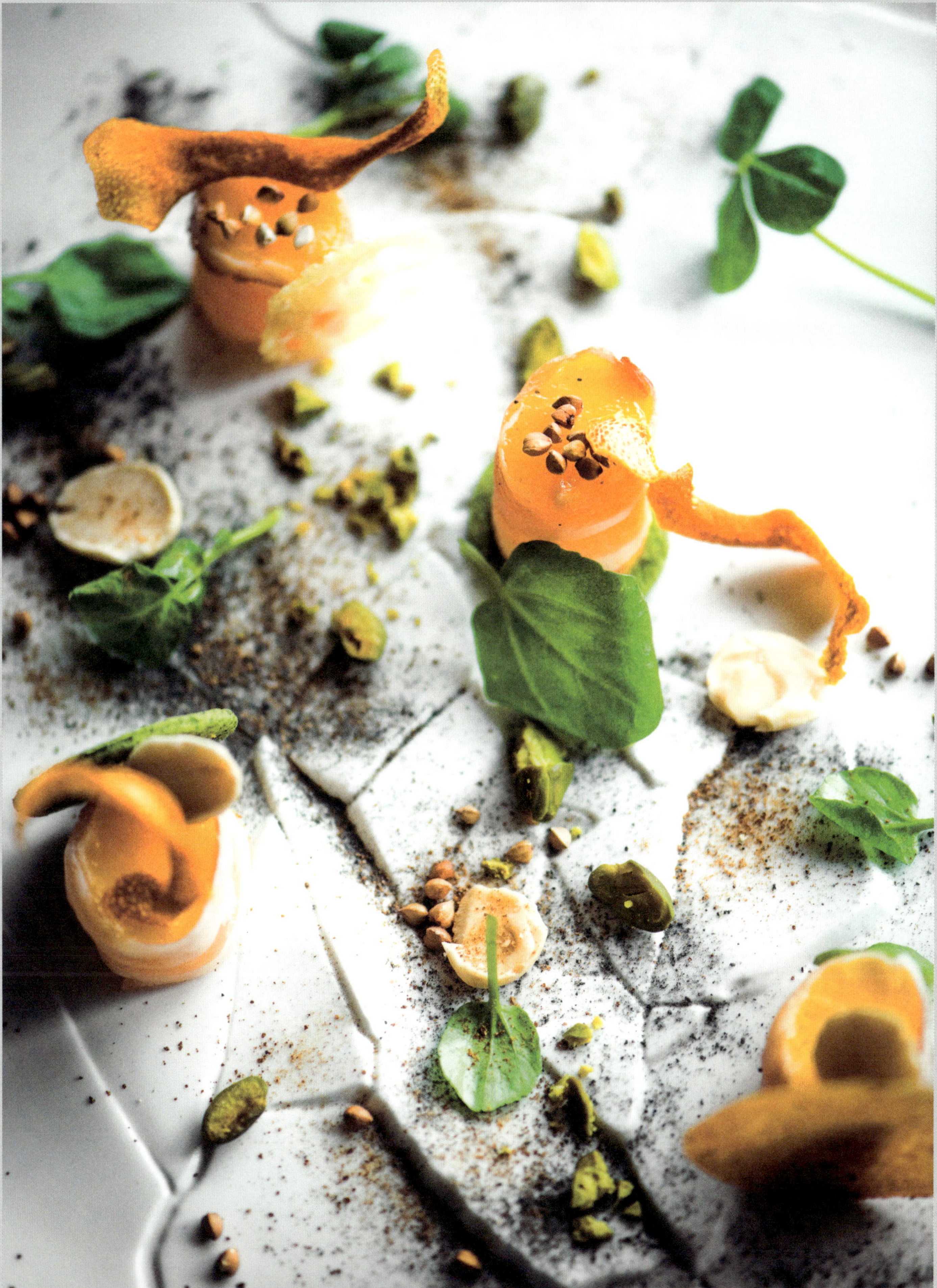

CLASSIC DISHES

BRUSSELS HERITAGE:
MEULEMEESTER'S QUAIL'S EGGS

INGREDIENTS

8 quail's eggs ·
100 g raw grey shrimps ·
100 g cooked grey shrimps ·
1 g agar agar ·
100 ml concentrated shrimp bisque ·
50 g mustard ·
50 g Emmental cheese ·
100 ml chicken stock ·
some chervil ·
shrimp powder ·

Wheat beer mousseline
3 egg yolks ·
200 ml clarified butter ·
40 g lemon oil ·
50 ml wheat beer ·
pinch of salt ·
juice of 1 lemon ·
1 siphon with 2 cartridges ·

METHOD

Peel the raw and cooked shrimps. Dry the skins of the cooked shrimps and grind them to a powder. Infuse the skins of the raw shrimps in oil to make shrimp oil.

Add the agar agar to the bisque and boil for three minutes; add the mustard and pour onto a baking sheet. Leave to rest. When it is completely cold, beat the mixture until it has the consistency of a gel.

Grate the Emmental cheese finely and spread out on a Silpat baking mat. Bake at 170 °C for 8 minutes.

Soak the eggs in spirit vinegar for 20 minutes so that they are easier to peel. Boil them for 2 minutes and 51 seconds in boiling water then transfer them immediately to ice-cold water.

Peel the eggs. Roll the eggs in shrimp powder and keep them warm.

Wheat beer mousseline
Melt the butter with the oil.

Add the egg yolks and the beer and then add the salt. Beat to a mousseline and add butter, season to taste with salt, lemon juice and wheat beer. Pour into the siphon and cook at 60 degrees in a bain-marie.

Chop the raw and cooked shrimps and form into a patty, mixing the chervil and shrimp oil through it. Place the patty on the bottom of a plate; lay the halved soft quail's eggs on top; pour over some of the reduced shrimp bisque; place a couple of pieces of Emmental tuile on top and add a little mustard gel.

Serve the wheat beer mousseline separately.

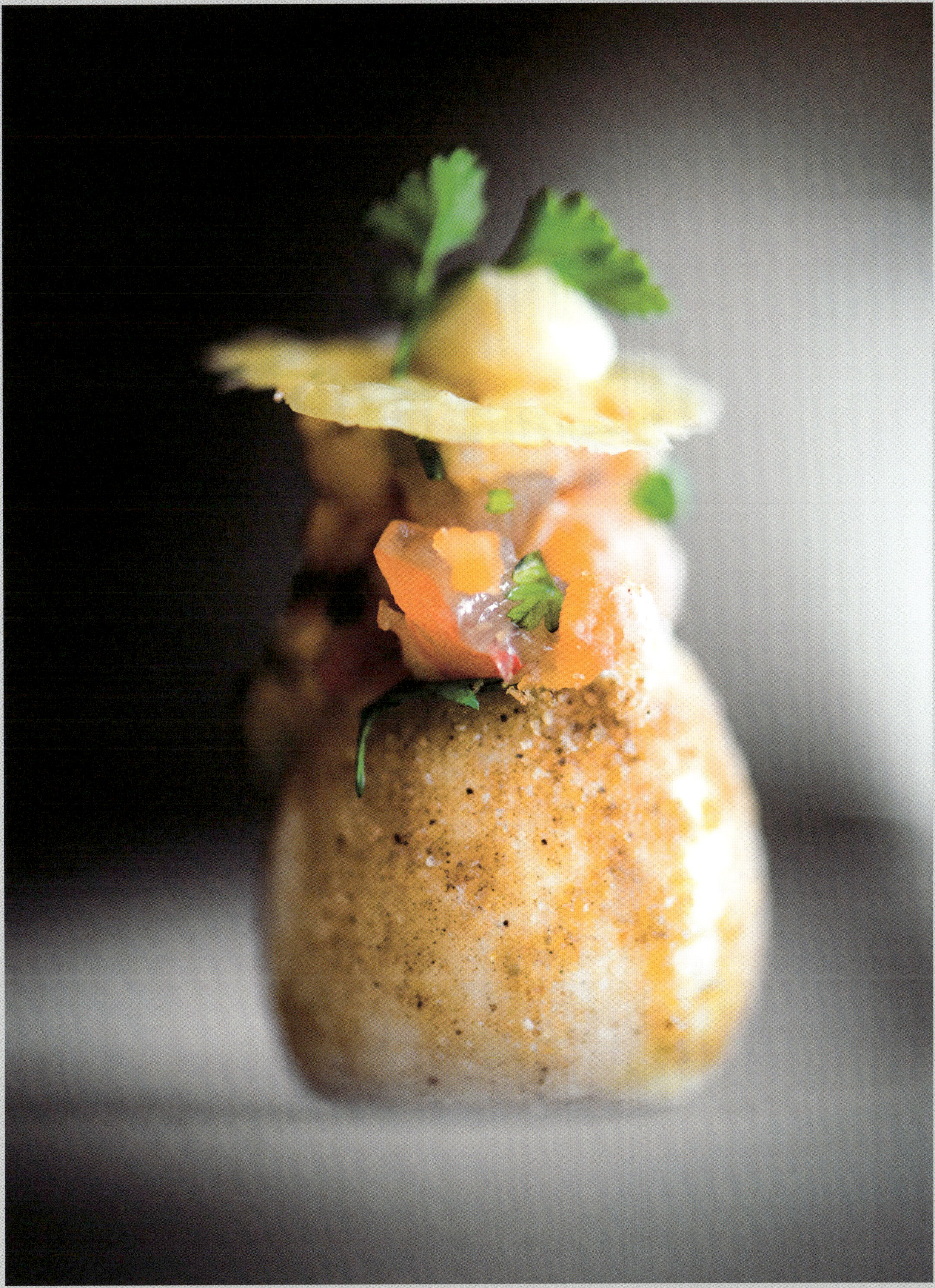

CLASSIC DISHES

INFUSED EGG YOLK CRÈME

●●●●●○

INGREDIENTS

4 eggs ·
500 g water ·
4 g fresh vervain ·
4 g fresh lovage ·
1 g lapsang souchong ·
5 g soy sauce ·
15 g dashi ·

METHOD

Bring the water to the boil and infuse the herbs and the tea in it for three minutes before adding the soy sauce and the dashi. Set aside.
Cook the eggs in their shells for 35 minutes at 68 °C then plunge them immediately into ice-cold water.
Break the eggs and separate the white from the yolk. Place the egg yolks in the infused water for 24 hours.

The next day:
Serve the egg yolk lukewarm with some garden herbs and pickled vegetables. Pour some stock over the top.

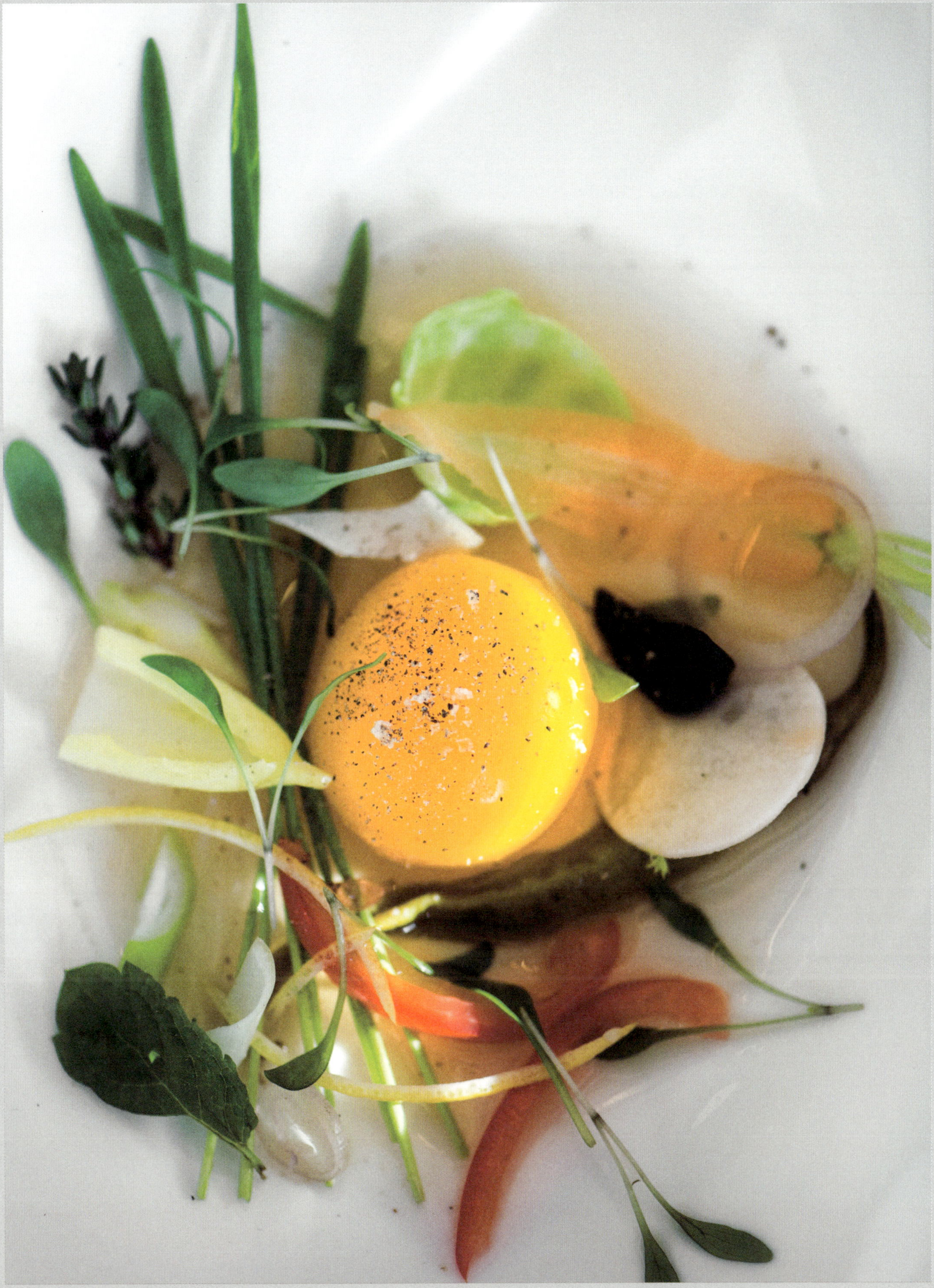

CLASSIC DISHES

EGG YOLK RAVIOLI WITH TRUFFLE

●●●●●○

INGREDIENTS

Fresh pasta
250 g semolina made from hard wheat ·
250 g flour ·
3 egg yolks ·
10 g butter ·
olive oil ·

Sauce
100 ml truffle juice ·
20 g truffle skins ·
50 ml chicken stock ·
50 g double cream ·
70 g truffle butter ·
some grated Parmesan cheese ·

METHOD

Fresh pasta
Make the pasta by mixing both types of flour with the egg yolks and the butter until you have a homogenous dough. Wrap in cling film and place in the fridge to rest.

Sauce
Mix the truffle juice, skins, the stock and the cream and reduce for 5 minutes before adding the Parmesan cheese and the butter; season to taste. Emulsify using a Bamix immersion blender.

Feed the sheets of pasta dough through the pasta machine until they are 1-mm thick, being careful not to let them dry out.

Place one egg yolk and a slice of truffle on a piece of pasta and seal the ravioli, making sure no air is trapped.

Heat water to a temperature of 65 °C and place the ravioli in it for five minutes. Plunge the ravioli into boiling water for 20 seconds.

Arrange on a plate and pour the sauce over it.

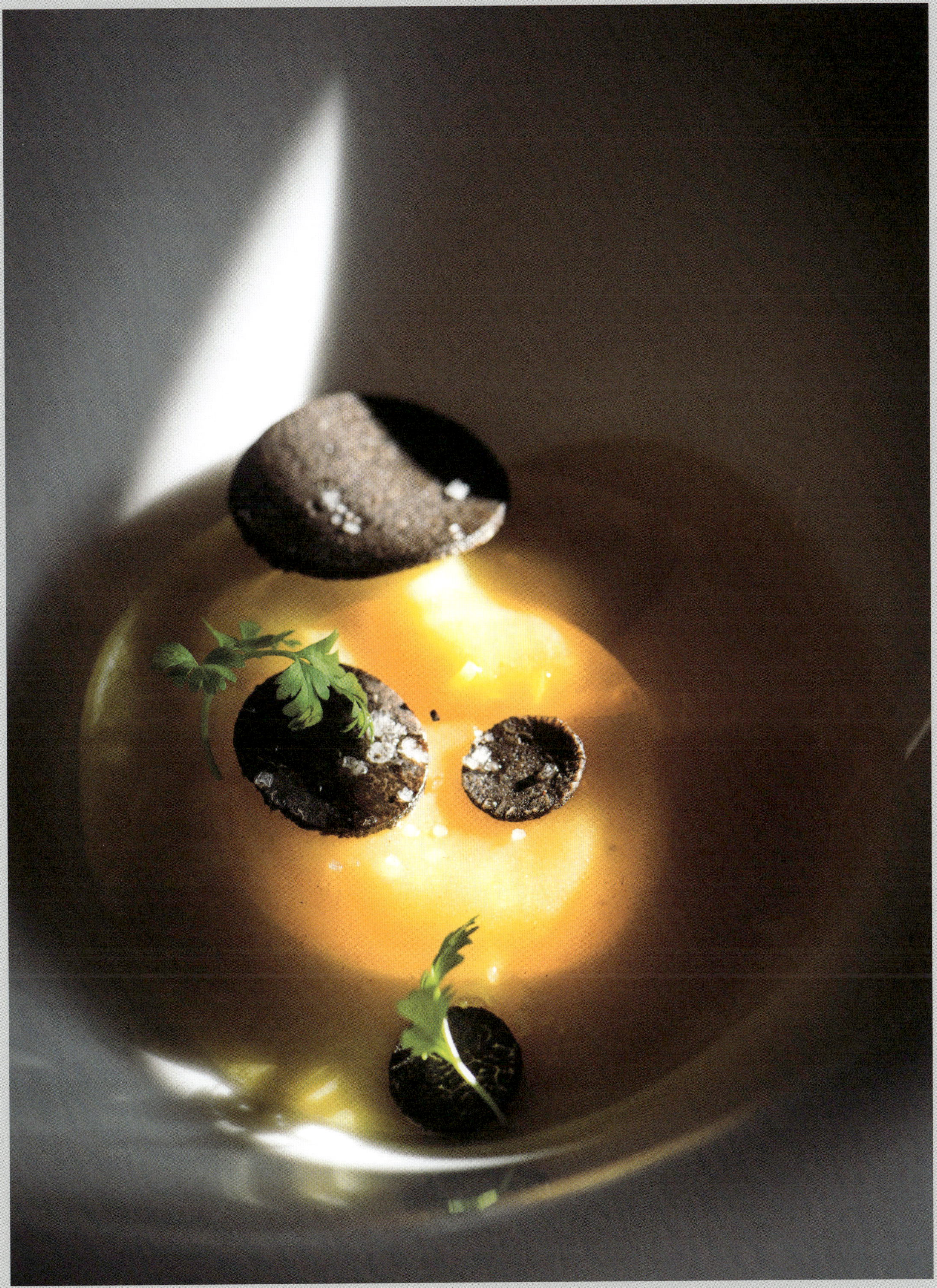

CLASSIC DISHES

ILE FLOTTANTE

INGREDIENTS

200 g egg whites ·
2 g fine salt ·
80 g hazelnut oil ·
40 g caster sugar ·

For the crème anglaise
250 g whole milk ·
2.5 g Earl Grey tea ·
40 g sugar ·
4 egg yolks ·

Cocoa tuile
320 g water ·
80 g glucose ·
200 g butter ·
600 g caster sugar ·
10 g pectin ·
40 g cocoa powder ·
200 g cocoa mass ·

METHOD

Add the salt to the egg whites and whisk; add the oil and pour into a high, rectangular Araven box. Cook in a microwave oven for 75 seconds at 1000 W power.

Crème anglaise
Heat the milk to 80 °C and infuse the Earl Grey tea in it for three minutes.

Add the sugar to the egg yolks and whisk to the ribbon stage. Add to the milk and stir continuously until you can run your finger down the spatula and leave a trail. Cool on an ice-cold slab.

Cocoa tuile
Mix the water, the glucose and the butter and bring to the boil. Add the sugar and the pectin and continue to boil. Add the cocoa powder and pour onto the cocoa mass.

Place two tablespoonfuls of crème anglaise in a deep plate, place a few cubes of île flottante on top and decorate with a few hazelnut shavings and some cocoa tuile crumbled on top.

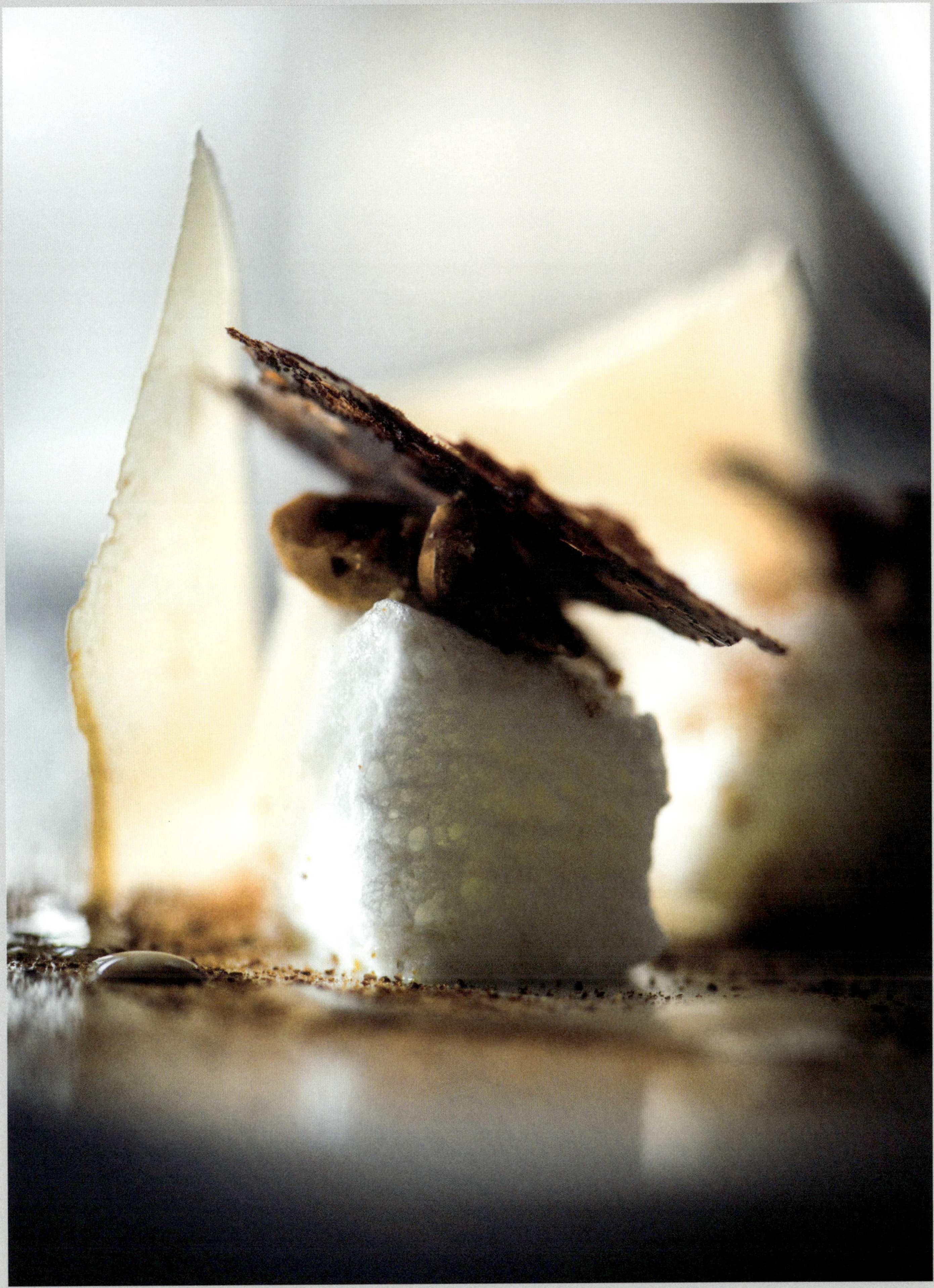

CLASSIC DISHES

BRUSSELS HERITAGE:
MANON REVISITED

● ● ● ● ● ●

INGREDIENTS

White chocolate ice cream
500 g milk ·
120 g egg yolk ·
150 g cream ·
125 g caster sugar ·
200 g chocolate Opalys (Valrhona) ·
5 g fine salt ·

Frozen cardamom powder
250 g cardamom water ·
75 g 30 Baume syrup ·
150 g yogurt ·
50 g lemon juice ·
½ sheet of gelatine ·

Ganache with coffee
225 g pouring cream ·
25 g glucose ·
25 g trimoline (invert sugar) ·
50 g cracked coffee beans ·
305 g Opalys chocolate (Valrhona) ·

French meringue
100 g egg white ·
200 g caster sugar ·

METHOD

White chocolate ice cream
Melt the chocolate; whisk the egg yolk and the sugar to the ribbon stage, boil the milk and let it thicken with the egg yolk and sugar 'ribbon' until it reaches 84 °C. Pour over the chocolate and add the salt. Leave to set, preferably in a Pacojet.

Frozen cardamom powder
Make cardamom water by infusing 60 g green cardamom in 500 g water for two hours at a temperature of 5 °C, preferably vacuum-sealed.

Soak the gelatine.

Mix all the ingredients together, adding the gelatine last.

Ganache with coffee
Boil the cream, the glucose and the trimoline and add the coffee. Infuse for 15 minutes. Pour over the chocolate and leave for 24 hours to crystallise. Weigh the ganache and add the same weight of pouring cream to it. Bind in a food mixer.

French meringue
Beat the eggs in the food mixer, add the sugar in three lots and form into the shape of a half shell.

Temper some white chocolate in the form of a shell. Place a tiny quenelle of the white chocolate ice cream inside and place a piece of ground ganache in the meringue shell.

Assemble the two halves into a ball and brush with cardamom powder.

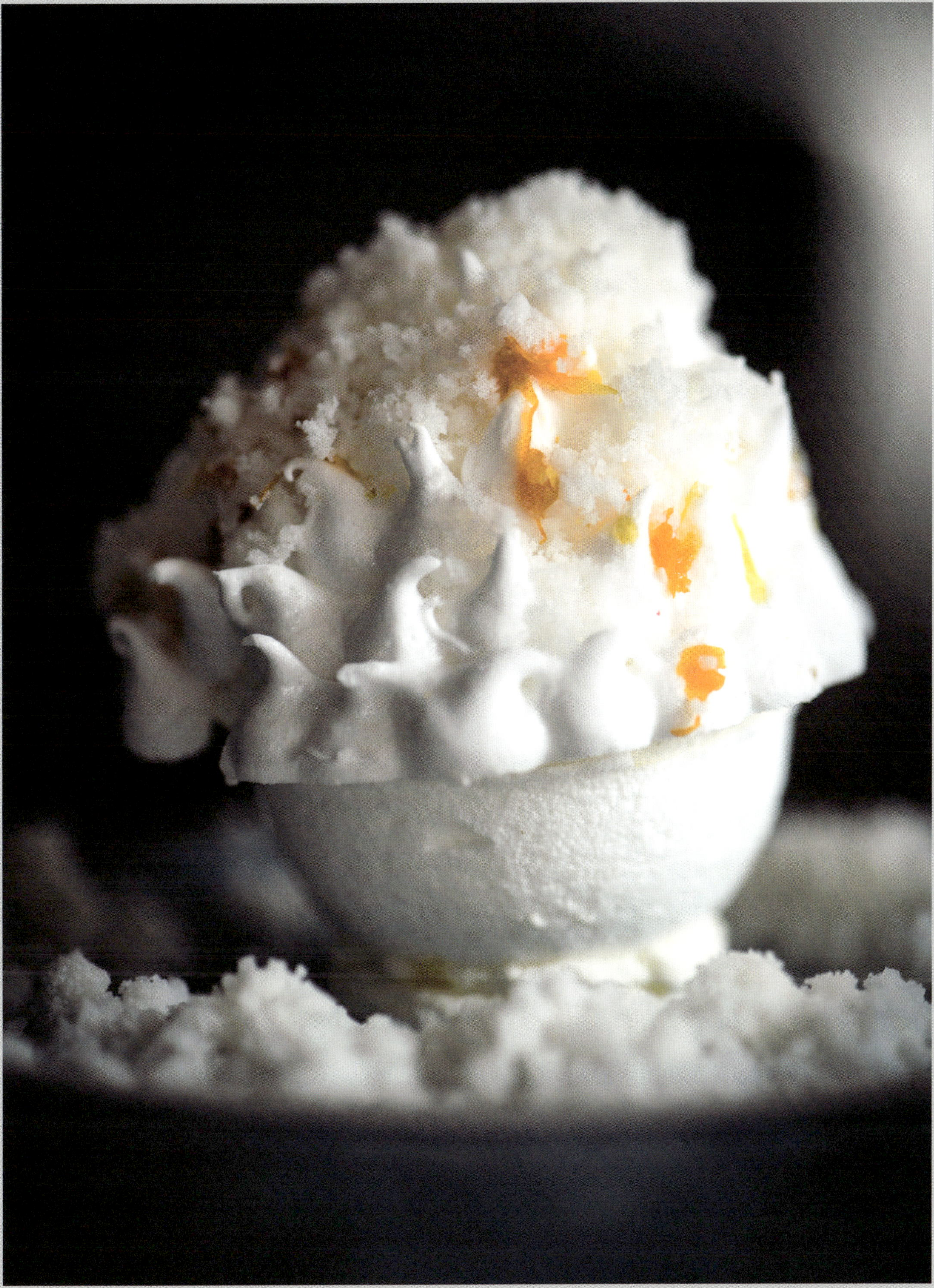

Giel's inexhaustible hunger for knowledge about artisan gastronomy has made him an excellent all-round chef.

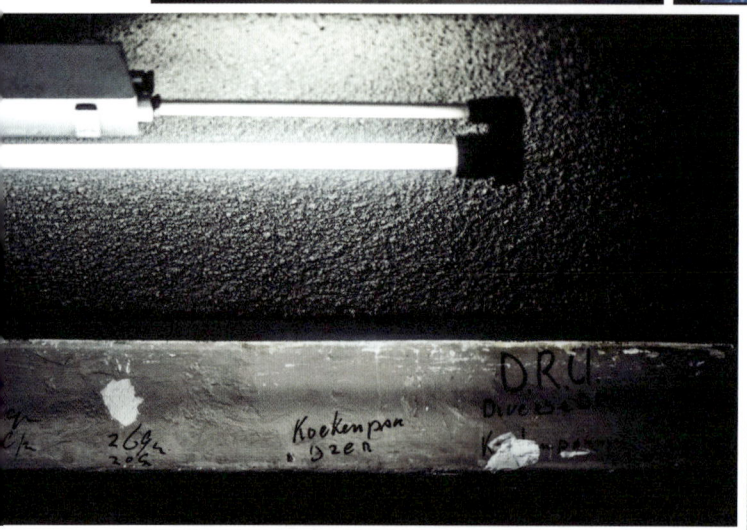

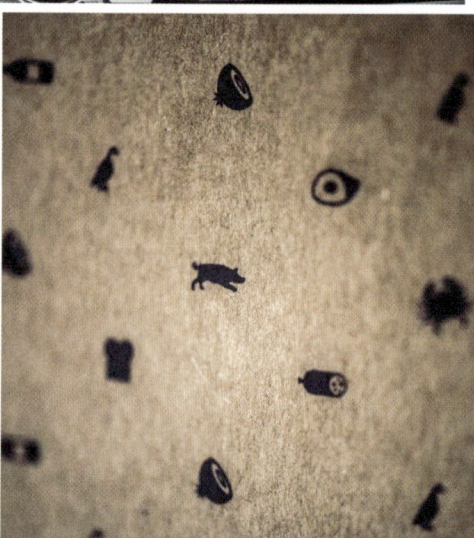

CLASSIC DISHES | 160

→ Giel Kaagman

Giel Kaagman

Apart from being a very talented chef, Giel is also a skilful craftsman. He has been working in kitchens in Belgium and the Netherlands since he was 12. He discovered his greatest sources of inspiration in Amsterdam, in the city's best Italian restaurant, Toscanini, and the iconic restaurant, Borderwijk, where he worked for many years as a chef. My dream meal would be one in which John Segers and Wil Demandt join forces and give their all. Both are iconic, mythical figures in the gastronomic scene who have already shaped and inspired a huge number of top chefs.

Giel's inexhaustible hunger for knowledge about artisan gastronomy has made him an excellent all-round chef; he is remarkable when it comes to charcuterie and especially in making informal dishes enthralling. He can transform apparently simple dishes into formidable gastronomic experiences. His experience at the best Italian restaurant in the Netherlands is naturally an enormous asset when it comes to keeping cooking natural, with few frills; no-nonsense but to the point.

The menu is his restaurant Kaagman & Kortekaas truly fires the imagination; choosing a dish stresses you out big time and ideally, you want to try everything. His cooking is rough but refined, exciting and stimulating, but above all it has a superior sense of finesse and elegance. He is a chef who has clearly found his own style and he carries his teachers purely as guardian angels on his shoulder, never copying them but using their wisdom to spice up his own creations: the perfect marriage of contemporary nouveau rough and skilful classics.

CLASSIC DISHES

DUCK EGG, NORTH SEA CRAB, JERUSALEM ARTICHOKE, BOTTARGA, BLACK LOVAGE

●●●○○

INGREDIENTS

5 duck eggs ·
2 North Sea crab legs ·
1 bunch of parsley ·
1 fresh bulb of garlic ·
2 Jerusalem artichokes ·
1 bunch of black lovage ·
1 fish roe from a grey mullet or tuna (bottarga) ·
4 duck carcases ·
red wine (for deglazing) ·
grated horseradish ·
200 g butter ·
200 g foie gras ·
dash of cognac ·

Condiments
Maldon sea salt, black pepper, extra virgin olive oil, salt, tabasco, lemon, argan oil, bouquet garni, balsamic vinegar, Pedro Ximenez vinegar, white wine vinegar

METHOD

Duck egg
Poach the egg in water just below boiling point for two minutes. Serve with Maldon sea salt and black pepper.

North Sea crab
Steam the North Sea crabs for 20 minutes at 90 °C or poach them for 20 minutes in court bouillon. Remove the crab from its shell. Season to taste with olive oil, chopped parsley, tabasco, lemon juice, garlic and salt.

Jerusalem artichoke
Bake the Jerusalem artichokes at 190 °C with 20% steam for 25 minutes. Cut them lengthwise, spoon out the flesh and deep fry the skin at 160 °C until it stops bubbling and is crisp and salty. Season the flesh to taste with argan oil, salt and pepper and serve hot.

Black lovage
Wash, pick over and dry the black lovage then cut it into wafer-thin chiffonade.

Bottarga
Preserve the grey mullet roe or tuna roe in sea salt for two weeks (vacuum-sealed). Dry the roe for four weeks by hanging it in a well-aired room.

Foie gras sauce with horseradish
Brown the duck carcases and deglaze with red wine. Put the carcases in a pan and add enough water to cover them. Bring to the boil, removing scum at regular intervals. Add a bouquet garni and boil for at least 4 hours until the bones have shed all their gelatine into the stock. Push through a sieve and reduce to 20%. Add balsamic vinegar, Pedro Ximenez vinegar, white wine vinegar, freshly grated horseradish, butter, foie gras, cognac, salt and pepper.

Arrange everything nicely on a plate.

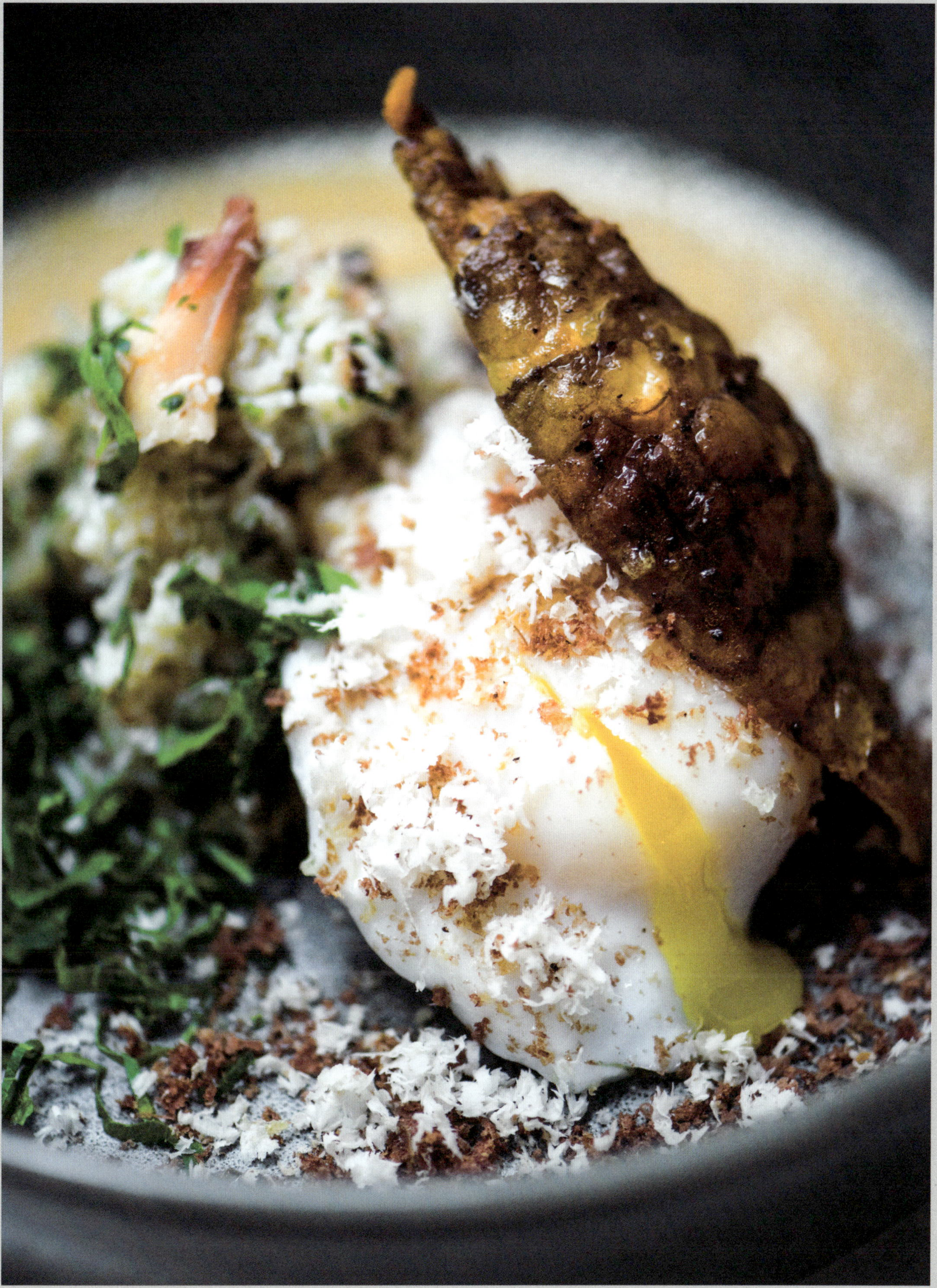

CLASSIC DISHES

VEAL, ZEELAND OYSTER, 63 °C EGG, KOHLRABI, CRYSTALLINE ICE PLANT, HAZELNUTS

INGREDIENTS

5 eggs ·
200 g organic veal, topside ·
3 kohlrabi ·
1 fresh garlic ·
pickle (see method below) ·
7 Zeeland oysters ·
2 egg whites ·
100 ml groundnut oil ·
50 g hazelnuts ·
100 g crystalline ice plant ·

Condiments

Maldon sea salt, extra virgin olive oil, sherry vinegar, micro capers, black pepper, salt, cream 40% fat content, lemon, cornflour, white wine vinegar

METHOD

63 °C egg
Steam five eggs in their shells for 50 minutes at 63 °C then chill in the fridge. Remove the shells, use only the egg yolk and serve with Maldon sea salt.

Veal tartare
Cut the topside into tartare shapes using a sharp knife and season to taste with olive oil, sherry vinegar, capers, salt and pepper.

Kohlrabi crème
Peel and wash a kohlrabi; boil it à point in salted water, drain, then puree in a ThermoBlender with a splash of cream, garlic, salt and pepper.

Kohlrabi pickle
Peel and wash a kohlrabi. Using a Japanese mandolin, slice it into wafer-thin strips; arrange the strips neatly in a vacuum bag with the pickle liquid and vacuum-seal. This method ensures that the kohlrabi is instantly impregnated and can be used immediately.

Marinated raw kohlrabi brunoise
Peel and wash a kohlrabi; dice it brunoise and marinate in olive oil, garlic, salt, pepper and lemon juice.

Oyster emulsion
Open three Zeeland oysters, blend the contents with two egg whites, lemon juice, pepper and white wine vinegar. Add 100 ml groundnut oil, stirring continuously.

Fried oysters
Open four Zeeland oysters, pat them dry, dredge in cornflour and fry for about one minute at 180 °C until crisp.

Hazelnut
Roast the hazelnuts at 160 °C for 10 minutes. Leave to cool then chop roughly. Season to taste with a little good olive oil and Maldon sea salt.

Crystalline ice plant from Texel
Serve the ice plant as it is.

Arrange everything nicely on a plate.

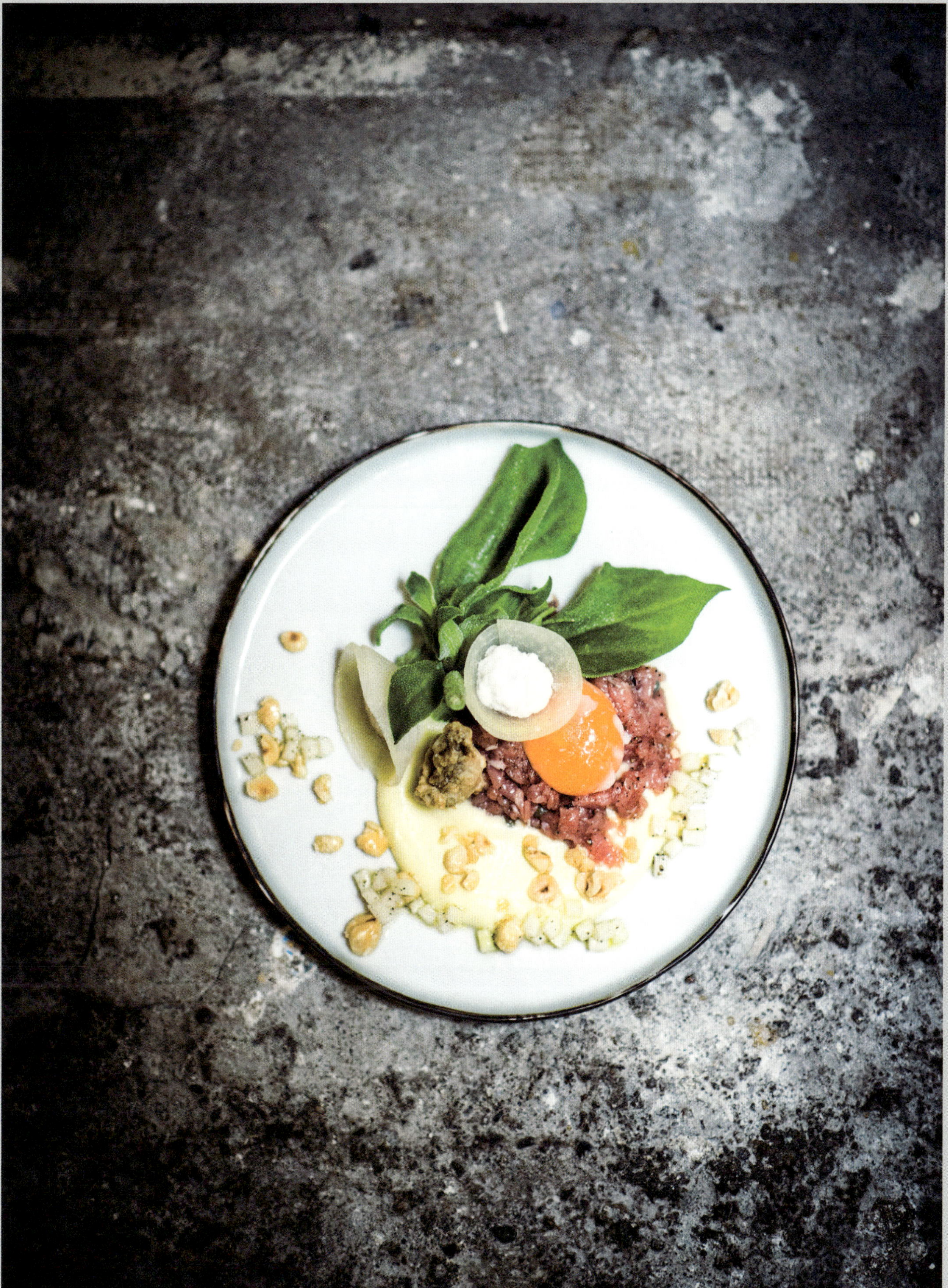

CLASSIC DISHES

COLD SMOKED WILD FJORD SALMON, EGG YOLK CRÈME, RADISHES, HERRING ROE, PORK SKIN, SALTED PRESERVED LEMON, PICKLE

●●●○○

INGREDIENTS

250 g cold smoked wild fjord salmon ·
1 bunch of Ajax radishes ·
1 green radish ·
1 large red radish ·
pickle (see method below) ·
100 g egg yolks ·
200 g pork skin ·
1 salted preserved lemon (see method below) ·
mustard spinach ·
1 pot of herring roe ·

Condiments
coarse sea salt, sugar, dill tops, black pepper, fennel seed, olive oil, salt, French mustard, groundnut oil, coarse sea salt

METHOD

Salmon
Clean and fillet the salmon; marinate it in coarse sea salt, sugar, dill tops, black pepper and fennel seed under a heavy weight for two days. Smoke the salmon cold for 48 hours. Carve the salmon into half-centimetre slices and serve.

Radishes
Wash the Ajax radishes and cut lengthwise. Season to taste with olive oil, salt and pepper. Use the same technique for the green and red radishes as described for the kohlrabi, i.e. pickling (see p. 168). Use a Japanese mandolin to cut the radish into wafer-thin slices and vacuum-seal (impregnate) with the pickle liquid.

Egg yolk crème
Vacuum-seal 100 grams of egg yolk and cook in a steamer at 63 °C for 70 minutes. Chill in a bowl of ice water and season the yolks to taste with French mustard, salt and pepper.

Pork skin
Boil the pork skin in salted water for about 90 minutes. Drain, pat dry and remove the remaining layer of fat with a scraper. Place on a sheet of greaseproof paper in the oven heated to 80 °C and leave to dry for 24 hours with the oven door closed. Once the pork skin is dry, it can be fried in groundnut oil heated to a temperature of 200 °C. Watch it closely because it cooks very quickly. Sprinkle with salt before serving.

Salted preserved lemon
Wash the lemons and make small cuts with a sharp knife all over them. Put them in preserving jars and cover them with coarse sea salt. The process takes quite a long time: at least a month. Another much quicker method is to vacuum-seal segments of lemon with coarse sea salt. This only takes two days. Rinse all the salt off the lemons and cut out the flesh. Now you are left with the skins. Cut off the white part of the skin. Slice into julienne strips and place in a jar filled with good oil.

Mustard spinach
Wash the mustard spinach, pat dry and cut into julienne strips.

Arrange all parts attractively on a plate and finish off with herring roe.

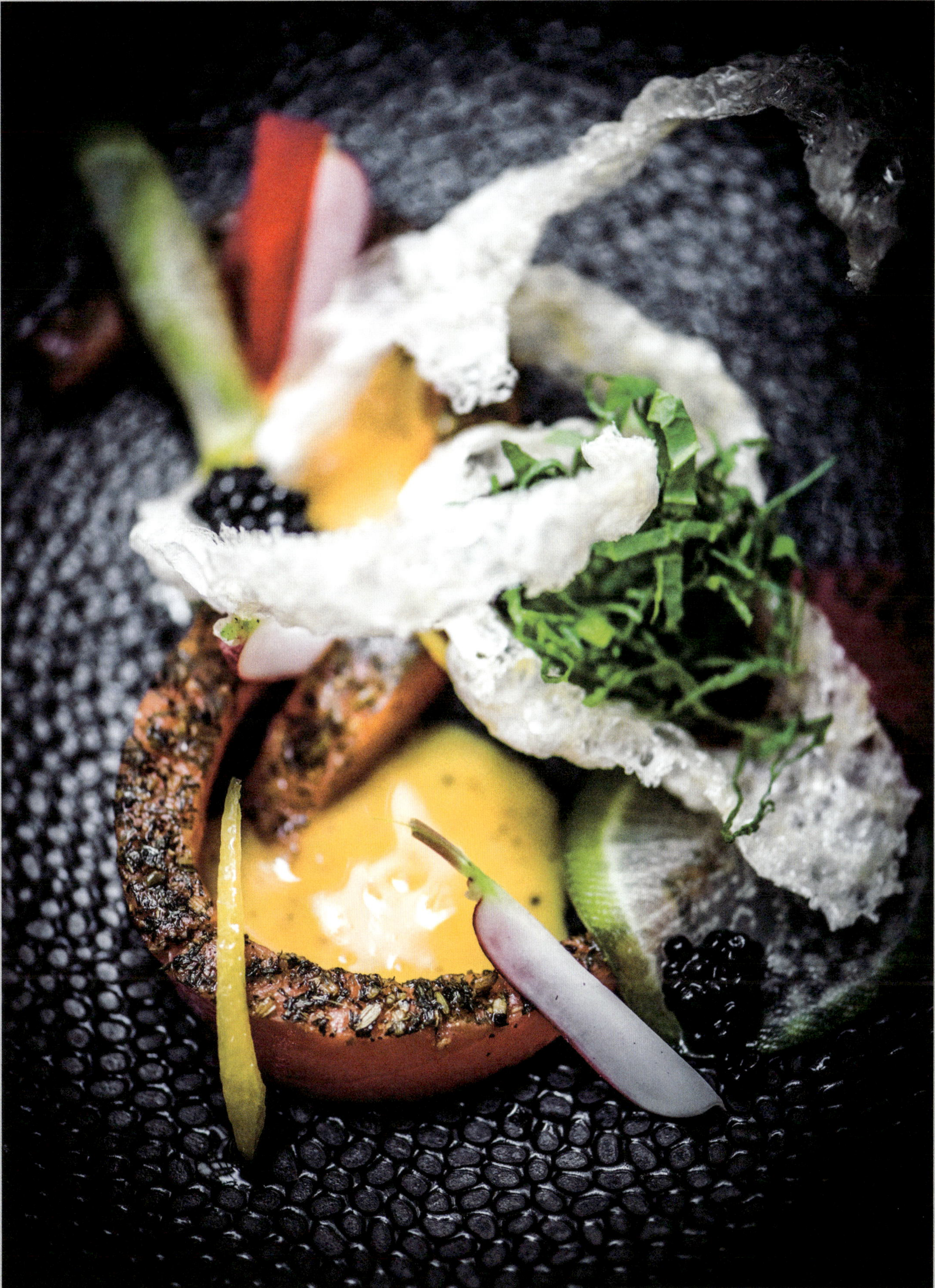

CLASSIC DISHES

MARROWBONE, NORTH SEA SOLE, KAFFIR LIME, MASHUA, BLOODWORT, MOLLICA FRITTA

●●●○○

INGREDIENTS

4 marrowbone quarters, cut lengthwise ·
1 large North Sea sole ·
300 g butter ·
2 kaffir limes ·
4 eggs ·
gastrique* (see method below) ·
2 slices of sourdough bread ·
300 ml olive oil for frying ·
pickle* (see method below) ·
2 yellow mashua tubers ·
2 red mashua tubers ·
1 small box of red vein sorrel as decoration ·

Condiments
Maldon sea salt, salt, flour, tabasco ·

*pickle
1.5 litres of clear natural vinegar ·
1 litre of water ·
500 g sugar ·
bay leaf ·
peppercorns ·
star anise ·

*gastrique
300 ml white wine ·
100 ml white wine vinegar ·
2 shallots, finely chopped ·
peppercorns ·
bay leaf ·

METHOD

Marrowbones
Cook the marrowbones for 20 minutes in a fan oven heated to 170 °C. Caramelise using a gas burner until they brown nicely (Maillard reaction). Sprinkle with Maldon sea salt.

North Sea sole
Clean the sole and fillet the fish into four pieces. Sprinkle with salt, dredge in flour and fry in melted butter until golden. Sprinkle with Maldon sea salt.

Kaffir mousseline
Make compound butter: melt the butter with the grated rind and juice of the two limes. Leave to infuse for at least an hour and then filter the milk protein (sediment) out of the butter. Separate four eggs, beat the yolks lightly with 100 ml gastrique and cook in a bain-marie. Gently stir the clarified, filtered kaffir butter a drop at a time into the egg yolk and gastrique mixture and season to taste with tabasco and salt.

Mollica fritta
The is the Italian way of making croutons. Mollica means 'crumb' and in this case we are using sourdough bread. Cut the crusts off the slices of bread, put the bread in a food processor and make fine crumbs. Cover the breadcrumbs with 300 ml of olive oil and cook in an oven heated to 160°C for 40 minutes. It is important that the crumbs are covered completely with the oil. Drain the bread and sprinkle with salt.

Mashua
Mix all the ingredients for the pickle. Slice the mashua tubers very thinly using a mandolin and marinate them for a few hours.

Gastrique
Reduce to 100 ml.

Arrange everything around the hot marrow bones and garnish with a few vein sorrel leaves.

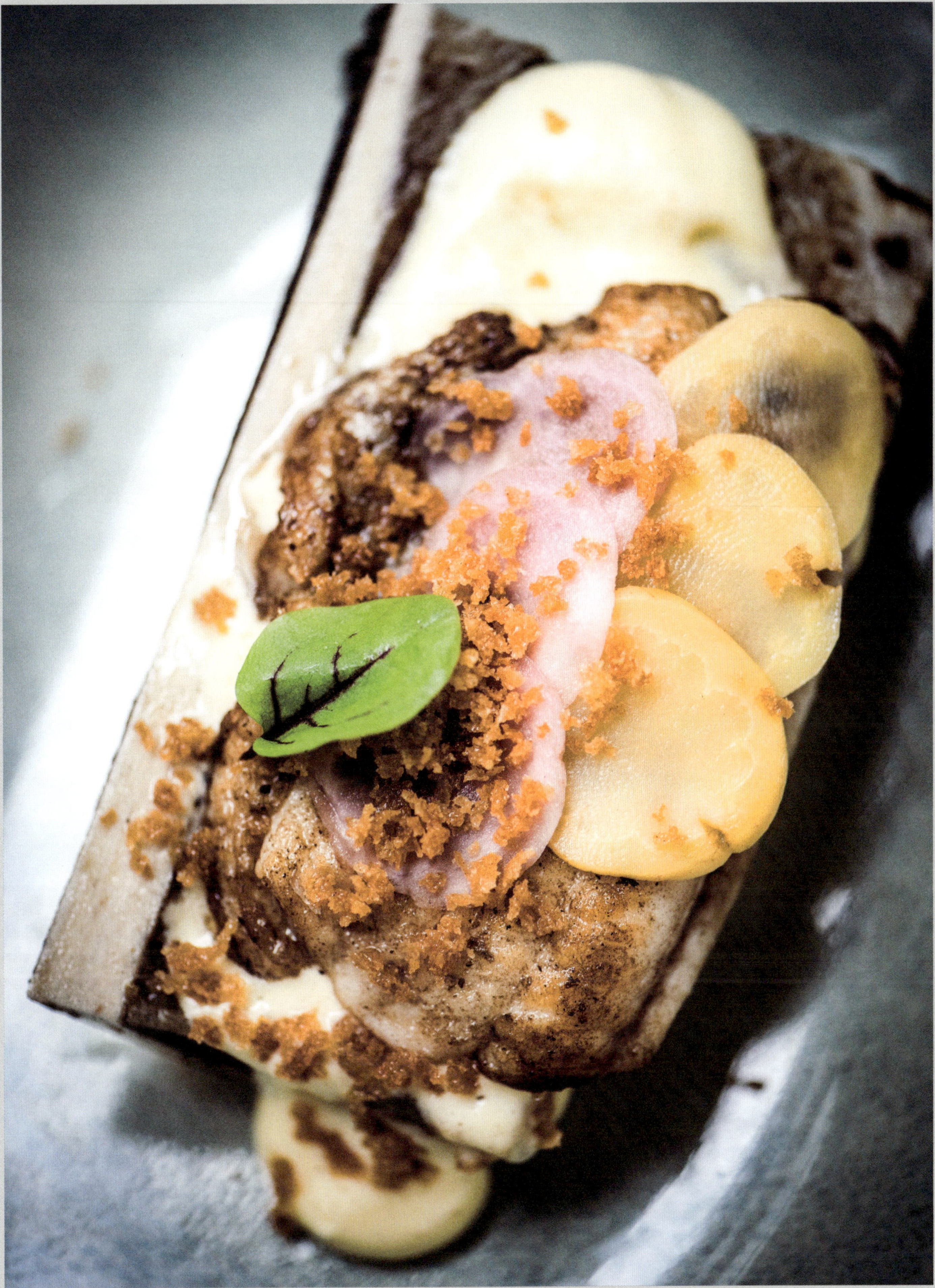

CLASSIC DISHES

EGG YOLK, WHITE CHOCOLATE CRUMBLE, COCONUT, GRAPEFRUIT, TARRAGON SORBET AND LEMON BALM

INGREDIENTS

Egg yolk
400 g sugar ·
100 g salt ·
½ bunch of dill, chopped ·
6 egg yolks ·

White chocolate crumble
40 g sugar ·
100 g flour ·
5 g salt ·
85 g unsalted butter ·
120 g white chocolate ·
20 g cocoa butter ·

Coconut biscuits
500 g grated coconut ·

Grapefruit
2 grapefruit ·
500 g sugar water (250 g sugar and 250 g water) ·

Tarragon sorbet
100 g sugar ·
200 g water ·
1 tsp glucose ·
2 sheets of gelatine ·
6 bunches of tarragon (freshly picked) ·
200 g ice water (cooled in the fridge) ·

Lemon balm
1 bunch of lemon balm (freshly picked) ·
350 g spinach (washed) ·
300 g sugar water (150 g sugar and 150 g water) ·

METHOD

Egg yolk

Mix together the sugar, salt and dill. Put half of the mixture in a bowl big enough to place the yolks two centimetres apart. Separate the eggs and place the yolks carefully onto the sugar mixture. Distribute the rest of the sugar mixture over the egg yolks; cover the bowl and place in the fridge for 10 hours. After 10 hours, carefully take out the egg yolks and dust off the excess sugar around the yolks.

White chocolate crumble

Put the sugar, flour and salt in a mixing bowl. Melt the butter in a pan and then add the melted butter to the mixture in the bowl. Mix everything together then bake in the oven at 120 °C for 20 minutes. Melt the chocolate and the cocoa butter in a bain marie and add it to the baked mixture. Mix everything together and put it into the freezer for two hours. After two hours, remove the crumble from the freezer and break it into small pieces. Whizz it in a Magimix until it is crumbly. Store the crumble in the freezer until needed.

Coconut biscuits

Put the grated coconut in a Thermomix and spin at the highest setting until the coconut has melted. Spread it out between two sheets of greaseproof paper and place in the fridge until it firms up. Break it into pieces of a suitable size.

Grapefruit

Cut the grapefruit into segments and remove the flesh. Put the skins in a pan of cold water (just enough to cover the skins) and bring to the boil. As soon as the water boils, sieve the skins. Repeat this six times. Place the skins in a pan with the sugar water and bring to the boil. Simmer gently until the skins caramelise. Sieve them, place the skins on a rack above a drip tray and leave them to dry in a well-ventilated place for two days. Once they are dry, cut them into thin strips.

Tarragon sorbet

Put the sugar, glucose and the water in a pan over a low heat and dissolve the sugar and glucose. Remove from the heat and dissolve the soaked gelatine in it. Blanch the tarragon six times, chill and spin in a Thermomix with ice water to make a coulis. Sieve the sugar water through the coulis and divide among Pacojet beakers. Freeze them and then stir before using.

Lemon balm

Spin the lemon balm and the spinach in a Thermomix and add the sugar water. Spin at the highest setting until it becomes a coulis. Chill in the fridge.

Arrange everything decoratively on a plate.

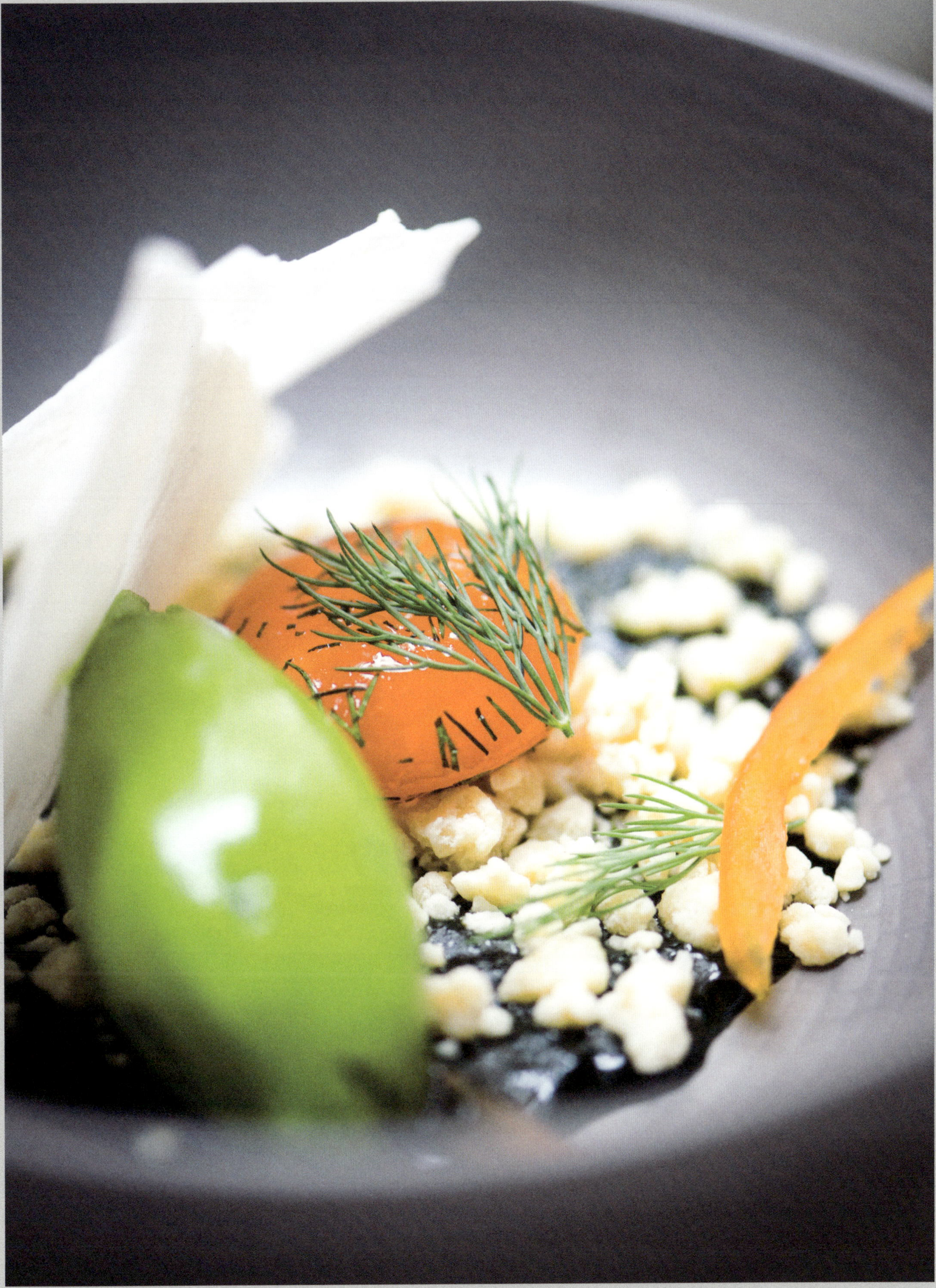

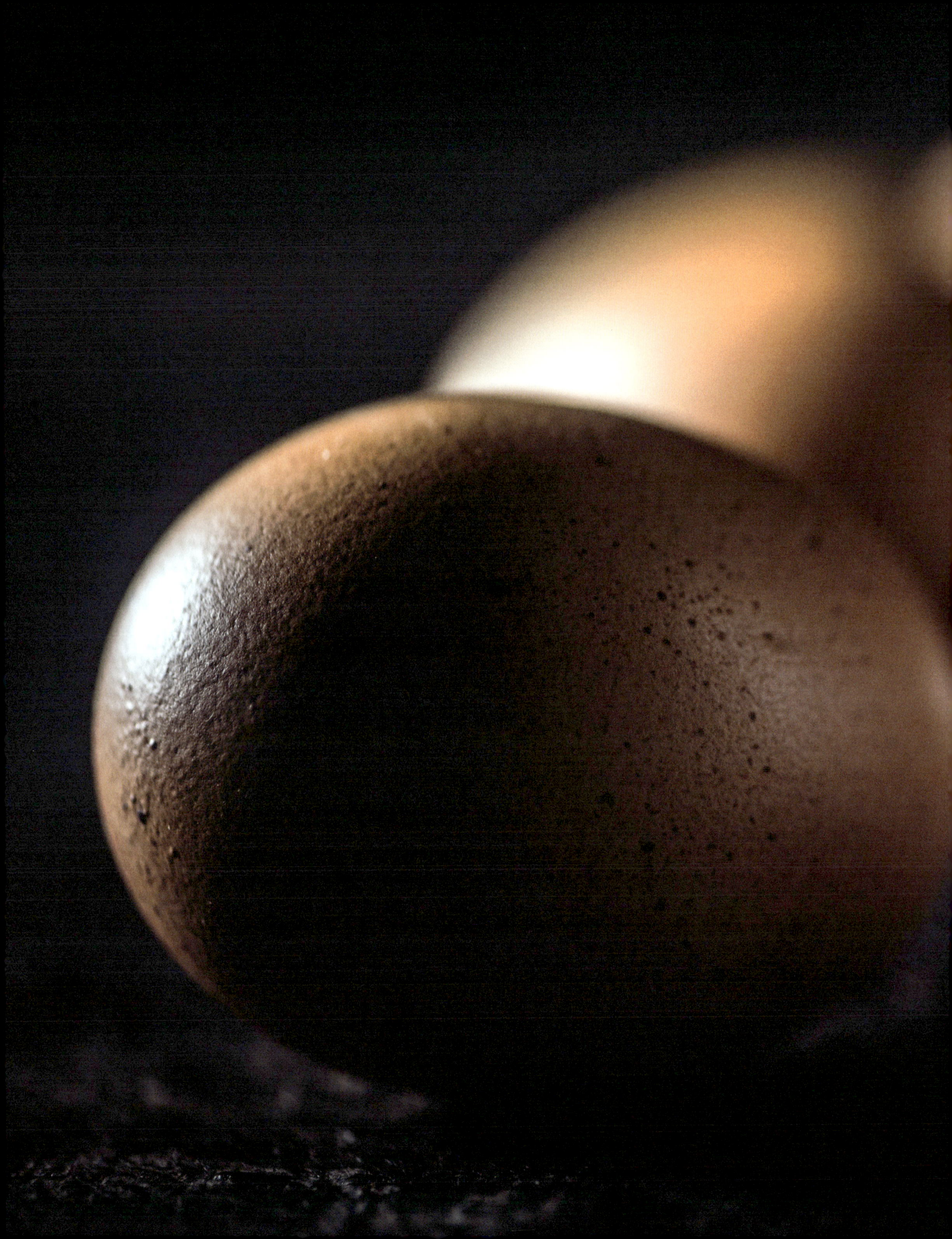

COCKTAILS

A COCKTAIL OUT OF A VET'S HANDBOOK

The cocktail, according to every American, is without doubt a completely American invention. But what do the Americans think is so American about a drink containing English gin, Italian vermouth or French absinth, mixed by an Irish or German immigrant bartender? The egg is the only American ingredient...

The British had a hand in all this. Sometime during the 17th century, the drinking culture in London changed and people began moving away from their ales and ciders. King William of Orange had a major dilemma in 1688. Years of good harvests had ensured that the granaries were full to bursting and so prices were low. He decided to reduce the tax on distillation. The following year, some two million litres of neutral spirits were produced from grain by British distilleries (just a reminder – the most common causes of death at that time were diseases such as cholera, dysentery, typhus, etc. caused by the poor quality of the drinking water. That was why people drank as much alcohol as possible, often starting at breakfast time). This colossal amount of alcohol filtered into the pharmaceutical industry. Sometime later a medical patent was taken out on Stoughton's Elixir. It was an alcohol-based, medicinal bitter and had been registered since 1712. By 1720, London

COCKTAILS

distilleries alone were producing about 80 million litres of various alcoholic drinks. An estimated 25% of habitable houses in London had active distilling equipment.

It had long been thought that the word cocktail appeared for the first time in 1806 in a newspaper in Upstate New York. But in 2005, the word was discovered to have appeared in a newspaper in Vermont in …1803 and, sure enough, in 2010, the word 'cocktail' was discovered in an edition of the Morning Post and Gazetteer printed on 20 March, 1798. William Pitt was quoted as mentioning 'a less French drink, a cock-tail' in an article about the Axe and Gate tavern, on the corner of Downing Street and Whitehall. What he meant exactly was a mystery since the word 'cocktail' had then only been used for mixed-race horses with a bobbed tail. There was however a sort of medication for horses listed in vet's handbooks at the time; it consisted of water, gin, grains and ginger.

The Professor

The main pro-American argument can be found in the work of the legendary Jerry Thomas, aka the Professor. Hailing from Connecticut, he wrote the first book about cocktails in 1862. Thomas is considered to be the father of modern bar and cocktail customs, but he conducted his research for his innovative book in… London. His dream was to work at the All Nations restaurant. The site is now occupied by the Albert Hall, but back then a famous restaurant stood there, run by the French chef, Benoît Soyer. Instead, he was able to start work at the American Bowling Saloon in Chelsea. American tourism in London was growing spectacularly and the American Bars in the British capital were crammed. Young creative bartenders mixed lots of interesting new drinks that the tourists took back to the USA with them. After a few years they were reintroduced to Europe as truly authentic American drinks.

The first British book about cocktails didn't appear until 1869: *Cooling Cups and Dainty Drinks* by William Terrington. His opening recipe included the very first use of the word 'cocktail' when he introduced a gin cocktail containing gin, ginger syrup, aromatic bitters and some water.

American Bars were prevalent in Europe at the beginning the the 20th century. The one in London that captured the most imagination was the one in The Savoy. Ada Coleman had come from Claridge's and had so many new ideas and charisma that immortality became one of her ingredients. She and Ruth Burgess formed an inseparable pair: they became the face of The Savoy until the US passed the 18th Amendment to the Constitution which introduced Prohibition. That naturally brought more tourists to London to drink, but Prohibition made Coleman and Burgess' position untenable, because women were forbidden from working in American bars. Harry Craddock was their replacement and became a big star. His *Savoy Cocktail Book* published in 1930 is still legendary. But the American Cradock also had a secret: he had been born in Stroud,

Gloucestershire. He had lived in the US for some 20 years and was married to an Irish immigrant but only received his naturalisation papers in 1916, just four years before he went to London as a great foreign talent.

Shake before use

Exactly when raw eggs started to be used in cocktails is not very clear. The reason why, on the other hand, is known. The use of fresh, unpasteurised egg white in particular is a delicious addition which gives a cocktail a rich, creamy structure and good, firm foam. Unpasteurised egg white is almost completely free of odour or flavour so its use chiefly adds to the texture. Just as in a mousse or in a meringue, lemon juice and some kind of sugar syrup are also incorporated into cocktails containing egg white. When this mixture is shaken it becomes frothy. In contrast to a mousse in which egg white acts as a setting agent, it remains liquid in a cocktail due to the alcohol.

Egg white may not add much flavour to a cocktail, but it does add a physical sensation, and that lovely frothy layer – which always puts me somewhat in mind of a latte – provides bartenders with numerous creative opportunities. They can use it – as baristas do – as a pristine canvas. Egg white mostly consists of water and proteins, little more, and when an egg is beaten or shaken, the main protein ovalbumin explodes, so to speak. Proteins can 'capture air' so that they form foam. The only difference is that you don't use a kitchen robot to do this, but a shaker.

It is less common to use egg yolk or even whole eggs in cocktails. When you do, you get an additional flavour component and it makes a sort of light emulsion, similar to advocaat or eggnog.

The Waukesha Plaindealer

Jerry Thomas wrote about whiskey sour in his *Bartender's Guide* of 1862: 'How to mix drinks'. This seems to be the first official mention of whiskey sour in a publication. We do know that sailors in the British Royal Navy drank something at sea that sounds very like whiskey sour. Drinking water was not always available on long sea voyages and so vast quantities of alcohol were consumed. British sailors, also called Limeys, consumed a lot of lemons and limes when at sea to avoid all manner of diseases. They were mixed with alcohol and then sugar and water were added to make it palatable.

Bizarrely, an article about whiskey sour appeared in a local paper in Wisconsin in 1870, The Waukesha Plaindealer, and even more strangely there was a story about a certain Elliot Staub in 1872 who had invented a drink, a whiskey sour, in a bar in Iquique which was then part of Peru.

Oh yes, 25 August is National Whiskey Sour Day in the United States!

The brunch capital

New Orleans is viewed as the brunch capital of the world. One of my favourite brunch cocktails is the Absinthe Suissesse. Little is known about it, but the drink was probably invented before absinth was prohibited in the US in 1912. Its strange name makes me fantasise about how the drink came about. I can visualise a Swiss lady barhopping in New Orleans. She drinks her absinth or pastis with milk. A clever bartender takes this as the basis for a decadent cocktail which I have also seen served as a dessert cocktail. Vanilla ice cream was used in that case.

The Ramos gin fizz on the other hand has a pedigree that originates in New Orleans. Henry C. Ramos first concocted it in the Imperial Cabinet Saloon in 1880. It is a cocktail you need to shake for a very long time, sometimes even 15 minutes, to get the right consistency. Henry Ramos bought a bar, The Stag, in 1907, and during the Mardi Gras carnival in 1915, a whole army of 35 shaker boys spent all day working to satisfy the demand for this drink. To guarantee the immortality of his Ramos gin fizz, Henry released the original recipe just before the Volstead Act ushered in the beginning of Prohibition in 1920. He hoped that people would copy his drink at some later date. Nowadays, the Ramos gin fizz is one of the favourite city drinks in New Orleans.

Don't flip

The Oxford English Dictionary tells us that in 1695 a flip was a mixture of beer, rum and sugar, heated by a red-hot iron. The extreme heat caused the drink to foam and this foam (flipping) gave its name to the mixture. In due course, eggs were added, the sugar content was increased and the beer was removed. From then on, the mixture was served cold. Jerry Thomas was the person who added the egg to the recipe for the flip.

Yannick Draeyers

Nowadays, you're more likely to find a team making and creating cocktails for a top cocktail bar, in this case Cocktails at Nine in Antwerp, because together, several talents are simply more inventive. Cocktails at Nine is an exceptional cocktail bar in every sense. The 200-year-old building in the shadow of the monumental cathedral exudes class, refinement and distinction, as does its owner Graham Herbert. He always puts me in mind of the perfect gentleman Sean Connery personified as James Bond.

With the renaissance of the cocktail trend in Europe, sipping a perfectly balanced cocktail has become hip and trendy and tackling classic cocktail receipes is increasingly the done thing. People like Naushad Rahamat, Dries Botty, Patrick America and of course Yannick Draeyers are contributing more and more to an evolution in the classic cocktails, by making subtle changes to sometimes ancient cocktail recipes and as such, making them their own.

Top talents like Draeyers are obviously not two a penny and their performance is restricted to the very best cocktail bars. It amazes me time after time how tiny, subtle adjustments can transform a cocktail from an ordinary drink to a sublime creation with depth and nuances.

ABSINTHE SUISSESSE

INGREDIENTS

3 cl absinthe Un Emile ·
30 ml Absinthe Un Emile ·
5 ml Pastis Henri Bardouin ·
15 ml Crème de menthe ·
20 ml lemon juice ·
2 dashes Peychaud's Bitters ·
1 egg white ·

METHOD

Put all the ingredients in a cocktail shaker, whisk the egg well and then add ice.

Shake well and pour into a glass without any ice in it.

Garnish
Add Peychaud's Bitters to the mixture.

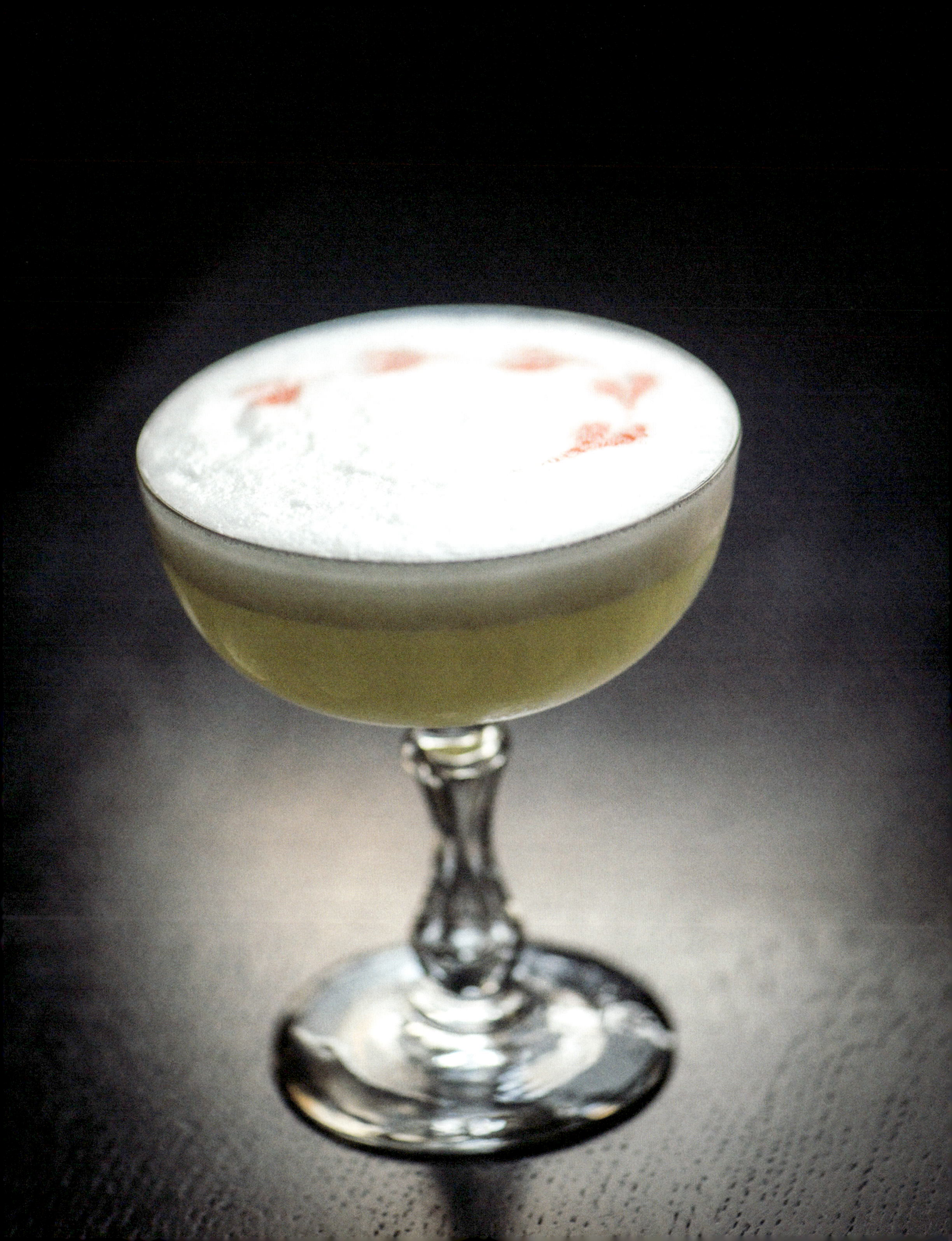

WHISKEY SOUR

●●●○○○

INGREDIENTS

50 ml Bourbon whiskey ·
30 ml lemon juice ·
20 ml sugar water ·
1 egg white ·

METHOD

Put all the ingredients in a cocktail shaker, whisk the egg white well and then add ice.

Shake well then pour into a glass filled with ice cubes.

Garnish
Garnish with a slice of orange.

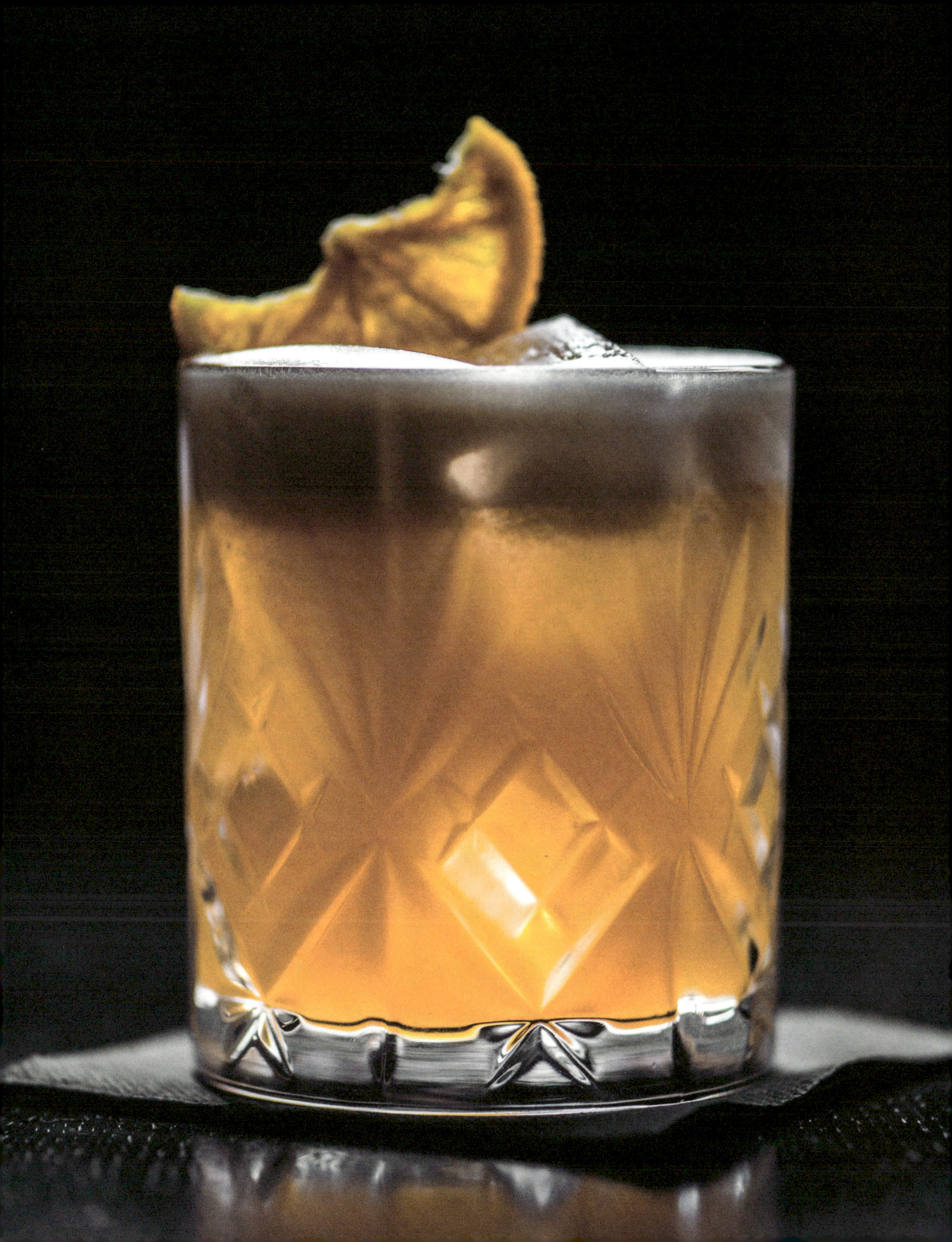

BRANDY FLIP

●●●○○○

INGREDIENTS

50 ml brandy ·
20 ml sugar water ·
20 ml double cream ·
1 egg ·

METHOD

Put all the ingredients in a cocktail shaker and shake well. Pour into a chilled glass with no ice.

Garnish
Garnish with grated nutmeg.

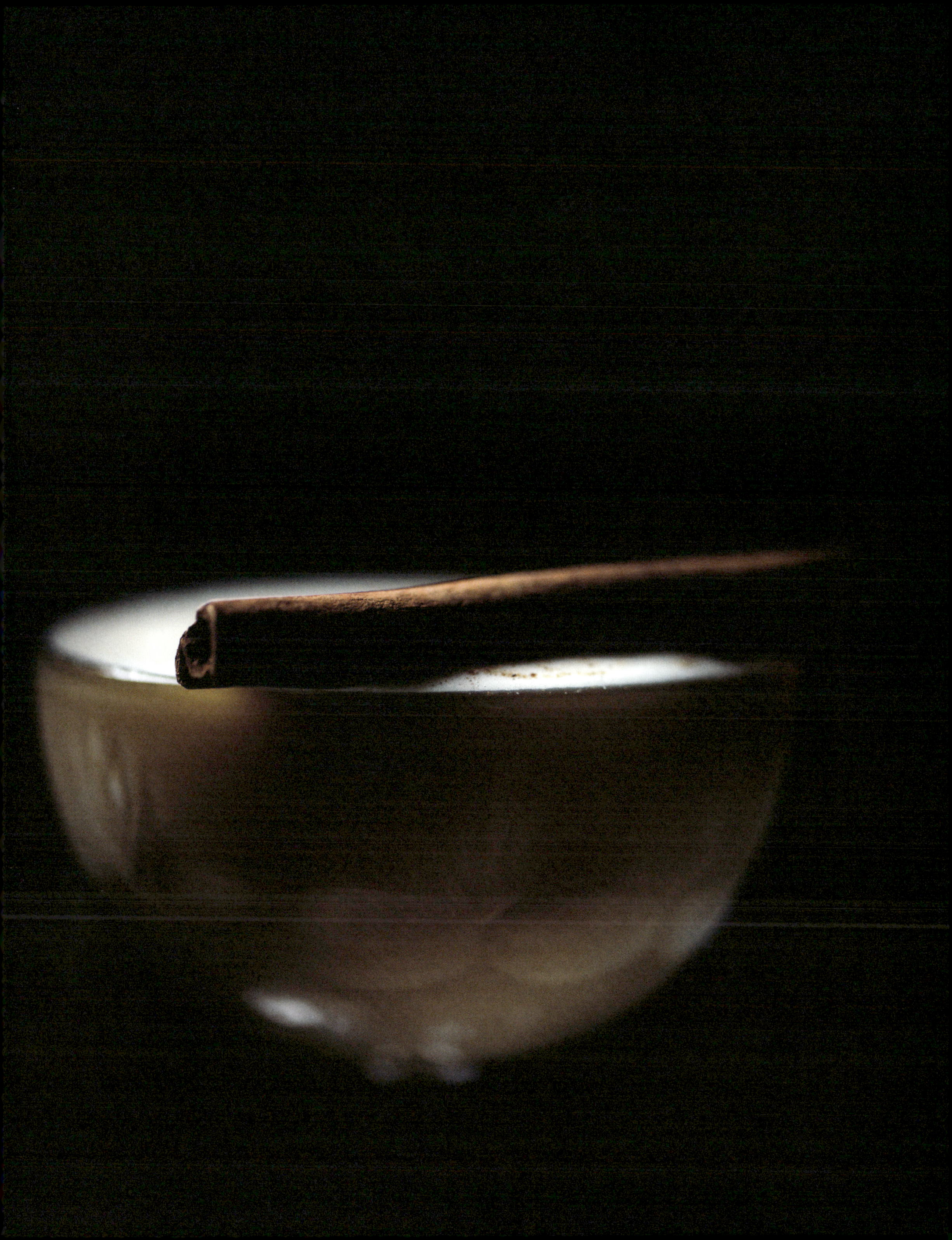

COFFEE COCKTAIL

🍥🍥🍥🍥🥚🥚

INGREDIENTS

45 ml cognac ·
15 ml Pedro Ximénez sherry ·
15 ml Amontillado sherry ·
10 ml sugar water ·
1 egg ·

METHOD

Put all the ingredients in a cocktail shaker and shake well. Pour into a chilled glass with no ice.

Garnish
Garnish with grated nutmeg.

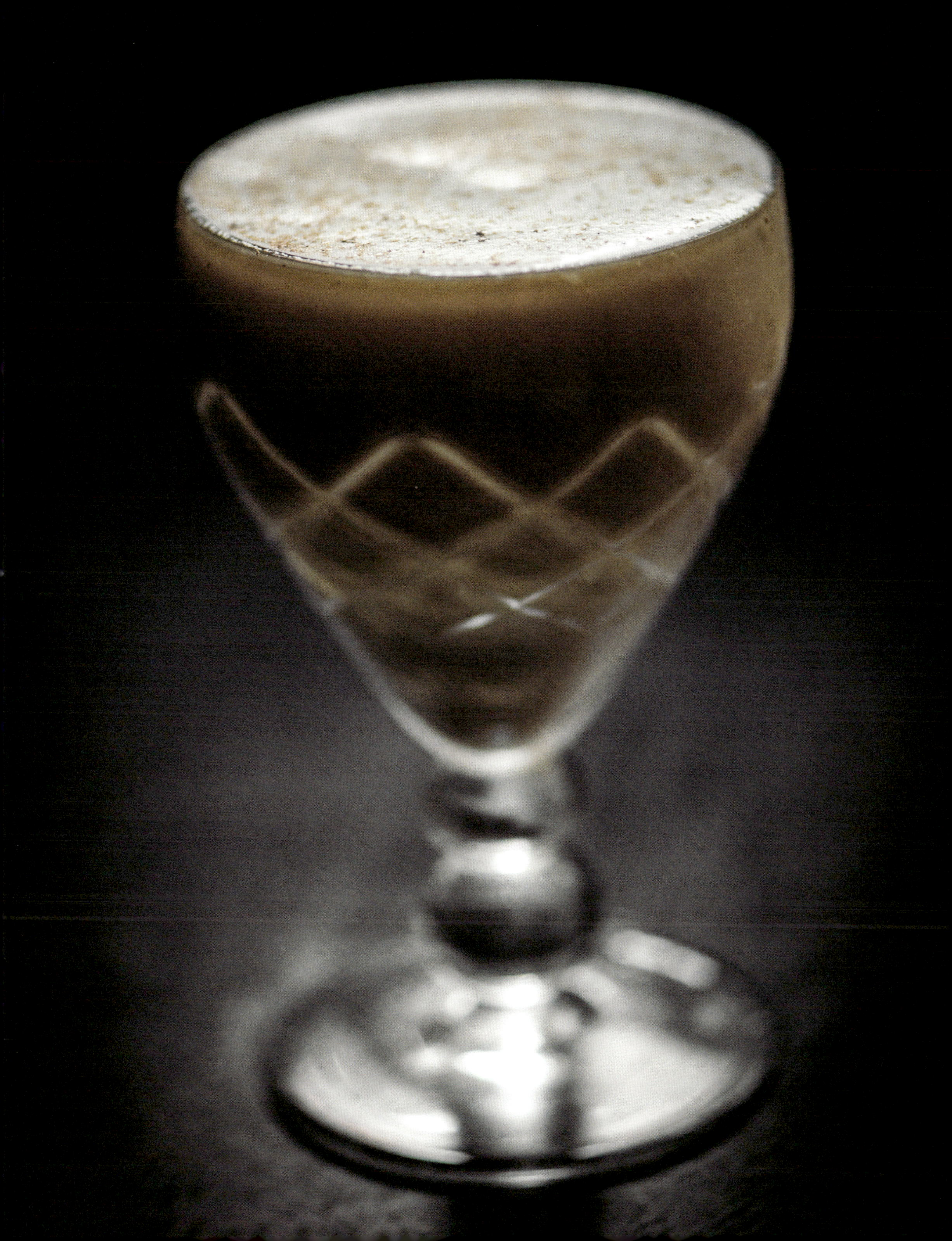

RAMOS GIN FIZZ

●●●●●○

INGREDIENTS

50 ml gin ·
15 ml lemon juice ·
15 ml lime juice ·
20 ml sugar water ·
2 dashes orange blossom water ·
1 egg white ·
30 ml cream ·
soda (to finish off) ·

METHOD

Put all the ingredients in a cocktail shaker and shake continuously for about seven minutes to get the perfect structure. Pour into a tall tumbler with no ice.

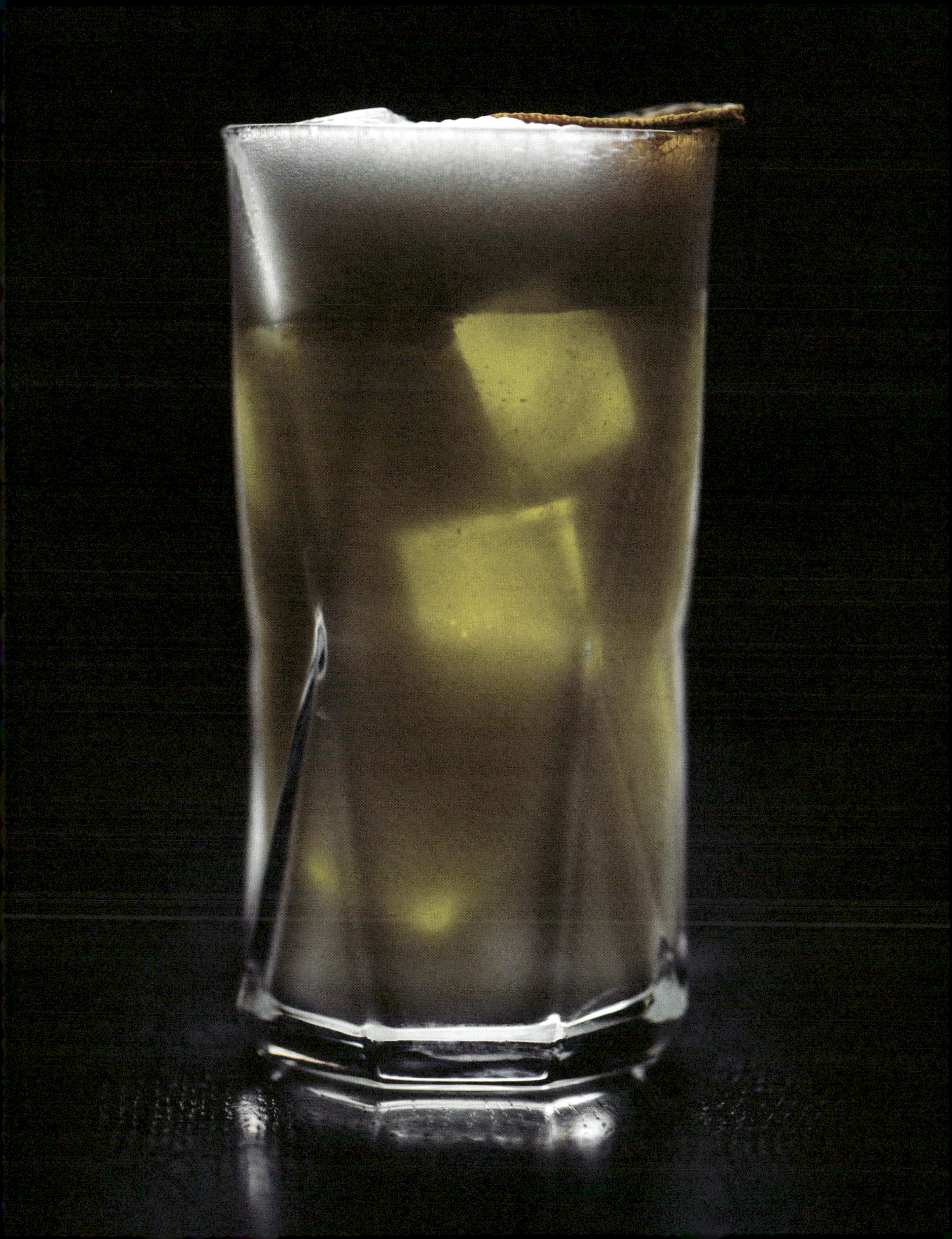

LIQUIDS (AND HERBS AND SPICES)
Volume Conversions: Normally used for liquids only

Customary quantity	Metric equivalent
1 teaspoon	5 ml
1 tablespoon or ½ fluid ounce	15 ml
1 fluid ounce or ⅛ cup	30 ml
¼ cup or 2 fluid ounces	60 ml
⅓ cup	80 ml
½ cup or 4 fluid ounces	120 ml
⅔ cup	160 ml
¾ cup or 6 fluid ounces	180 ml
1 cup or 8 fluid ounces or half a pint	240 ml
1 ½ cups or 12 fluid ounces	350 ml
2 cups or 1 pint or 16 fluid ounces	475 ml
3 cups or 1 ½ pints	700 ml
4 cups or 2 pints or 1 quart	950 ml
4 quarts or 1 gallon	3.8 l

Note: In cases where higher precision is not justified, it may be convenient to round these conversions off as follows:
1 cup = 250 ml // 1 pint = 500 ml // 1 quart = 1 l // 1 gallon = 4 l

WEIGHT
Weight Conversions

Customary quantity	Metric equivalent
1 ounce	28 g
4 ounces or 1/4 pound	113 g
1/3 pound	150 g
8 ounces or ½ pound	230 g
2/3 pound	300 g
12 ounces or 3/4 pound	340 g
1 pound or 16 ounces	450 g
2 pounds	900 g

OTHER NON-LIQUID INGREDIENTS
Weights of common ingredients in grams

INGREDIENT	1 CUP	¾ CUP	⅔ CUP	½ CUP	⅓ CUP	¼ CUP	2 TBSP
Flour, all purpose (wheat)	120 g	90 g	80 g	60 g	40 g	30 g	15 g
Flour, well sifted all purpose (wheat)	110 g	80 g	70 g	55 g	35 g	27 g	13 g
Sugar, granulated cane	200 g	150 g	130 g	100 g	65 g	50 g	25 g
Confectioner's sugar (cane)	100 g	75 g	70 g	50 g	35 g	25 g	13 g
Brown sugar, packed firmly	180 g	135 g	120 g	90 g	60 g	45 g	23 g
Corn meal	160 g	120 g	100 g	80 g	50 g	40 g	20 g
Corn starch	120 g	90 g	80 g	60 g	40 g	30 g	15 g
Rice, uncooked	190 g	140 g	125 g	95 g	65 g	48 g	24 g
Macaroni, uncooked	140 g	100 g	90 g	70 g	45 g	35 g	17 g
Couscous, uncooked	180 g	135 g	120 g	90 g	60 g	45 g	22 g
Oats, uncooked quick	90 g	65 g	60 g	45 g	30 g	22 g	11 g
Table salt	300 g	230 g	200 g	150 g	100 g	75 g	40 g
Butter	240 g	180 g	160 g	120 g	80 g	60 g	30 g
Vegetable shortening	190 g	140 g	125 g	95 g	65 g	48 g	24 g
Chopped fruits and vegetables	150 g	110 g	100 g	75 g	50 g	40 g	20 g
Nuts, chopped	150 g	110 g	100 g	75 g	50 g	40 g	20 g
Nuts, ground	120 g	90 g	80 g	60 g	40 g	30 g	15 g
Bread crumbs, fresh, loosely packed	60 g	45 g	40 g	30 g	20 g	15 g	8 g
Bread crumbs, dry	150 g	110 g	100 g	75 g	50 g	40 g	20 g

ADDRESSES

de Gulle Waard
Meester A.th. ten Houtenlaan 4
NL - 7102 EH Winterswijk
+31 543 513 133

Bon Bon
Tervurenlaan 453
BE - 1150 Brussels

Hof van Cleve
Riemegemstraat 1
BE- 9770 Kruishoutem

Kaagman&Kortekaas
Sint-Nicolaasstraat 43
NL- 1012 NJ Amsterdam

Hangar
Aambeeldstraat 36
NL - 1021 KB Amsterdam

Mokja
www.mokja.be

Sinem Usta

Divin by Sepi
Verschansingstraat 5-7
BE -2000 Antwerp

Joost Arijs
Vlaanderenstraat 54
BE - 9000 Ghent

Mmei 5 Flavors
Volksstraat 37
BE - 2000 Antwerp

Dim Dining
Leeuwenstraat 1
BE - 2000 Antwerp

Dishoom Cafe
12 Upper St.-Martin's Lane
UK - London WC2H 9 FB

www.lannoo.com
Register on our website and we will send you regular newsletters containing information about new books and exciting, exclusive offers.

Colophon

Text: Luc Hoornaert
Photography: Kris Vlegels
Design: Grietje Uytdenhouwen
Translation: Kay Dixon

If you have any comments or questions, please contact our editorial office: redactielifestyle@lannoo.com.

© Lannoo Publishers, Tielt, Belgium, 2017
D/2017/45/370– NUR 440-442
ISBN: 978-94-014-4125-4

All rights reserved. No part of this publication may be reproduced, stored in a retrieval system, and/or transmitted in any form or by any means, whether electronic, electrostatic, magnetic tape, mechanical, photocopying, recording or otherwise, without the prior permission in writing of the publisher.

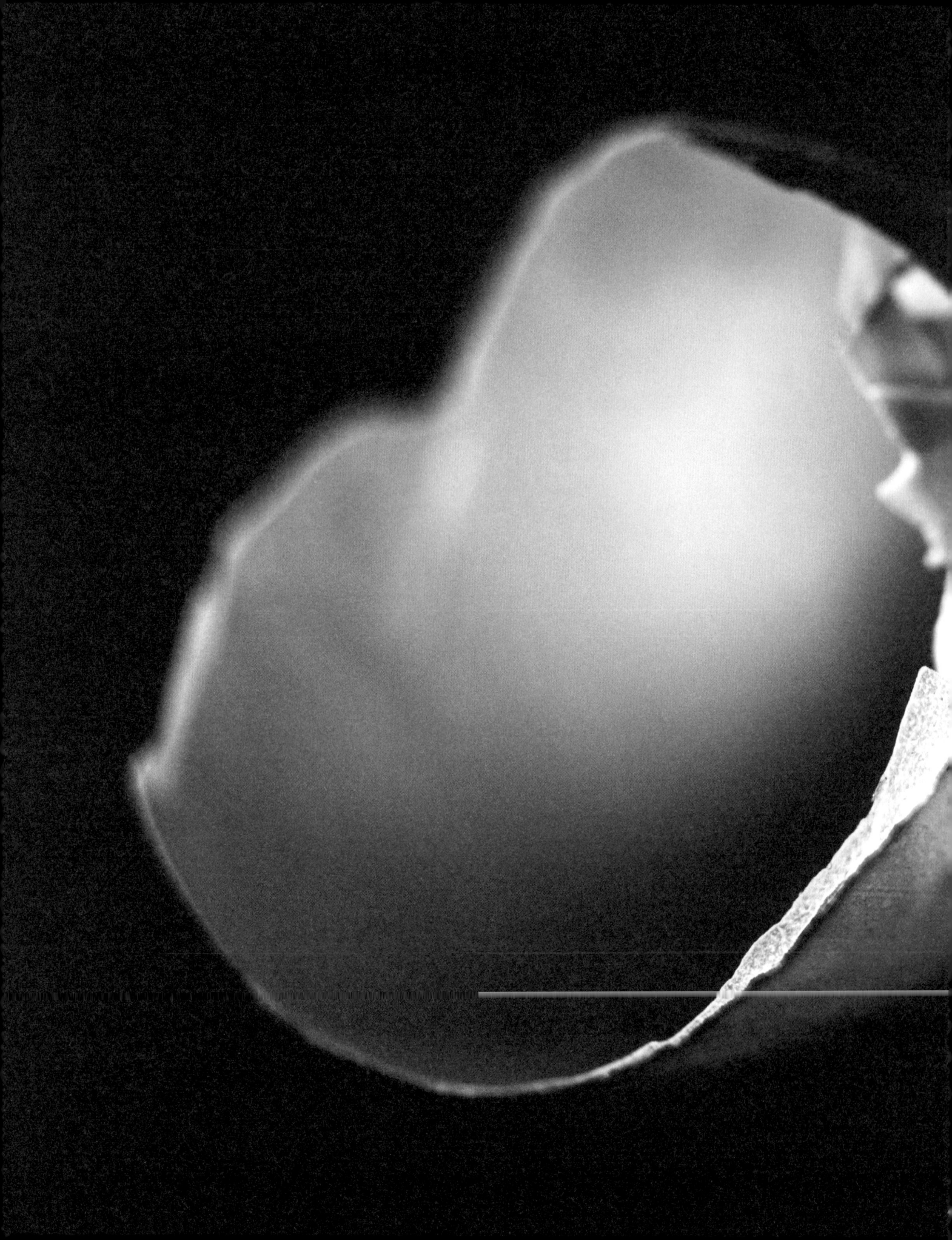